The Travel Writer's Guide

Revised 2nd Edition

Gordon Burgett

Prima Publishing
P.O. Box 1260
Rocklin, CA 95677
(916) 632-4400

Typography by Col D'var Graphics
Copyediting by Candace Demeduc
Production by Janelle Rohr, Bookman Productions
Cover design by Paul Page Design, Inc.

> **Library of Congress Cataloging-in-Publication Data**
>
> Burgett, Gordon, 1938–
>   The travel writer's guide : how to earn at least twice what you spend on travel by writing newspaper and magazine articles / Gordon Burgett.—Rev. 2nd ed.
>   p. cm.
>   Includes bibliographical references and index.
>   ISBN 1-55958-561-7
>   1. Travel—Authorship. I. Title.
> G151.B86   1994
> 808'.06691—dc20   94-20626
>   CIP

95 96 97 98 RRD 10 9 8 7 6 5 4 3 2 1

Printed in the United States of America

How to Order:

Alleline Vadeau

ACKNOWLEDGMENTS

The encouragement for this book really came from the thousands who haved attended my travel writing seminars these past 15 years, mostly in California. Their curiosity, excitement, and desire to learn has been a continually gratifying inducement to keep the how-to information easy to understand, directly applicable, and current. The result you see on these pages.

But I also want to thank those who make it possible for me to travel, lecture, and write. To my daughters, Shannon and Kim, whom I never want to disappoint; Virgil Cooper, my computer guru; Liz and Linda, who keep the business flowing while I journey; and to Shirley Summer, who made the visit to Germany (used as an example on these pages) fun and intelligible, the latter through her mystical linguistic skills.

CONTENTS

INTRODUCTION

Much has happened in the world in general that affects travel since this book first appeared in 1991.

Computers are playing a more direct role in the submission of travel copy. Air courier jobs are more available and an inexpensive way for travel writers to get abroad. So I've added new segments to address each in Part Five. New article topics also abound: ecotourism, gay travel, car rentals, air miles, letters of credit, and more. So the "300 Ideas for Travel Articles" chapter in the first edition became "365 Ideas for Travel Articles" here, one for each day of the year.

As I said in the first edition, travel writing can open up a new world of opportunities for you at the same time that it reveals new vistas to your readers. This book talks about both wonders.

The opportunities open to you as a successful travel writer include the mastery of a new skill, that of writing for publication. This in turn requires the attainment of other skills, such as interviewing, marketing, and editing. And by plying your new trade you can increase your income, secure in the knowledge that the same skills used in writing about travel can be used to write about any other wonder for the reading world!

Better yet, travel writing can be great fun, take you to any part of the globe your desire and purse will reach, pay you far more than you spend, let you share with others the joy and awe of seeing new places, and even allow you to deduct from your taxes the expenses necessary to conduct this wonderful business!

That too is what this book is about: the step-by-step process of travel writing for publication in magazines and newspapers.

This is a show-and-tell book. The basic text, the how-to element, is the "tell." The "show" comes by example, usually at the end of a chapter, to illustrate the points made. Any books mentioned in the text can be found in the bibliography along with others of interest.

The example in this book is based on an actual trip to Germany that I have converted into a travel writing model for these pages. The site is arbitrary—it could have been almost any other used for the 1,600 articles I've had in print. I picked Germany because the places mentioned are truly spectacular and because Europe in general is such a common direction for most North American readers. The principles used in selling articles about any location would be the same.

There is a final joy that I hope to impart to you through this book. That of taking raw facts and observations and crafting from them a new and totally personal element: an article at once as singular as a snowflake and as useful as a word map. For writing is also an art and an article is a creation. By helping to create new artists, this book might even help elevate you and your readers to a higher creative plain. If that sounds a bit presumptuous, it is really only a modest hope that you, the reader, putting into practice what these pages share, will make a reality.

PART ONE

An Overview of Travel Writing

CHAPTER 1

Travel Writing: The Professional Way for Professional Results

I've got $500 and the whole summer free!" announced a young school teacher at my travel writing seminar in San Francisco when I asked if anybody was going to try their hand at some articles right away.

"I've only got $10 and a coupla hundred *days* left," retorted an old-timer loudly to the laughing back row. "What do *I* do?"

Write. Your travel articles can pay for your trips, reap you a fat profit, and allow you to deduct the travel costs from your taxes.

Choose where you go, how long you stay, what you do. And when you return (or while you're on-site), by sharing what you've seen, heard, and learned, you can develop a skill and sharpen a trade that can bring you more profits, more sights, and more new knowledge— until your days do run out or you put yourself out to pasture. With luck, an exotic pasture.

Who benefits the most? You *and* your readers. If you do your job well—if your writing is honest and balanced and embodies the full measure of life as you see it—readers learn about other people and places without taking a step. And beyond the obvious benefits of fun and profit to yourself, you perform a valuable function through good travel writing: You help bring all humanity closer together.

In a step-by-step process, this book shows you how professionals profit from travel in print and how you too can do the same. There are some basics: You must be literate. Clarity of expression is a plus. Curiosity is mandatory. And some hard work is the order of the day. In addition, five points apply to the whole field of travel writing. Let's take a look at them.

1. TRAVEL WRITING SELLS

Great news: Nothing is easier to sell in the writing world than travel! It's estimated that one million articles are published each year. Somebody writes them. They get paid. They could be you.

First, think magazines. They are the travel writer's best market. They pay from several hundred to several thousand dollars per article, photos extra, and you only write for them when you know they are interested. (More on that later.)

Divide magazines into two categories: consumer (called "slicks") and specialty/trade. Consumer magazines are sold on the racks and by subscription. Almost all of them use travel regularly.

Some are standard, well known magazines, like _Travel & Leisure_ and _National Geographic_. Others are less well known: _Accent, Adventure West, Cruise Travel Magazine, The Islands, Mature Traveler,_ and _Touring America_. Some are published by travel-related sponsors, like *Amoco Traveler* and *VISTA/USA* (by petroleum companies).

Still others have a theme or purpose that involves travel. Those include RV/motor home publications (*RV Times Magazine, RV West Magazine, Western RV News*); in-flight magazines (*American West Airlines Magazine, American Way, Sky, Tradewind, USAir Magazine, Washington Flyer Magazine*); and publications about automobiles, motorcycles, aviation, camping, cruises, food and drink, nature, photography, geographic locations, and many more.

Examples of the more obvious consumer magazines are easy to find. Libraries subscribe to them, supermarkets and newsstands sell them, dentists age them and leave them in their waiting rooms. However, a less obvious market, the specialty/trade magazines, may be hungrier, and sometimes, though rarely, may pay better.

Some of these specialty magazines are easy enough to imagine: They are for people in the travel trade, like *Star Service* (guide to accommodations and cruise ships), *Bus Tours Magazine, National Bus Trader, RV Business,* and *Travelage West* (for travel agency sales counselors). But others take more creative thinking. For instance, let's imagine a magazine called *The Plumber's Journal,* and let's say you want to go to Guatemala. While there you research the Guatemalan plumbing trade. Upon returning you write an article ("Plumbing in Guatemala"), which *The Plumber's Journal* buys because its readers are interested in all facets of plumbing—plumbing trends, plumbing history, plumbing how-to, and even plumbing in exotic places. For them yours is a plumbing piece; for you, an article that helps support your habit: traveling on a full stomach with a cooperative wallet.

If you know a field well—as a teacher, architect, gardener, plumber, or whatever—you can provide those specialty/trade publications with solid articles from new or unusual sites. You have an advantage over the rest of us: In addition to the consumer magazines open to us all, you have access to those magazines that cater to your area of expertise. You know what the readers of those magazines would enjoy reading more about, the special vocabulary they use, and how they might benefit from that knowledge.

You needn't be a specialist to write for those pages, however. I've sold to horticulture publications (I can't get weeds to grow); stamp collectors' newsletters (my collection is a roll of unused 29-centers); the Lions, Rotarians, Phi Tau, and Kiwanis publications (says Groucho, "I wouldn't join a club that would have me"), children's pages (though I haven't been around small children for years), many academic journals (do they give doctorates in spelling?), and, yes, _Modern Bride_, repeatedly, though I'm a devoutly outdated and, in my near-dotage, single male.

Let me share two quick examples to sharpen your vision for spotting those harder-to-find trade and specialty markets.

Although a friend of mine normally covers Portuguese-speaking Africa, Diu, and Goa, she was given an assignment in Beirut (in the days when it was a glittering resort town). While in the area, she decided to visit Egypt to see the pyramids. Surprisingly—since she was a seasoned traveler who preferred going it alone—she signed on with a tour group.

When she boarded the tour bus she found it full of architects fresh from a world conference in Athens. Whipping out her stenographer's notepad, she began interviewing. By the end of the tour she had spoken with them all, plus squeezed in three rolls of color slides. The result, some months later, was over $2,500 from sold freelance articles—almost all to architectural magazines!

Three points worth noting. One, she had never read an architectural magazine before, had trouble spelling *Egypt*, and hadn't planned to write about her Egyptian side trip. She simply took advantage of a reportable situation.

Two, she gained her architectural expertise from the experts she interviewed and from follow-up research and magazine reading after her trip. (To write successfully for this or any expert group, the article must work: What you write must be accurate as well as interesting to the reader.)

Three, she let the architects lead the interviews. Rather than trying to imagine what an editor would want, she asked the architects at the pyramids, "Why is this particularly interesting to you?" From their answers and related comments, she built (and sold) articles based on in-depth listening.

The second example is of an agriculture major from the University of Illinois who took his wife on a belated wedding trip to Japan some time after he had graduated. Although he'd never been in print before (nor to my knowledge has he since), he turned one day's digging into seven articles and about $1,500 (helping to pay for his trip!).

He became interested in the intensive form of farming in Japan, in contrast to the more extensive system practiced in the Midwest. He wanted to share that with his college ag cronies, now scattered around the country, so he decided to write an article.

Cleverly, he persuaded the Ministry of Agriculture in Tokyo to "lend" him an English-speaking employee. The two then spent a day visiting three model farms, where our writer toured, pinched, bowed, tasted, interviewed, and photographed. When he returned home he actually wrote two different articles and sent them to 20 regional (mostly county) agricultural magazines, all outside each other's distribution range. Seven bought, six paid, all used photos—and knowledge was spread.

Anybody can write for architectural or agricultural magazines. The articles simply must work, the information must be correct, and it must meet the readers' needs.

The hardest part for beginners is to let their minds expand to see those less obvious markets, then dare to approach them with a good idea or article.

After consumer and specialty trade magazines, newspapers are the third market for travel articles. Usually newspapers don't buy much from freelancers. They are largely staff written, with most of the rest picked up from syndicates and wire services. Freelancers are a headache for most editors, and they have enough headaches already.

Except for travel. It costs far less to buy a travel article and photos from a freelancer than to send a staffer half way around the world. So this is a particularly receptive market that responds quickly and pays promptly, though modestly, once the words have appeared in print. More about newspapers in Chapter 12.

2. THINK AND ACT LIKE A PROFESSIONAL

More than half the battle is thinking and acting like a professional, of wearing the suit while you grow into it. In fact, it's unlikely that unless you do—unless you sell, then write like a pro—you'll ever become one.

Although the world is full of people who can write well, editors have trouble finding responsible, energetic, and accurate people who can observe, listen, and research—and then write well and deliver their product in a timely fashion. In other words, professionals who give what they promise when they promise in a reliable, usable form.

If you're going to compete with professionals like these, you must do it from the moment you get to the starting line. And keep doing it from then on.

If you aren't literate you just aren't in the race. That's not fatal. Millions of Americans, most of who are literate, have no desire whatsoever to be in print and they still lead exciting, positive lives. Join them and do something else very well.

Just as important as being literate, is the ability to sell. This is something you can learn to do: it's akin to wearing the right shoes, training the right way, and eating the right foods before you enter a race. Likewise, selling your travel writing has its own rules and methods.

This book will show you how to get in the race in the first place—and how to win every time. Professionals win with every article they put in print. Which takes us to our next step.

---

3. WRITING IS EASIER THAN SELLING

If you can make a place, an idea, or a people come alive, wrap your prose around a central theme, keep the paragraphs short, write clearly in words that readers understand, be accurate, and help readers experience your experience with all their senses, you won't have much problem with the writing. And the more you do it, the faster and sharper you'll become. But that is only half the battle—selling is definitely the other half.

How do you sell your work? Begin by examining the magazine or newspaper in which you'd like to appear. What did the editor just buy? What was the topic? How was it treated? What was the ratio of fact, quote, and anecdote? What angle did the writer take? Any humor? How much? What kind of photos accompanied the piece?

Who took them? How many sentences per paragraph? What made the piece "work"?

Remember, you can be the greatest writer in captivity, bursting with electric text and sparkling dialogue, but unless you sell those words you're an outsider looking in, pockets hanging. The old adage (which I made up about a decade back!) that "amateurs write, then try to sell; professionals sell, then write" is true. But it took me, a kid in Illinois writing up a storm, a long time to learn it. I believed that editors wanted to see what they were buying *before* they actually bought it. Wrong! (And I've got the rejection slips to prove it.)

What I didn't know was that professionals promised an exciting piece *before* they took a trip. They got the editor's interest and tentative approval, gathered the information and photos on their travels, and tailored their piece to the magazine's readers—they sent off customized prose and got back a customized check.

They then sold that same piece again and again! And they rewrote it into other articles. And they sold other items based on the same trip to newspapers. After spending $1,500 and a few weeks in some magic spot, they ended up with $4,500, a great trip, and lots of deductions. This makes for success, and selling is as much a key to it as writing.

---

4. DO MOST OF THE WORK BEFORE YOU GO

Although this may sound odd, it makes good sense. Get most of the work done before you reach your destination, then you'll have lots more time to enjoy the place!

How do you do this? By studying the writings of others. By combing encyclopedias, geography books, maps, press releases, and the odd item in the library's vertical file.

By checking out videos or watching TV shows or travelogues. By talking with others who were there. By reviewing the *Reader's Guide to Periodical Literature* (or its computer equivalent) and the newspaper indexes; then reading the articles themselves.

In Chapter 2 I'll show you how you create a solid information base before you take the trip, so that you spend most of your time on-site adding to, correcting, and expanding that base. Plus gathering invaluable observations, taking photos (an important feature of travel articles), talking with locals, and blending left brain–right brain elements into a full-dimensional manuscript that includes facts, quotes, anecdotes, and photos.

Every research hour well spent at home is another hour uncommitted once you're there.

5. DOUBLE OR TRIPLE YOUR INCOME BY TRAVELING SMART

Occasionally you'll have time for only a short visit to one place. But if you have more time at your disposal, as a travel writer you can greatly increase the amount of articles you write (and the money you make). By planning well you can include many stops coming and going, with enough time to branch out locally from your destination. Not only is it far less expensive to do this than visit the same number of places separately, but each stop can be lucrative.

Let me explain by example. Suppose you live in or near Los Angeles and want to write a piece about Reno, Nevada, some 470 miles north. If you have little time, you'll fly directly there, gather what you need quickly, and fly back.

But if you have more time, you can jump in the car and head to Santa Barbara, "where the Westerns were

born and the stars now hide." Check out La Purísima
Mission near Lompoc, the best preserved and recon-
structed in the chain; then stop at Solvang, the Danish
village a few miles east. Pismo Beach, San Luis Obispo,
and Morro Bay are travel havens along the way. Then
head up Highway 1 to Hearst Castle, the San Antonio
Mission (half-hidden behind big Sur), and the "17-Mile
Drive" in Carmel.

Stories beg to be written about Monterey, once the
state capital. Santa Cruz and nearby seaside villages are
throwbacks to beatnik days, and San Jose, in the throes
of a massive downtown rebuilding, glistens with
unwritten articles.

In San Francisco find tightly focused pieces on
Brazilian restaurants, bed-and-breakfast inns tucked
away in the city, ferry boating, or the fortifications near
Lake Merced.

Cross the Golden Gate Bridge for a matching article,
"The Other Highway 1," from Marin to Leggett, a day
or more of the wildest, snakiest, prettiest stretch of sea-
hugging road imaginable. Write about it and the places
along the way: Point Reyes, Fort Ross, Mendocino, and
more.

From there it's either up the "Valley of the Giants"
(a road lined with towering redwoods) to Arcata or
Eureka, or back down to Highway 20, Marysville, and
the fabled Feather River. Why not swing north to Oroville
and its magnificent dam, and a few miles more to
Cherokee (a shard of a town but still full of early mining
tailings, a museum, and a full cemetery)? Some of
America's only diamonds were found there.

The back roads will take you to Nevada City and
Grass Valley, through Truckee (where, in 1846, the
Donner Party became stranded and turned to cannibal-
ism), then off to Squaw Valley, Lake Tahoe, and finally,
an hour later, to Reno!

On the way back head a bit north to Highway 49 (the "Road of Gold") and Camptonville, with its magnificently preserved hydraulic mining remains. South then to record and photograph the remnants of the gilded age: to Coloma, where gold was first found at Marshall's mill; to Hangtown (Placerville), Amador City, Jackson, Angel's Camp; to Columbia, where a gold town has been completely preserved.

You may want to stop in Sacramento, since the highway passes nearby, and later head east to Yosemite. Go through the park to the highlands, continue on to Mono Lake, and snake skyward to Bodie, a silver ghost town that rings with authenticity and photographic charm. Then home to Los Angeles and a much deserved rest!

This could apply to any sector of America...or the world! I've simply shown you how a straight-line trip can be bent and expanded to pick up another 20 articles coming and going. What I call "pocket-trip stories"— two to three hours of on-site work each (well researched in advance), most of the time spent interviewing, taking sharp photos, and capturing the impressions and sense of the place in a notebook, to be molded later into compelling copy for magazines and newspapers.

You start at the end, the purpose of your trip. Determine how many days you need to do it properly, add another day or two, then pick up the other stories on both sides, determining what you can add coming and going by the time, money, and energy you have available.

By conducting your travel writing venture professionally, you'll be able to have great success and fun too. It's an ideal job. As long as you, your legs, and your curiosity hold out, you can be desk-free, poking around wherever in the world you want, and getting paid for doing what you'd otherwise gladly pay to do!

THE TRAVEL WRITER'S TASKMASTERS

Even though it *is* an ideal job, it's also more than fun and games. Four taskmasters watch your every merry turn: travel editors back home, the clock, your working budget, and—the most exacting of all—the reader.

Locate "Big Ben" in Bangkok, encourage readers to tramp across Lapland in shorts and sandals, or extol the virtues of seeing "the real New York" by strolling downtown at 2:00 A.M. and that will be your last advice in any magazine or newspaper foolish enough to print it. Irate readers become red-penned writers, which puts editors on notice: Buy more from you and that red could become the pink of their dismissal slip.

Obligations of a Travel Writer

Your job is to tell the truth. Sounds good, doesn't it? Virtuous. Yet just telling the truth won't sell articles. You must dip into the vat of truths and pick out those that create an article about a place, event, or topic that editors want for their pages, that readers will eagerly read, and that, in the blending of smaller truths, still remain true in their totality.

Let's look more closely at the first two qualifications: (1) what editors want for their pages and (2) what readers will eagerly read.

What Editors Want

Magazines and newspapers exist to inform the public, either the general public or people with special interests. There are general public magazines like *Newsweek* and the *Smithsonian Magazine*; special interest magazines like *Skydiving* and the *Mustang Monthly*; general newspapers like the *Christian Science Monitor* and the *New York Times*; and specific newspapers like the *Santa Barbara News-Press* and the *Des Plaines Suburban Times.*

No matter what type of publication—general or special interest—editors want articles that will attract and keep readers, that will entice them to buy the magazine or newspaper from the newsstand and later to order a subscription. Editors also want complete accuracy: places mentioned that are identical to places in reality, names correctly spelled, quotes as they left the speakers' mouths. And they usually want prose that evokes the time and place in telling detail—the smell and feel of a place, a sense of the actors and action. In short, words that come alive to paint pictures of people and places.

What Readers Want

One of the best ways to determine what readers want is to first determine who your readers are.

If you are writing an article for the general public about the beaches lining the California coast from Santa Barbara to San Francisco, you should ask yourself: Why would readers of the *Chicago Sun-Times*, say, read this? What are their expectations? What do they want to know from my words and photos? What does the editor expect?

You can make educated guesses about the readers' expectations. If you have access to earlier *Sun-Times* issues, you can see what kinds of similar articles the editor bought to give you an idea of what the editor wants.

You can also put yourself in the readers' shoes. What would you want to read if you were in Chicago or were thinking of heading west to actually see those beaches? Your list might look like this:

Readers' Expectations List

1. How many beaches are there?

2. What do they look like? White sand? Rock? Dunes? Swamp mud?

3. Are they continuous? If not, what separates them? Can you hike over or around the separations? If so, how far? How much of the total shoreline is continuously accessible?

4. Where is it safe—or best—to swim? Where are dangerous riptides usually found? Any problems with sharks, jellyfish, or other unpleasant critters? Where? Seasonal?

5. Is any of the beach inaccessible for other reasons? Military preserve? Nuclear generators? Private land?

6. Are the beaches accessible by car? Four-wheel-drive truck? On foot only?

7. Is it possible to leave a vehicle at one spot, hike a long way, and get back to your vehicle by other means?

8. What are the best times of day and seasons to visit this beach? When are other people there? What are they like? Friendly? Hermits? How much of the beach is underwater or impassable during high tide? How can you find out when it will be high tide?

9. Is a particular beach reasonably flat or is it steeply sloping into the sea? Does that make it harder to hike along?

10. Can you camp at or near these beaches? Should arrangements be made in advance? What are the busy/open seasons?

11. Is food available at any of these beaches? Which?

All year? Can you cook on or near the beaches? Any restrictions?

12. Is it dangerous to stay at these beaches at night? Or leave your vehicle unattended while hiking during the day?

13. Can you surf between Santa Barbara and San Francisco? Where? Are rental boards available? Where? Cost? Security required?

14. What kind and amount of clothing and sunscreen is needed on these beaches? Can you go barefoot or do you need shoes? Sandals or sandproof running shoes?

15. If you could pick the three most interesting beaches, offering the widest variety of activity, beauty, and flora/fauna, which would they be? Why? How can one specifically get to these three sites?

16. Following up on (15), the next three? What are the three worst places—and why?

General public readers would eagerly devour a story incorporating this information, whether in Chicago or elsewhere, if the facts are accompanied by quotes, visuals, anecdotes, and other telling details that add color and spunk.

Special interest readers require more tightly targeted stories. If your goal is an article in *Sea Kayaker* rather than the *Chicago Sun-Times*, your readers' expectations would naturally center around the sea and kayaking. To fulfill these expectations, you would first make yourself familiar with sea kayaking in general (read back issues of the magazine itself, for instance). You'd then want to find out where along this coast sea kayaking is done (which would lead you to the zone extending from Nipomo to Morro Bay). To complete your survey, you would interview any sea kayakers you could locate. All this would allow you to devise a set of questions from which you'd later compose a query to the editor. The result could be an article of fresh interest to the readers of *Sea Kayaker*.

This chapter provided you with an overview of the travel writing profession and of how travel writers go about their business. The rest of this book deals with the nitty-gritty of the profession—in hopes of providing you with the knowledge and tools to begin your own career or hobby of travel writing.

PART TWO

Before the Trip

CHAPTER 2

Getting Organized

Many travel writers never take the "big trip," a major excursion undertaken for fun and profit. Instead they specialize in one region, almost always where they live, probably where they were born, and about which they know best. Sometimes they write about other regions as well, usually in conjunction with a business or family trip.

Yet because the big trip requires the fullest use of all the travel writer's professional skills, this book will focus on it. For writing jaunts of a more modest scope, pluck what you need from the spread of skills described in these pages.

At this point I'd like to introduce a checklist that shows you all the steps needed for a big trip: preparing for it, taking it, and writing and then selling your articles about it. We'll spend the rest of the book bringing each step to life. (Any terms not explained in the checklist—*query letters, query responses, feasibility study*)—will be defined later as needed.)

Big Trip Checklist

1. Select a place you want to visit, can afford, and where there is likely to be sufficient material for

Ft. Lauderdale

many articles. If you route yourself wisely almost any site qualifies.

2. Determine whether the time you can travel is the best time to go to that particular site. If it will be under water, scorchingly hot, buried in unskiable snow, or just plain miserable, pick another season in which to visit.

3. Assuming your trip is well timed, figure out precisely how many hours or days you need to travel, how much time you want to spend at the ultimate site, what percentage of the time you should allot to writing-related tasks, and how much idle time you want or need.

4. Plot a rough travel itinerary, remembering to select sites for articles en route, if possible.

5. Research everything reasonably accessible about your ultimate destination(s) and any of the locations you plan to visit en route. Research articles that have been written about these sites, in which publications they appeared, what topics and angles they chose, and so on. Then complete a feasibility study, composing as many market lists as you have subjects to sell.

6. Develop both a writing and a sales plan. Leave ample time between the initial planning and the trip itself (as much as six months is advisable) because you will need to send queries and receive responses, a process as vital to your status with the IRS as it is to the direction and success of your writing.

7. Send query letters to the top magazines on your lists. If you receive a rejection, move on to the next publication on that list, querying until you get a "go-ahead."

8. When you receive positive replies, study the last three issues of each publication and draw up a rough outline of the kind of material each seems to prefer: facts, quotes, anecdotes, types of photos (black-and-white [b/w] or color, vertical or horizontal, people or scenery, etc.). Take this outline on-site with you.

9. If the publications have someone you can contact at the site, get letters of recommendation or introduction. Get other letters of introduction as well, if they are commonly used in the area. These letters can be from government officials, the clergy, academics, friends—anyone who has useful contacts or can open doors in the country you'll visit.

10. Before leaving double-check everything related to your trip: itinerary, tickets, layovers, equipment, writing tools, clothes, glasses, immunizations, medication, and so on.

11. Go and have fun! You should be so well prepared that all you have left are the interviews, verifications, and plenty of photo taking. (a) Complete the work on your queried go-aheads first, then gather material for later newspaper articles or magazine post-trip queries. (b) Acquire any local printed material you can use, to read now and pluck from later. (c) Fill your notebook(s) with quotes and anecdotes; verify facts. (d) Take many, many photos (far cheaper to toss out the losers than to fly back for that "one key shot").

12. Back home get your photos developed: proof sheets for b/w's, paper-mounted slides for color.

13. Write your queried go-ahead articles. Take time to compare your final rough draft with the articles in the latest issue of the magazine. Edit, write, edit,

write, then send the package (text, photographs, maps, etc.) to the editor. Do this for all the go-aheads before or by the deadline(s).

14. Send post-trip query letters regarding those sites you visited or those topics you investigated but did not query beforehand. You may need to do some of the same research that you did for the queried articles, including a full feasibility study, of which the market list is a part. As you receive positive responses to these queries, write the copy, select the photographs, and sell them.

15. In the meantime write your newspaper travel articles and other nonqueried pieces and send them out, taking care not to glut a market. For example, if most of your articles are about the Amazon, send them to the newspapers every few months, or even every month, but not three articles at once! Alternating with your Amazon pieces, submit those written about other sites.

16. Submit your published pieces for reprints or query for rewrites. Look to syndications that sell abroad for resales too. If you have scraps of facts left over, work them into fillers (items of one page or less) and get those out. Find a market for your good, unsold photographs (read *Photographer's Market* to see what can be done with them).

17. Gather and itemize your receipts for tax purposes.

Next, let's focus on four key areas from the Big Trip Checklist that are vital to planning our big trip. First, you must pick a destination and make an itinerary, determine how long you can stay, decide how much money you can afford to spend, and select writing tools you'll need. Second, see what is available in print about that area: articles, books, guides, and maps—then review them. Third, you must create a writing plan, and fourth, a sales plan (the last two areas will be covered in Chapter 3).

WHERE TO GO AND WHAT TO TAKE

Where and When

Choosing a destination is often the easiest part. Make a wish list and shoot for the top. Time and money will then determine how far up that list you actually go!

Almost anywhere in the world can yield good copy. In fact, where you go is less important than your ability to discover those topics that will appeal to editors and readers. I apply a simple rule of thumb: What grabs my attention or piques my curiosity will do the same for others.

Given the above, the time of year that you travel can influence the salability of your articles. Some sites work well all year whereas others are definitely tied to the seasons. Yosemite offers copy for articles about cross country skiing in the winter, surviving inner-tube river rides in the spring, sheer outdoor magnificence in the summer, and superb riverbed hiking in the fall. But Siberia in the winter or Panama during the rainy season are hard to sell to even the most generous editor—unless you discover a secret delight that any editor would be happy to reveal to his or her readers.

As with choosing a destination, your length of stay is also determined by the uncommitted time you have and the funds you can spend.

I use two guides to measure desired trip time in advance: how many hours I like to work each day and how many on-site hours I feel each article requires. I like to work four hard hours a day, preferably in the morning, during which I observe, gather information, and take photos. In addition, I figure six hours of on-site time will be required for each major article. So if I send out a flock of query letters each suggesting an article about a different topic, and four return with positive replies, I will need six half-day periods to gather the basic requirements, six full days there.

Why do I work only four hours a day? Because I want to have fun on the trip too. But I don't necessarily spend the rest of my time gawking or carousing. I might walk or cycle, camera and notepad in hand. Or enjoy a harp concert, interviewing and snapping photos as well as listening. Or visit a now-retired adventurer and tape our conversation. These activities could easily find their way into other articles.

Prudence also suggests that I add another day or two, in case I find a super article idea that simply begs for my full attention, in addition to the other commitments I've made in advance.

So now we're up to eight days at the prime destination. How many days then, if any, can I add for writing/touring stops coming and going? Or similar stops at places within easy distance of the prime destination?

Other points: (1) Remember that you can lose or add a day when you cross the international date line. (2) Jet lag is real: it reduces your ability to work and think at full capacity, so factor it in when traveling longitudinally. (3) Much of your first and last day can be spent simply getting to and from the airport, with delays at each step.

Given all these considerations, when you ask yourself how long you can spend, remember: Too much time is always better than too little.

Money

How much money can you afford to spend? How much do you have and how much will the trip cost? How much will you earn from it? And later, after you've created a clientele that gives you assignments and pays in advance, how much will you need up front? Answer those questions and you will know approximately how much capital you will need on hand.

At the outset assume that no editor is going to give you an advance, however eye-popping your query. At this point all the editor knows is that you have a good idea and can write a smashing query. If the article is as good, you'll be paid soon enough (by the editor's lights); if it isn't, thank God you paid for the trip yourself!

Since it's almost certain that you will pay for your first trips out of your own pocket, you must figure out what you can afford. Trim the sail to match the wind. Prepare an estimated budget, then adjust the distance and time on tour to match what you can comfortably afford to spend. You'll be nervous enough traveling afar to research and write for vaguely known editors and unknown readers without mortgaging your house and car!

What must you take into consideration when planning your budget? Suzanne Hogsett's *Bargain Travel Resource Book* (Travel Easy, 1991) offers an easy-to-use worksheet, which I've slightly modified in Figure 1.

It used to be that whatever you calculated, it was wise to bring about a third more in traveler's checks, just in case. Now, with credit cards acceptable worldwide, that wisdom is a bit dated, although a few hundred dollars in twenties come in very handy in small, rural towns where the cards (or you) may be suspect. I've included a line for emergency money in The Estimated Budget Worksheet.

Once you know the approximate cost and the length of time of your trip, get out a map and a schedule book and block out the area you can afford to visit and the time you can afford to invest.

Figure 1 Estimated Budget Worksheet

```
FIXED COSTS
Airfare (_____ per person x
       _____ people)                    $ _____

Train, bus passes, etc.                 $ _____

Car rental                              $ _____

        TOTAL FIXED COSTS              $ _____

VARIABLE COSTS
Transportation (tickets for
   train, boat, bus, subway,
   taxis, other, including
   costs for transport porters
   and other personnel)                 $ _____

Food (restaurant meals,
   groceries, nonmeal drinks,
   snacks, other)                       $ _____

Lodging (hotel/motel, camp-
   site, hostel, family, other,
   including costs for hotel
   porters and other
   personnel)                           $ _____

Sightseeing (admission fees,
   sightseeing tours, other)            $ _____

Entertainment (movies,
   plays, shows, other)                 $ _____
```

*Rental car additional
   expenses* (gas, tolls,
   parking, other) $ _____

Shopping $ _____

Other expenses (equipment
   rental, lessons, other) $ _____

Pre- and post-trip expenses
   (immunizations, passports,
   and visas; guidebooks and
   maps; clothes, luggage, and
   travel goods; camera, film,
   and development; other) $ _____

   TOTAL VARIABLE COSTS $ _____

Multiply the Variable Costs
   by 1.2 to allow for a
   margin of error of 20%:

           TOTAL ADJUSTED
           VARIABLE COSTS $ _____

Add the Total Fixed Costs
   and Total Adjusted
   Variable Costs:

           TOTAL ESTIMATED
               TRIP COST $ ===============

Personal Items

What remains of the preplanning is figuring out which
personal items and writing tools you will need on your
trip.

First, keep in a safe place all tickets and documentation
(passport, visas, tourist cards, personal identification

cards, credit cards, letters of introduction, vaccination certificate). Check these regularly before and especially during your trip to make sure they haven't been stolen. In addition, pack all necessary legal papers, plus a driver's license for a car rental and a copy of your car insurance, if valid in that area.

If you're traveling abroad, bring at least $15 in small currency to tide you over until you can get your American dollars exchanged for the local currency. I bring about $20 in U.S. singles, which are the best kind of tip in some countries.

Bring a watch that you know how to operate, since time changes are the bane of travel writers. A reliable, inexpensive alarm clock is also valuable and makes an appreciated tip for the maid at the last hotel.

One umbrella per person if it might be wet, proper attire for normal and inclement weather, and always a second pair of comfortable shoes are other essentials.

Remember to include prescriptions for all medicine, lest you be jailed as a junkie, and if you wear glasses, bring a second set, or at least a recent lens prescription should the first set get lost or damaged.

Pack at least one full set of proper, conservative business clothes (including a tie for men) for interviews and other similar occasions.

Business cards are very useful abroad. They can include personal information as well as professional (you can have "Professional Travel Writer" set in bold type at the top!). You might also bring evidence of your intent, that is, query, go-ahead, or assignment letters. Even a copy or two of recent articles in print.

Tools of the Trade

As a travel writer you will need a camera, two if possible: one for color slides and one for b/w's, 35mm or larger.

Plus filters, a sturdy carrying case (or two), plenty of film, and waterproof/weatherproof coverings are essential.

In addition, tape recorders, small and battery-run, are very useful for interviewing and keeping personal observations. Include an extra set of batteries and plenty of cassettes, particularly if they are an odd size.

You will also need file folders (which you may be able to buy locally). Steno pads too, and perhaps some large manila envelopes to hold receipts, booklets, and anything worth keeping that you pick up.

I like to carry an old manual typewriter, worth no more than $25, to bring my notes up every evening. I tape the purchase receipt inside its cover and, at that price, it will pass customs in any country.

You will have additional needs, idiosyncratic to you. Mine include running shoes, trunks, and sweatbands. Remember—you're not headed to boot camp or a monastery! Bring whatever you need to turn your working trip into a thoroughly enjoyable adventure!

THE RESEARCH PLAN

There are two very important reasons why you need to study what's been said about your destination before you go. The first, so you have solid information about potential articles around which you will write your query letters. The second, so you can use your time most effectively once you're there.

Some of the sources you will use are predominantly factual: maps, weather charts, hotel and tour lists, encyclopedias, even promotional sheets and fliers from tourism bureaus and the countries themselves (although the objectivity of the latter may not be absolute!).

The more subjective accounts can be particularly helpful. These are usually articles written by other travel writers like yourself. Going as far back as ten years, locate all accounts in print through the *Reader's Guide to Periodical Literature* (or its computerized equivalent, both located in your library's reference section), academic indexes, and the respective newspaper indexes (we'll discuss this in greater detail in the next section). Make a copy of each article.

Then draw a large grid on a sheet of paper. On the left side list all the attractions mentioned in the articles, top to bottom. Along the top, each heading a vertical column, list an article, its author, publication, and date, from the oldest to the most recent. In each box indicate whether the particular attraction was mentioned in the particular article. Put a plus or minus to show a strong positive or negative reaction. Add any key words the author used about it: "Not worth the time," "Spectacular," "See at night," and so on. This exercise will show you what other travel writers thought was worth seeing, how reactions have changed over time, and may reveal lesser-known features you might also want to investigate.

Before leaving home you will know what you want to see at a particular site, the restaurants and hotels worth exploring, local cuisine you should sample, seasonal activities to consider, items to buy, problems others have encountered. Between the objective fact sheets and the more subjective reporting you'll be able to prioritize your time.

At this point you'll also be able to ask two important questions: "Is the promised article feasible to write?" and "Is it feasible to sell?"

You can answer the first question now (we'll address the second in Chapter 3). If your research has unearthed a solid article about your topic—all the better if several have seen light—you can rest assured there is something to write about.

Now you must read those accounts, add information from other sources, and based on these materials write three or four relatively short paragraphs about the topic in a query letter to an editor that promises more depth and a current review of the topic when you visit the site. Your letter says to the editor, by implication: Here is something your readers will want to know about, it exists, I will look into it more fully when there and can give a reliable, interesting, and accurate account of it when I return. Are you interested?

At this point let me share a 15-step process called "How to Prepare and Market Magazine Articles That Sell" from another of my writing books, *How to Sell More Than 75% of Your Freelance Writing* (Prima). You can use this checklist for any travel pieces you wish to compose.

How to Prepare and Market Magazine Articles That Sell

1. In one sentence, what is the subject of the article you want to write and sell?

2. Who would benefit from reading your article? Who would be most interested? What kinds of readers would select your specific subject from a variety of choices? Rank all those potential readers in order, placing those who would derive the most benefits first.

3. Which publications do these readers buy and read? Prepare a market list of those publications that are the most likely to buy your manuscript.

4. In addition to the publications checked in (3), it is necessary to review the broader publishing field for articles similar or identical to yours. Therefore, you must check both the *Reader's Guide to Periodical Literature* and specific subject indexes for at least the previous three years, then

(a) list the articles that are closest to your subject, in order, with the most similar first: subject, author, title, publication, page reference, length, and when they appeared. Where the subjects appear to be very similar, how does yours differ?

(b) cross-check newspaper indexes for the past three years and provide the same information.

5. Have the publications listed in (3) and (4) printed articles within the past three years that are similar to the one you propose?

6. After each publication, note the name of the person you should contact (editor, managing editor, etc.), with title and address. Then provide the following information about each publication:

(a) Does it pay on acceptance or publication?

(b) How much does it pay for articles as long as yours?

(c) Does it prefer a query or a direct submission?

(d) How often is it published?

(e) What percentage of it is written by freelancers?

(f) What is its preferred manuscript length?

(g) Is any other information provided that will affect its placement on your list?

7. Now rank your market list in priority order, based on when the buyers pay (on acceptance or on publication), how much, the frequency of publication, and the percentage of freelance material used per issue.

8. Read the latest issues of your target publication, front to back. Select the articles that are the most similar, in form if not topic, to the piece you will prepare. Outline each article. Write out the lead and conclusion of each, by hand. Attempt to

identify the publication's readers by age, sex, occupation, income range, education, residence, and other pertinent factors.

9. To verify the availability of resource information

   (a) read as many of the articles in (5) as necessary or possible, then list the sources of information found in each,

   (b) consult the card catalogue and list books you will refer to for factual information: title, author, call number, date of publication, and library, and

   (c) list the people you should consult for additional information and quotes, working with the reference librarian for information that you do not already have: their name, position, and current affiliation (if related to the topic), academic title and degrees (if relevant), and reasons for their being consulted.

10. From the information you've gathered on the specific target publication and the research you've done on your topic, select the material needed to write a professional query letter. Verify its accuracy.

11. Write a selling query letter to an editor of your target publication. If you do not receive a positive reply, write a query letter to the editor of the next publication on your list, and so on, one editor at a time, until an editor does respond positively. Repeat as much of (9) as necessary for each new publication queried.

12. When you receive that positive response to your query, plan your article to determine what is still needed to finish it.

13. Complete the needed research.

14. Write the manuscript in final draft form. Include, on separate paper, at least five additional, different leads.

15. Select the best lead, edit the draft, type a final manuscript (keeping a copy), and mail it, with illustrations (if needed and available), to the editor who gave you the go-ahead.

The most profitable hours for a trip are spent at home, often months before you pack. In those hours you gather information, ideas, opinions, quotes; you look at other articles, read books, and study photographs, slides, and video travelogues. It's called research. Better before the trip, so you know what you must see and where it is and why it's crucial for your articles, than after you're back!

Libraries

There are two kinds of libraries for travel writers: your own at home, and everybody's, in town or at a local university. To function as a professional writer certain resources are mandatory for your personal library. To begin, you need a dictionary, a thesaurus, and a general atlas.

The dictionary should be reasonably current and comparable to *Webster's New Collegiate* (or *New World*) *Dictionary*. Even though most word processing programs include a spell checker, real writers need to get their hands on real dictionaries. A writer avoiding a dictionary is like a pianist practicing on paper keys.

You need a thesaurus for the same reason. Good writing isn't hit-or-miss when it comes to words. It's precise, the right word for a specific meaning. Winston Churchill urged "short words rather than long, old words rather than new"—so use your thesaurus to find the exact word, and when appropriate choose the short, old, comfortable word.

Don't spend hundreds of dollars on a multicolored atlas that will become obsolete the next time an island changes its name. Buy an inexpensive atlas that gives you a current overview of continents, nations, and topographical features, then add to your information before the trip with more detailed maps (either from a library or a good map store).

You'll also need a current *Writer's Market*, which you can update monthly through the *Writer's Digest Magazine*, available at all public libraries. If you are pursuing photography with the same vigor, then *Photographer's Market* will also be needed.

You'd be surprised how often you'll turn to an almanac if you have one at hand. Buy either the current *Information Please Almanac* or the *World Almanac and Book of Facts*.

Those are the absolute essentials, unless your grammar is shaky. If so, add a basic English grammar handbook.

Travel writers in for the long haul tend to fall into two camps: generalists and specialists. Generalists add assorted, eclectic items to their shelf. Specialists stock up on everything available about a country, a region, or even city. Since collections like this grow over time, there's no reason to invest heavily in your home library at the outset, especially if you're lucky enough to live near a well-stocked public library or, even luckier, a good college or university library. What they don't have, they can get nationwide through interlibrary loan.

Why so much research? So you know what to expect and what to see before you go (and what to stress in your query letters) and so you won't have to spend hours on-site gathering this information. You'll also know what to look for and where to get more information when you return.

I always start with an encyclopedia, to get a quick, comprehensive overview of the area or subject. From the general encyclopedia—like the *Encyclopaedia Britannica* or the *Encyclopedia Americana*—I might move to a specific one. When checking into gray whales and their migration, for example, I continued with the *Encyclopedia of Science and Technology* to find out more about cetaceans.

Akin to the encyclopedia is a specific sourcebook for travelers called *Webster's New Geographical Dictionary*, ideal for the spelling of place names, the populations of cities and countries, and other such details.

While at the library you'll find its card catalogue (manual or computerized) a primary tool for your research. Check four things: the books in stock (and their call numbers), cross-references for your topic, any microfiche material listed, and any microfilm material noted. Follow up the cross-references (so you can find more books related to your topic) as well as the microfiche and microfilm items.

Then head for the stacks, browsing each call-number area to see if something else is there that wasn't catalogued or was listed under another heading but nonetheless meets your needs. Write down the key call information about each book and check out the most important ones.

You may have to use the library machinery to read microfiches (usually found at academic libraries) and microfilm (most often used for back issues of magazines and newspapers).

Beginners tend to ignore microfiche altogether, either because they don't know about it or haven't bothered to learn how to use it. Microfiche consists of transparent plastic sheets containing miniscule photocopies of book pages, which are read on a magnified light machine.

They are absolute boons to historians and as valuable
for travel and history. An example shows how.

A while back I was writing a series of articles on the
year 1876, when I noticed that three things dating from
that year had been preserved on microfiche in the library
where I was doing research. Two were guidebooks of
the 1876 Philadelphia Centennial Exposition, each many
hundreds of pages long with superb line drawings of
the exhibits, including the new Otis elevator, a
revolutionary new floor covering called linoleum, and
a novel sound machine being displayed by Alexander
Graham Bell called, later, the telephone.

Of equal interest on the third microfiche was the diary
of an Illinois lad, Jerry Bryan, who had gone to Deadwood
in the Black Hills, drawn by a new gold rush. The diary,
An Illinois Goldhunter in the Black Hills, was reproduced exactly as written. Where else could I have found
this firsthand account of actual events occurring on
August 2, 1876?

> About noon a man was found just a cross the creek
> Dead, cause of Death poor whiskey. An exciting day
> in Dead Wood. The fun commenced early this morning
> by a crowd of 20 armed men escorting a Murderer
> through Town. Just after dinner Wild Bill was Shot
> through the Head. Killed instantly. While the crowd
> was Debating whether to hang the assassin or not.
> Reports came from Crook City that the Indians have
> Surrounded the Town and that help was wanted. All
> those that could get Horses went down to render
> assistance. Just at Sundown a Greaser came in with
> an Indian head. This caped the climax. [Wild] Bill
> and evry thing else was thrown in the Shade....It is
> getting to dangerous here to be healthy. (Illinois State
> Historical Society, 1960)

"Wild Bill" was Hickok. Less than a month before he, his friend and fellow scout of earlier days "Buffalo Bill" Cody, and a prostitute named "Calamity Jane" had been camped together near Deadwood when they heard of Custer's "last stand."

I wouldn't have been able to add this colorful bit of history to my article if I hadn't been roaming through the microfiche. Another good source for authenticity and verve are old newspaper accounts, found on microfilm.

To infuse history into travel, check the *New York Times Index* for a particular date, plus some days before and after. See what was reported, then call up the microfilm copy of the actual edition. Local newspapers may also have indexes, and most have files or a morgue that they will let you use, particularly if you're a writer. Although the major indexes seldom list travel articles per se, news about specific locations in the United States is listed. Local files and morgues may index the travel articles they have used.

Most direct travel reference material, though, will come from magazines and books. The *Reader's Guide to Periodical Literature* covers most of the major consumer magazines and is both well indexed and readily available in libraries. When I went to the Amazon for a three-week writing trip I listed every article about Belém, Santarém, and Manaus, and also Quito and Bogotá (for stops on the way back). I then made a copy of the articles for my grid and for all the extra facts and observations they contained. (Some libraries now use the computerized *Magazine Index* instead of, or in addition to, the *Reader's Guide*.)

In-flight magazines (available on airplanes) usually aren't listed in the *Reader's Guide*, so I'll discuss them below in "Other Sources." Articles in thousands of other magazines, journals, and newsletters aren't listed in the *Reader's Guide* either. Most of these are academic and are listed in scholarly indexes available in college or university libraries. Almost every academic discipline has one: business, biological sciences, modern languages, literature, and nursing has three.

To locate books on your topic, check the card catalogue at your local library. For books not available locally but currently in print, check the *Subject Index to Books in Print.* You can get these books in one of three ways: check with nearby libraries, contact bookstores (which can order what they don't have on hand), or ask the reference librarian to check larger holdings to see if the book is available through interlibrary loan.

Although interlibrary loan is very effective, it should be your last recourse because it often takes too much time. Nevertheless, it can be a great asset. When I was writing my thesis in history, titled "The Mormon Battalion in the Mexican War," I needed a pamphlet that had been printed circa 1846 in Council Bluffs, Iowa. I discovered that only one copy was extant, in a college library in Walla Walla, Washington. They "loaned" me the original (rather than merely a copy), which I received in five days! (For this service you usually pay less than a dollar plus postage and copying charges, if necessary. A huge bargain!)

Even more effective, and forever helpful, are the "angels of the stacks," the reference librarians. If you do the base work—checking the catalogues, stacks, cross-references, and other obvious sources—they will help you zero in from there. Tell them you're a writer to whet their appetite even more. (Later, a copy of the printed article with a note of thanks for their help in making it possible is always appreciated.)

Another quick way to find other sources is to check the bibliographies of the sources you do use. Your library even has bibliographies of bibliographies! And biographical information abounds. My two favorites are the

Biography Index and *Current Biography.* Also check the many versions of *Who's Who.*

Larger libraries and academic libraries usually have a map or cartography section—windfalls for travelers since the topographic and other maps available here are often far more detailed and useful than those you can buy. Better yet, you can usually make copies to take with you. Ask for town, historic, or cultural maps as well.

Probably the least-known gold mine for travel writers is the "vertical file." More common in local libraries, this is a repository for the odd-sized things that don't fit well on the shelves: maps, menus, guidebooks, clipped articles, catalogues, photographs, and the like. I once found a woman's personal diary of an Ecuadorian train trip from Quito to Guayaquil that she had taken a decade earlier. Several years later I took the same trip! (Or tried to. When our train hit a burro and nearly tumbled into a canyon far below, we were hurried off. We hiked to the Pan American Highway and took a bus several hours back to Quito, Guayaquil unseen.)

Finally, the most useful items for a coming trip, current guidebooks, may or may not be found in your library— or may have a waiting list months long! However, these are usually available in bookstores so let's discuss them next.

Bookstores

Whether you're a well-heeled travel writer or a footloose student, somebody has written a guidebook for you. The trick is to find it, then use it.

You might try the library first. Amazingly my library once had the very copy I needed still wet from the press! But most of the time you will have to buy one from the bookstore.

The larger bookstore chains have travel sections that usually sell the better-known guidebooks, those by Frommer, Fodor, Waldo, and sometimes Fielding or Baedeker. Be sure to read the contents closely to see if the emphasis of a particular guide meets your needs. For museums, Baedeker is best, for low-cost housing, Frommer, and so on. Look for the most recent edition, of course. Most updates occur in the fall.

In this age of specialization, boutique bookstores are flourishing. Most cities have a travel/map store replete with dozens, maybe hundreds, of guidebooks to everything from backpacking the Bavarian Alps to busing over the Andes (a trip taken once!) to finding your way through Melbourne or Marrakesh.

Why are such guidebooks valuable for travel writers? Because they highlight the key attractions; give times, dates, and prices; list taboos; put some objective structure under the puffed prose of most articles you will read about the location; and can save you a bundle in housing and food costs. In addition and very important, in your query letter about a site yet to be seen, much of the information on which you base your proposal to the editor (and which you slant to the magazine's readers) comes from these guidebooks.

At the bookstore you can also buy phrase books for the area to be visited, if the folks for some reason don't speak English. Some bookstores even sell newspapers or magazines from other states or countries. Buy these too!

Other Sources

In-flight magazines contain excellent articles about the airlines' ports of call, plus events, calendars, cost comparisons, and other travel-related information. Alas, they are seldom found in libraries or listed in the magazine indexes. Sometimes an airline will send you a copy if you contact their main office. You might ask the reservation clerk at the local airport (if it is served by that airline) to snag a current copy. Or you might check the in-flight magazine section of *Writer's Market* for specific titles. You can then write to the respective editors and ask for copies.

The federal government has scores of books, booklets, pamphlets, and maps that simply await your request or purchase. The government publications section of a large library will have numerous guides to federal publications. You can also contact Consumer Information of the U.S. Travel Service (U.S. Department of Commerce, Washington, DC 20230).

When I was a student in Bahia (Salvador), Brazil, we were provided with a booklet about that country prepared by the State Department. It was right on target and full of how-to details. Check both the Departments of State and Defense (the latter, if our military is or recently was stationed there) for these publications.

For parks and outdoor activities, the National Park Service (Department of the Interior, Washington, DC 20240) is very helpful. Be specific about where you want to go and what you want to do.

State governments are eager to lure visitors and can provide detailed assistance. The same applies to cities, museums, historical societies, sports centers, and amusement parks. Write or call them; the general information number or address will get you routed to the right person.

Foreign countries are just as enthusiastic to help you tell others about their charms. Contact the travel promotion bureaus or the consulates in the larger U.S. cities (or the embassies in Washington, D.C.)—let your mail carrier bear the consequences! Request a current map at the same time, and a city map of a particular site, if needed. Glean the truth from this slick public relations material—and double-check the facts before you use them in print.

Maps can also be secured in person or by mail from auto clubs, like the American Automobile Association or the National Auto Club. If you tell them the route you have in mind, they can usually put together a packet for you. Sometimes they can handle a trip abroad as well.

Now that you have well researched your topic, you're ready to focus on the next steps: writing and selling your travel articles. You'll need to make writing and sales plans, both of which we'll discuss in the next chapter. And at the end of that chapter we'll look at an example of how to plan for a big trip, using the tools and guidelines covered up to that point.

CHAPTER 3

Your Writing Plan and Sales Schedule

THE WRITING PLAN

From your research you have (I hope) extracted specific topics that (1) you think others would like to know about and (2) you want to write about. List these topics under the heading "Pretrip Queries," and rank them according to your preference, placing the one you most want to pursue first. These are the topics you will actively market before you leave. Done right and with sufficient vigor, you should receive enough positive replies to ultimately cover your trip's expenses!

Now make a second list, under the heading "On-site Topics." Here you'll list potential articles to research while you're on-site; you'll query about these when you return and write them for sale later. Although it's always preferable to query about a topic in advance (especially for tax purposes), some topics simply cannot be queried at this stage. Usually there is too little written about them to create an honest query letter. Or the subject is so new that you're not sure there would be an article's worth of information when you arrive.

There can be other reasons too. Some years back when I was headed to Manaus and the Amazon I very much wanted to meet and write about a legendary jungle and river guide, the Bavarian adventurer Kurt Gluck. But I couldn't query for three reasons. One, almost nothing was in print about him at the time, though everybody on the Amazon knew tales of his exploits. Two, what I had heard about him as a college student in Brazil was about as believable as stories about Paul Bunyan, scant stuff on which to build a credible query. And three, guides have a way of being out guiding when you show up to interview!

So I put Gluck on my on-site topic list and sought him out the moment I arrived. I caught up with him just as he was about to take off—had I dallied ten minutes longer I'd have missed him entirely! We managed to squeeze in two days on the Rio Negro and the Solimões River, I as his boat boy while he showed the jungle and critters to very nervous tourists. I had plenty of time to interview him while we poled and putted about. I wrote query letters after my return, and many articles followed.

Some on-site topics will lead to exciting multiple sales. Others will be gossamer. Still others, nothing at all: rumor, factually wrong, or too dull. Given the last, pursue on-site topics until the first hint that no salable copy will result, then abandon them.

Pencil in a third list at this stage: "Newspaper Articles." Include anything that can be researched and photographed at the site. Newspaper pieces sometimes also take different slants from the go-ahead or on-site articles. You gather newspaper copy at the locale, then write about it when you return and submit it with a cover letter.

The three lists comprise your writing plan. Articles based on the positive replies from pretrip queries pay the cost of your trip, so pursue those most actively now.

Newspaper pieces are where you make your profit, and on-site items can be bountiful, blessed bonuses for post-trip queries and subsequent sales.

THE SALES SCHEDULE

When do I sell my articles? And how do I coordinate the research, preparation, and mailing to magazines and newspapers of original articles, rewrites, and reprints?

You sell your trip in four installments: (1) within three weeks of your return, you send articles to those magazines that gave you the go-ahead before you left; (2) to those magazines that respond positively to your post-trip query letters, you send articles three weeks from their reply; (3) to newspapers you submit articles accompanied by cover letters; and (4) you sell reprints—always after the item to be reprinted has actually appeared in print—and rewrites of articles already written.

Create a rough schedule for each trip that puts the selling opportunities (and other key steps) in a time flow. List the opportunities on the left and the dates or time periods on the right. (See the "Tentative Travel Itinerary" near the end of this chapter.)

Opportunities include (1) the feasibility study, (2) writing/sending pretrip query letters, (3) the trip itself, (4) writing/sending go-ahead articles from the pretrip queries, (5) writing/sending post-trip query letters, (6) writing/sending newspaper articles, (7) writing/sending rewrite query letters, and (8) writing/sending reprint cover letters.

Follow this schedule as closely as possible. Sometimes this may be difficult, especially when you don't have the luxury of, say, six months' anticipation (as we do for the Big Trip imagined here). You'll have to hustle to squeeze in your research, planning, and querying in the time you do have.

On the rarest of occasions an editor will want the copy rushed to print from the site, to beat a tight deadline, so the traditional three weeks after you return to prepare the manuscript won't work.

You have the most flexibility at the rewrite stage. Rewrites can be done the moment you return. You simply give a different spin to the material you gathered for your go-ahead articles. You can query for a rewrite as soon as you formulate the idea.

It's clear that most of what you write, from go-ahead articles to rewrites, comes from the success of your pretrip query letters. These should receive your utmost care and attention, because they are the seeds of your financial harvest. By knowing what you can sell before you leave you can custom design the articles, pinpointing precisely what you'll need once you arrive to make the writing work and saving hours of wandering-around time once you're on-site.

From these same pretrip go-aheads you should be able to rework several rewrites and reprints, even pulling out many of the facts for the newspaper pieces you'll write when you get home.

Most important, as we shall see in Chapter 4, pretrip queries lay the groundwork for later tax deductions. Simply sending queries proves that the purpose of your trip was to write (keep a copy of each query letter and response to prove it was sent!). And by getting positive replies, you prove that the intent of the editor was to seriously consider the article's purchase. Voilá!

Travel writers get one blessing that other writers don't: They can query well in advance of actually submitting their articles. In fact, they can begin querying as much as six months prior to their trip. The only stipulation is that they mention in the query (1) when they will go, (2) when they will return, and (3) when the editor can expect to have the copy in hand.

Sometimes departure and return dates are uncertain, so you must approximate. Nobody will be at the pier or airport checking. But you must be exact about when the editor will receive the article. Since three weeks is a magic time in article writing (the length of time it supposedly takes you to do a masterful job), you simply promise to put the material in the editor's hands three weeks after you return. If you're not sure when you'll be back, make sure that the promised date is three weeks after your *latest* possible return.

If you've already taken the trip, plan to have your copy to the editor three weeks from the date you receive a positive reply to your query—unless, very rarely, the editor wants it at another time.

Although we've touched on the basics of preparing a writing plan and sales schedule, these are complex tasks, mixed inextricably with the feasibility study and query letters. We'll address these topics more fully in Chapter 5.

Right now I want to show you how to plan for a big trip. I'll pursue pretrip queries and research those receiving positive replies before I leave. I'll also prepare a writing plan and a sales schedule. Then I'll be ready to go.

EXAMPLE: PLANNING THE BIG TRIP

I chose the new, united Germany for this writing jaunt because I had never been there before, it is now teeming with activity, and I think others want to read about it as much as I want to see it (see the map in Figure 2).

Figure 2 Germany

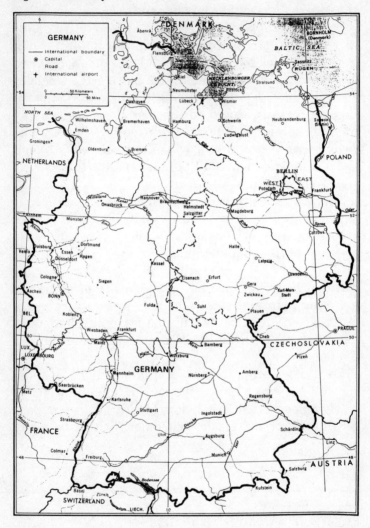

What was my thinking at the pretrip stage?

Time constraints dictate that this trip will be for two weeks maximum, and it has to occur in October because I want to include the Frankfurt Book Fair. This is a perfect time of year because I can hike in the Alps, after the summer flock has gone but before the snow and skiers arrive. I can afford to spend about $3,500, which should earn me at least $7,500 back. And since I will rent a car for the two weeks there what I bring as baggage is less important than if I had to tote it around Germany on my back or by train. I'll have no problem including a small, used typewriter to keep my notes current each night, plus my cameras, tape recorder, umbrella, and extra clothes. Mustn't forget my driver's license for the car rental.

If I'll be there 14 days and an article takes about a day and a half to research and photo, I can plan on nine magazine pieces, plus spin-off newspaper submissions later. I'll have to send different query letters for at least 9 different article subjects, or as many as 13 (adding half as many again), assuming that some queries, even if sent to all the markets in the order they occur on my prioritized list, won't result in positive replies.

Can I do it for $3,500? Time for a quick budget estimate, which I can adjust later as article ideas take form (see Figure 3).

Figure 3 Estimated Budget

FIXED COSTS		
Airfare (round trip, LAX-Frankfurt-LAX		$ 900.00
Train, bus passes, etc. N/A		0.00
Car rental		300.00
	TOTAL FIXED COSTS	$1,200.00
VARIABLE COSTS		
Transportation (boat trip)		$ 100.00
Food ($25 per day x 13)		325.00
Lodging ($60 per night x 13)		780.00

continued on page 54

Sightseeing	60.00
Entertainment (feeding interviewees)	125.00
Rental car additional expenses (gas & parking)	200.00
Shopping N/A	0.00
Other expenses	15.00
Pre- and post-trip expenses (film & processing; mailing)	300.00
TOTAL VARIABLE COSTS	$1,905.00
Multiply Total Variable Costs by 1.2 margin of error.	
TOTAL ADJUSTED VARIABLE COSTS	$2,286.00
Add Total Fixed Costs & Total Adjusted Variable Costs:	
TOTAL ESTIMATED TRIP COST	$3,486.00

As you can see, my budget just makes it! There is some slack, plus the $431 variable, which might not be needed at all if the winds blow a favorable dollar. Food is not cheap in Germany but breakfast (rolls and butter, a beverage, and sometimes cold cuts) is usually included in the hotel fee; one can also shop the local markets and eat for less. I assume that I may have to buy lunch or dinner for some people (to get interviews with them), so I've included entertainment costs. And the rental car might cost less than I've listed. On the other hand, there's nothing for a trinket for Aunt Tess (or anybody else). The boat trip may cost more, but perhaps I could shift some money from lodging and food. And the sightseeing fees might be more expensive. (Are beer halls considered sightseeing?)

How do I know these costs are representative? From a reliable travel agent who knows how to save my dollar; by following up Suzanne Hogsett's tips in *Bargain Travel*

Resource Book (Travel Easy, 1994); by looking through the current Fodor and Baedeker guidebooks in the bookstore; by asking people at the consulate; by reading other articles; and by talking to recently returned travelers (but be skeptical about what they say about costs—often their memories are faulty or costs have changed since they traveled).

How might I expect to earn $7,500 back? I figure I can get paid from four different fronts. To make this clear I write up an estimated earnings schedule.

Estimated Earnings

Magazine Articles	Nine sold at $500 each, including slides and photos	$4,500.00
Newspaper Articles	Eight different articles sold an average of 2.5 times each for $100 apiece	$2,000.00
Newspaper B/W Photos	Used with ten sales, at 1.5 photos per article and $12.50 per photo	$ 187.50
Reprints or Rewrites	Four magazine pieces sold at $250 each, including slides and photos	$1,000.00

The total income from sales would be $7,687.50, for a profit of $4,201.50. That's a 220% profit ratio over estimated costs. A low ratio, partly because of the high costs of traveling to and touring Germany. (Desirable ratios are in the 300% to 500% range, with 300% perhaps the average.) Three quick ways to improve the ratio: Be frugal, sell more, and sell to higher-paying markets.

Will I hold rigidly to these early plans? Maybe not. If I receive a go-ahead from a magazine paying $5,000 for copy and photos, I'd spend more than 1.5 days on it. Maybe a week. Or, based on my query replies, I might decide to zero in on one topic only, say hiking in the Alps, spend the entire two weeks gathering material for a dozen different but related pieces, and then focus on rewrites and specialty magazine articles when I return.

What's critical is that I have a general plan. I then send out query letters to test my plan and lay my tax deduction base (ultimately, neither I nor Uncle Sam care how I cover my expenses and earn a profit, as long as I succeed!). I start with a plan, then modify it if necessary.

Researching the Big Trip

Since I've chosen three specific focal points to see in Germany (Heidelberg, the Rhine, and the Black Forest/ Alps), and since arriving in Frankfurt is both far less expensive than other cities and is also closest to the three sites as a group, my pretrip research will be much simpler than if I'd simply said "Germany."

At this point, I head to the libraries (one local, the other at a nearby major university) and a specialty bookstore.

My local library offers a potpourri of resource tools: a computerized card catalog (but nothing newer than 1973 about Germany on the standard shelves related to travel or general description); a recently added newspaper index (alas, without many of the newspapers; Sunday copies only of the *New York Times*, for example, and those only a few years deep); a fairly comprehensive computerized magazine index (but the magazines kept only five years); the *Reader's Guide* intact and current; and a special, unlisted shelf section for travel abroad with the newest Baedeker's, a book by Robert S. Kane called *Germany at Its Best* (Passport Books, 1988), and

Craig Evans's *Trail Guide to West Germany* (Quill Paperback, 1982). Not too bad.

The university library is far more complete. Eight full trays of subject index cards (more than twelve hundred by the librarian's estimate). But at least 75% of them are in German! And most of the rest are very old, very academic, and very esoteric. Almost nothing about contemporary Germany, nothing at all since the reunification, and only a half-dozen books about travel or description. What they do have is interesting historically, particularly the earliest versions of Baedeker's guides, over one hundred years old.

The map library is a godsend: excellent topographical maps of each area I'd like to visit, to a scale of 4 cm = 1 km, including footpaths! These are particularly useful for hiking in the Garmisch-Partenkirchen and Mittenwald area of the Alps. Best yet, I can copy them on the spot!

The library also possesses a deep, reliable storehouse of periodicals and newspapers, on paper or microfilm.

My final expedition is to my local travel/map store, a hidden gem that can order what isn't on its well-stocked shelves. Here I find two up-to-date travel books about Germany that complete my background needs. (The university maps, though, are better than those available here.)

I read and skim the assortment of books from the three locations, check the few articles (copying what I may need later), and make reproductions of specific maps.

At this stage, from the assortment of available facts, I would normally prepare a grid, and from that grid select article topics that would serve as the heart of my pretrip query letters. I would also note other ideas that might find their way into newspaper print or later articles, queried when I return if anything materializes on site. Alas, no grid this time. Simply too little in print recently about any of the three focal points.

That's good news: Publications should be receptive to what I have to say, since each site is a legitimate travel prize. And bad news: I can't use others' observations to point me to the best stories. I'm on my own!

The Writing Plan for the Big Trip

Time now to ferret out nine good article ideas that I can cover well in two weeks, see if there are hints about what I might want to pursue in Germany and query about when I return, and come up with some newspaper subjects to cover on-site and write about later.

From my library research I see five likely article cores from the three sites I'd like to visit: Heidelberg; Frankfurt for the huge book fair; two cities nearby that are across the river from each other, Mainz and Wiesbaden; the Rhine River run from Rüdesheim to Koblenz; and the distant, mountainous area of Garmisch-Partenkirchen (and Mittenwald), which I'll call the hiking region.

Assuming two articles each from Frankfurt, the hiking region, and collectively from Mainz, Wiesbaden, and the river zone, plus three from Heidelberg, let's figure out the logistics first. Could all that be fit into the time frame? Yes, it will fit snugly if done this way:

Tentative Travel Itinerary

Days 1–4   Arrival, to Heidelberg (October 2–5)

Days 5–6   Frankfurt, at Book Fair (October 6–7)

Days 7–9   Mainz, Wiesbaden, Rhine River (October 8–10)

Days 10–13   Garmisch-Partenkirchen and Mittenwald (October 11–14)

Day 14   To Frankfurt, departure (October 15)

Article topics. What will the articles be about? Preliminary reading suggests the following topics:

Heidelberg: (1) *Das Schloss,* a spectacular castle that looms over the historic old center and Neckar River, with moats, gardens, the world's largest wine barrel, sunken walls, and staterooms, reachable by steps or cable car, with a day's worth of hiking on the *Königstuhl,* the mountain that looms over the castle.

(2) "Student Princeville," a look at what remains of the setting of Sigmund Romberg's operetta, site of the nation's oldest university and four museums. Arm-linked bands of playful students still comb the streets each night, beer halls their usual destination.

(3) Following in the footsteps of Mark Twain, as reported in *A Tramp Abroad* (1880), to see how Heidelberg (and the Rhine nearby) has changed. A humorous piece in keeping with Twain's commentary.

Frankfurt: (1) The Book Fair, with eighty thousand participants, not only the largest of its kind in the world but the latest in a historical tradition of fairs held in Frankfurt. Focus on the ten huge buildings in the *Messe*; zero in on one kind of display for a niche publication, like art, juvenile, calendar, or engineering books.

(2) One of Europe's little-heralded but top art centers, with three buildings to feature: the *Städelsches Kunstinstitut* (art museum that includes works by Rubens, Rembrandt, van Eyck, Botticelli, Monet, Picasso), *Liebighaus* (world-class collection of sculpture), and the *Museum für Kunsthandwerk* (a decorative-arts museum).

Mainz, Wiesbaden, Rhine River: (1) Tie-in to the Book Fair, since Mainz was the home of Johann Gutenberg, of movable-type and Gutenberg Bible (1455) fame. A visit to the Gutenberg Museum is the focus here, with its copy of that book and hand-illuminated Bibles that preceded it, and the presses of that and subsequent ages on display. Link with the baths, casino, and charm of Wiesbaden.

(2) Rüdesheim and Lorch, other upper-Rhine towns seen on a short river cruise to Koblenz, past the castles, monasteries, and Riesling vineyards, through the land of Lohengrin, narrow streets, and small museums.

Garmisch-Partenkirchen: (1) Hiking in the German Alps, starting with a four-mile jaunt to Grainau for the beautiful views, then the two most colorful gorges, the Partnachklamm and the Hollentalklamm, reaching the first on the tiny Graseckbahn cable car to an inn, then on to the narrow, deep, breathtaking trek aside the boiling torrents. Later, around the peaks that fringe the city, near the 9,782-foot *Zugspitze*, to the Hollen-Tal area, to enjoy the pines alone.

(2) Garmisch-Partenkirchen may be the world's top winter sports center, with skiing in every direction, the magnificent Ski and Ice Stadia from the 1936 Olympic Games, and sun almost every day. In October the cities rest up for the coming hordes, so the pace is comfortable, the towns' historic features can be appreciated, and nearby Mittenwald, on the Austrian border, beckons, tucked into the sheer face of a mountain and brimming with Bavarian buildings and dress. Will also mention Oberammergau a few miles off, site of the Passion Play every decade.

On-site topics. (1) Pull together material from all of the Frankfurt, Mainz, Wiesbaden, Rhine River, and Heidelberg articles to show how visitors can put together two or three super pocket trips if they have some extra days and are passing through Frankfurt.

(2) If I can gather enough material, create an instant orientation piece. What every German city seems to have, how to use the train station as the center, how to survive, the 20 key phrases that will keep you going, and so on.

(3) Drawing from the *Schloss* in Heidelberg, do a piece on Germany's castles, touching the ruins on the Rhine,

and indicating those open for visitation, staying, eating, and the like.

Newspaper articles. Since newspaper articles must also be fresh, I would surely write about Heidelberg, Frankfurt, and Garmisch-Partenkirchen. I would naturally include information gathered for the magazine articles, both queried and to-query. But I would also work in enough different information, quotes, and anecdotal material to create new copy.

In addition, perhaps a piece on Wiesbaden, city of the Romans and the public baths, and Mainz, across the river. "A place to visit if you're in Frankfurt with a day to kill." Take the tram from the airport to Wiesbaden an hour away, then another tram (which runs every 20 minutes) across the river to Mainz.

Perhaps an item on the autobahn, how it works—or, during rush hour on Friday, how it *doesn't*. The speed limits, open zones, the many rest and washroom stops along the way, and so on.

Another curiosity is the honor system used on Frankfurt's tram and bus systems, where you buy a pass but nobody checks or collects it. And what happens if you are caught in violation. Plus how well the whole thing works, and why.

Strolling the streets at night is fun to write (and read) about, whether in the big cities or the smaller Bavarian towns. What there is to do, where the locals go, what kind of fun you can have, concerns for safety, and more.

Since newspaper pieces are short (1,200–1,350 words is ideal), I may come up with 15 more topics on-site that I can later convert into good newspaper material. I plan the newspaper items least and last since they either flow out of the magazine research or they become obvious to me on-site and I gather what I need at the time.

The Sales Schedule for the Big Trip

Now I must figure out when I will foist these Teutonic masterpieces on the unsuspecting travel editors of America. And how I will get all the disparate parts of my master writing/selling scheme to work as a lucrative whole.

So it's time to develop a rough schedule for this trip that puts the selling opportunities (and other key steps) in a time flow, something like this:

Selling Itinerary

Opportunities	Date
Feasibility Study	April–October
Write/send pretrip query letters	April–October
Trip	October 1–15
Write/send go-ahead articles from pretrip queries	October 16–November 7
Write/send post-trip query letters	November 8–30+
Write/send newspaper articles	November 12–December 15+
Write/send rewrite query letters	December 1+
Write/send reprint cover letters	After articles are in print

This is my sales schedule! And it seems like a lot of lucre to extract from two weeks. A lot of reworking and reselling of the same information as well. I'd better get hustling and find some super ideas for those major magazine articles!

CHAPTER 4

Taxes and Rights:
Law and Strategy

TAXES

At this point it's a good idea to address taxes, before planning and taking the Big Trip. Your goal is straight-forward enough: How can you take your travel writing expenses as a business deduction? The answer is no less complicated: Do it, but be sure that you have full documentation to prove that your writing is indeed business related.

I'm not a tax expert, so please resolve any tax questions with an expert or the IRS. (This is a disclaimer!) What follows comes from reading the experts, checking with the IRS, following my own advice and faithfully paying taxes for years, and receiving invaluable assistance from an actual but in these pages anonymous IRS auditor (who attended my travel writing seminar and now allows me to bounce tax questions his way). And using plain old common sense.

For starters, the IRS allows you to deduct business expenses, but generally does not allow deduction of costs to pursue a hobby. Should you be brought in for an audit concerning your writing-related deductions (which is highly unlikely unless your numbers are grossly out of balance or they spin the wheel and it's your turn), the first question will surely be: "Was this a hobby or a business?"

Make your writing a *business*. You can have a regular job plus any other job that your energy, skills, and time permit. Uncle Sam encourages many jobs. Report your primary income, for which your employer deducts withholding and other taxes, on Form 1040. Report your other businesses, including writing, on Schedule C, using a separate schedule for each business. (If they are closely interwoven, like writing and photography, they can be included on the same form.)

All writers, like all businessfolk, have certain obligations related to properly filing their Schedule C. You must report, and be able to prove, all the income and expenses generated by your writing. That means that since you will almost always be paid by check, you should keep the stub of each payment. If that isn't clear enough, write the date, amount, and item sold on it. If paid another way, resist the inclination to simply pocket it. Note it on a sheet of paper, with the name and address of the payer, and report it as well.

Expenses can generally be recorded in one of four ways. (1) When paying by check, write on the memo line in the lower left-hand corner how that payment relates to writing, such as "writing/research" or "writing/supplies." (2) When using a credit card, get a receipt at the time or, if unavailable, note at the end of the month on your bank credit-card reconciliation sheet those items related to writing and how they are related. (3) If you pay by cash, get a receipt, even if you must prepare it yourself. Indicate on it the amount paid, what is being bought, and the date, then have the recipient sign it. (4) Keep a booklet with you or in the glove compartment of your car in which to faithfully note car expenses (include the date the car is used for writing-related activity, the mileage or odometer readings, and how it relates to writing) and those other expenses for which no receipt is possible: public phone calls, parking meters, coin-operated copy machines, and so on.

What kinds of expenses can writers in business generally deduct? Paper, pens, envelopes, stamps, other mailing costs, newspapers and magazines, typewriters and word processors if used primarily for business (you may need a log to prove this), the paper and software needed by the computer, a printer, cameras and tape recorders, a specific and clearly defined place to conduct the business (if in your home, check the IRS pamphlet for details), phone calls needed for writing, travel, and anything else the business requires.

At issue is whether the expenses were necessary for writing and for the proper operation of the business. Keep notes on why or how each expense was necessary should it be challenged in an audit years later. Entertainment expenses are a good example. If you and a few writing cronies slip out for lunch and a libation, that's hardly deductible. But if you take a client out to dinner to discuss your writing a newsletter for his firm, note the details on the receipt and claim it.

An auditor will be interested in your accounting, your receipts, and the volume of business you do, to see if yours is a legitimate business or simply a hobby that you'd like your not-so-rich Uncle Sam to subsidize. To help satisfy the auditor, keep a mailing record on which you record, faithfully, every query letter or actual manuscript you send out, the response (noted each time there is communication sent or received), and any income earned, with the date. The income should be matched by the check stub. These communications should be provable with copies of your queries or manuscripts and editors' responses.

What is the auditor seeking? Proof that you generated enough business activity, in the beginning, to at least potentially earn back your expenses; later, more income than expense. The guidelines now state that you should show a profit three years out of five. The IRS allows tooling-up costs and doesn't expect a profit (or conceivably even an income) the first year. But businesses can't lose money forever. Good documentation, a serious attempt to become solvent and profitable as quickly as possible, and prudent business practices count heavily in determining whether you are in business or enjoy an unprofitable hobby.

As a travel writer you must prove that the intent of your travel is to produce income. That the travel is a necessary expense to do business and not just a scheme to deduct a few years of globe-trotting. This is best done by planning your trip like other professional travel writers: in detail, in advance, and on paper, with plenty of proof as to why you are going, when, and what business results you expect.

Let's plot out a model trip now so you can take all your proper deductions. Start six months before the expected date of departure. Determine where you will go, create a realistic budget, and then complete a full two-pronged feasibility study (see Chapter 5). The goal of that study is the preparation and mailing of query letters to editors of the magazines most likely to print articles about your trip.

Query letters are a double blessing. Whatever the response, the letter itself states, or at least undeniably implies, that your intent is to travel to write articles, with the rough dates of travel noted. These letters clearly show that the purpose of your trip is business related.

Better yet, positive replies to query letters justify the expenses required to prepare the articles promised. Your goal is to try to get enough positive replies *before* you leave to cover your anticipated budget. Although editors almost never give assignments to new writers, their "let me see it," "send it to me," "send it on speculation," or anything similar and positive is, if followed up professionally, almost tantamount to a sale. You must incur travel costs to complete the promise. So by complying in good faith by submitting the manuscript or material promised in the query, the expenses involved *are* deductible, whether or not the articles are purchased.

How much can you deduct for each such positive query response? Deduct what the article costs to prepare, which can be determined either by exact costs or by taking the total costs of travel and operational expenses and prorating them to specific articles or projects.

There are four more ways you can earn your trip. One is to develop stories on-site, query about them when you return, and write when you receive the positive replies to those queries. The second is to gather information at the site and prepare newspaper travel pieces from it when you return, since newspaper travel editors generally don't accept queries, preferring to see the actual copy. The third way is to either resell the queried articles already written and sold, assuming the second or reprint rights are yours (more about rights later), or to rewrite those articles and sell them to different publications. And the fourth is to sell photos and illustrations to accompany the copy gathered on the trip.

All of which should result in far more income than expense, meaning that the costs related to the writing and photography are deductible—and the profits are taxable!

But what if you have no track record as a travel writer (or a writer at all)? Say you take a trip somewhere exotic and suddenly decide to become a writer, doing all the professional activity after you return? You can deduct only what you earn, up to the total of the writing-related costs.

Why? Because you didn't clearly establish the intent of the trip first, then back it up with sufficient documentation (query letters).

Again: Plan in advance, send out good query letters, establish a paper trail proving that the purpose of the trip is to write, then write and sell. Four things will let you survive an audit: sales, documentation, your businesslike approach, and the obvious volume of income-generating activity. The bonus? You'll probably bring in far more money than you spent!

EXAMPLE: THE TAX PLAN

My purpose is to earn back at least twice as much as my costs on the trip to Germany, and I wouldn't object at all if I could triple them. But I would object if I couldn't deduct the legitimate business expenses incurred gathering the raw data just because I hadn't convinced my taxing Uncle that what I was doing was very much a business.

So my first task, well before leaving, is to get a bevy of sharp, successful query letters in motion. I plan to write nine magazine pieces, a heavy load for a two-week trip, so I will write at least 9 queries, each about a different potential article, to nine editors. (Actually I'd probably send 13 different queries, since from that I'd more likely receive nine go-aheads before I leave.)

My querying goal is twofold: (1) to get each editor to say something positive indicating that he or she would buy or at least seriously consider buying the manuscript proposed, when submitted after I return, and (2) to at least equal the projected cost of the trip in potential income from those positive replies.

Why? Querying shows my intent: to travel to Germany to write articles. It promises the articles as a result of taking the trip and paying the necessary expenses to get there and secure the information (expenses like food, lodging, photography, and additional travel). It justifies the costs for a business purpose.

To make my tax plan clear, I'll diagram it (see Figure 4). The diagram defines my tax strategy, which is both perfectly legitimate and good business.

During the trip I also intend to create additional magazine articles, which I will query about when I return. I'll send other post-trip queries for rewrites of the articles queried before departure, to sell them in a different form to other magazines.

When I return I also intend to send at least eight different newspaper articles, each to many newspapers simultaneously. And, after the trip, I will sell reprints (or second rights use) of magazine articles to other publications once the articles have been in print (see below for a discussion of rights).

It's not enough, though, just to intend to do this. I must have sufficient documentation to prove that I did indeed execute a business plan. Therefore, I will keep a copy of every query sent plus a copy on the respondent's letterhead of every reply. And I'll do the same for all subsequent query and cover letters and replies to them.

As important as the number of items sold and money earned is the professional process by which the income is sought, to prove your business is legitimate and diligently pursued. To assist in this documentation, I keep a mailing record and files for each query/response. Although I list every query or direct manuscript submission on my mailing record, on page 71 is an abbreviated and exerpted form, with an entry for each of the five kinds of submissions.

Figure 4 Tax Plan Diagram

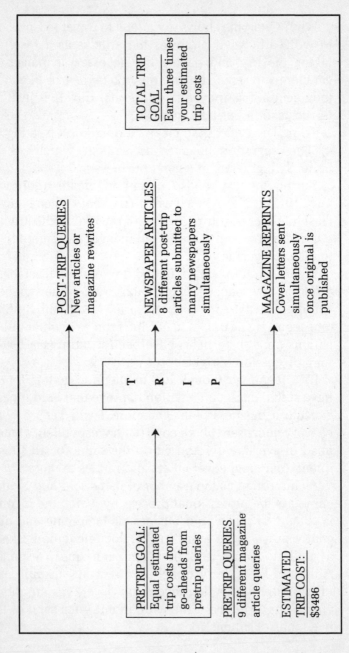

PRETRIP GOAL:
Equal estimated
trip costs from
go-aheads from
pretrip queries

PRETRIP QUERIES
9 different magazine
article queries

ESTIMATED
TRIP COST:
$3486

T
R
I
P

POST-TRIP QUERIES
New articles or
magazine rewrites

NEWSPAPER ARTICLES
8 different post-trip
articles submitted to
many newspapers
simultaneously

MAGAZINE REPRINTS
Cover letters sent
simultaneously
once original is
published

TOTAL TRIP
GOAL
Earn three times
your estimated
trip costs

Mailing Record

5/8	Q/ *Schloss*/Heidelberg	BBB Magazine
11/10	Q/ Pocket Trips	CCC Magazine
11/15	Wiesbaden/Mainz	DDD Newspaper
12/1	Q/ Moats at *Schloss*	EEE Magazine
12/25	*Schloss* reprint	FFF Magazine

The mailing record shows, respectively, the pretrip query, a post-trip query, a newspaper article, a rewrite of the pretrip query (after its resulting article has been in print), and a reprint of the article from the pretrip query.

On my actual mailing record I would have many more entries between most of these dates, and under each unrejected entry would be more information: date and type of reply, date of manuscript submission, information about the number and type of photos sent, other correspondence or exchanges, the date accepted or rejected, and the amount paid. For example, over a period of many months the first entry might look like that below.

Specific Mailing Record Entry

5/8	Q/ *Schloss*/Heidelberg	BBB Magazine

    6/1 —looks good, send
         ms
    11/7 —ms, 100 slides sent
    11/11—send caption 2
         slides
    11/12—2 expanded captions
         sent
    11/23—accepted ms/4 slides
    12/5 —check arrived, $585
    2/15 —article in March
         issue

The second part of my tax plan is to keep a daily accounting of expenses on the trip, plus all related costs before and after. I will keep receipts for each of those expenses in a large envelope, plus local driving and incidental expenses in a notepad in the glove compartment of my car. I will also note the currency rate every time I exchange money, to later convert the German expenses into U.S. dollars.

RIGHTS

Let's talk about rights as they pertain to travel writing, leaving further exploration of the legal pastures to those books written specifically about them, like Bunnin and Beren's *The Writer's Legal Companion* (Addison-Wesley, 1988).

Copyright first. When you write something it belongs to you. In a common law country when you create property (say a book or an article) the rights to that property are yours. But only that property: the actual words in the order in which they are written. You cannot copyright an idea, only the way you express it.

Moreover, if taken to court you will be required to prove that you wrote it first, if that is what is challenged. This will be easier if you register your work with the Library of Congress. You can call (202) 287-9100 at any hour and leave a message for them to send their registration forms to you, or you can contact your congressperson to receive a copyright packet.

You will be asked to submit two copies of the manuscript with a registration form and $20 to register your opus. Do as indicated for scripts, books, tapes, software, music, and lyrics. However, you may not want to bother with this for your articles. They are seldom worth the cost of taking a thief to court, frankly. And if you keep a clear paper trail—query letter, response, mailing record, and copies of the published article itself—you are in good condition anyway.

Can others use your words? Without your permission, they can use the facts and opinions you express, but not your exact words in the order you wrote them, except in small amounts (usually a paragraph is about the limit, but less if the original work was itself shorter, such as a poem or lyrics). And the source—you—must always be acknowledged. But ideas and impressions can't be copyrighted: they are in the public domain, for all to use. In fact, you probably used others' ideas and facts to help write your article!

Other rights attach to travel writing as well: all rights, first rights, and second or reprint rights.

These rights are defined as a contractual relationship between the author and the publisher that define what the publisher is buying. If a publisher buys your article on an "all rights" basis, for example, that means that the publisher can use your piece in that exact form (with some leeway for modest editorial rewriting) as often as he or she wishes, forever.

Although that sounds terrible, in truth it isn't bad. For one thing, there are few all rights buyers any longer, and they usually pay better. So sell it to them, then rewrite the piece! All they bought were the words in the order in which they were written. Do a major rewrite and resell the facts and ideas elsewhere. Two tips: Come at it from a significantly different angle the second time, changing the title, lead, and conclusion. And *don't* sell it to the original buyer's chief competitor. Hawk it to other fields!

Most publications buy first rights, meaning that they have the right to use that article first in their publication. You may not sell it again until it appears in print in the publication that purchased first rights. On rare occasions your manuscript is not used. In these cases you must have the rights returned to you by the publisher before you can sell first rights again.

Once your article has appeared in print, you are free to sell it to any other publisher on a second or reprint rights basis. (The terms are used interchangeably and mean the same thing.) Second rights means that it has been in print before and you are offering, on a nonexclusive basis, the opportunity to other editors to use the work on their pages. You can send a cover letter attached to a copy of the printed article that (1) promotes the contents of the article; (2) offers the article for sale, stating three points that the reprint buyer needs to know: who bought the first rights, when the article appeared in print, and that you are offering reprint or second rights; and (3) offers for purchase the photos that accompanied that article plus any other photos not bought or used by the original editor.

How specifically might these general guidelines on rights affect travel writers?

In the magazine field, the process is straightforward. Sell all or first rights to the best possible market, then sell reprints to all those who will buy them. The latter are almost always those who pay on publication.

Newspapers are usually interested in circulation or distribution rights, presuming that you will handle your own minisyndication and thus will not sell to other syndicates in the United States. Newspaper distribution usually extends in roughly a 100-mile circle from the city of publication. Generally you can sell to any newspaper outside that circle, with the exception of the national newspapers. (See Chapter 12 for a more complete discussion of newspaper submissions.)

Of course you can always write different articles about the same site or trip and sell each to a different market. Just keep them clearly different. And to avoid undue confusion, don't ever sell the exact same article to a magazine *and* a newspaper. Trust me, you'll see why as we go along.

Newcomers labor unduly over rights, spending tortured nights and queasy days afraid that their gilded words will be lifted and converted into billions of purloined dollars. Or that they will be sued if they use any two words in tandem. Forget all that. Follow the simple rules just outlined. And worry instead about turning out words so good that editors will want to print them and others will fight to steal them. By then you'll know that 99% of your fears are baseless. And all the energy so spent is unprofitable.

EXAMPLE: RIGHTS

The *Writer's Market* indicates the kind of rights each publication buys, so I act accordingly.

I query, then sell them what I promised in the letter. Let's say that one magazine stated that it bought all rights. That's it. I can rewrite that piece but the original is theirs. Say the rest bought first rights. If the subject lends itself to it and there are other interested markets, I'll try to sell those articles as reprints once they've appeared in print.

I don't quibble over rights. I'm much more interested in what publishers pay! I don't quibble there either, until I've been on their pages long enough that some expenses should be picked up. Then I'll simply make a straight request. If they don't pay enough I don't query them at all, no matter what rights they buy.

CHAPTER 5

Query Letters: The Magic Key to Magazine Sales

Magazines are your best market for travel articles. They pay more than newspapers, buy both slides and black-and-white (b/w) photos, and often help with travel expenses after you've written for them a while and earned their confidence.

Whether the publication is a travel magazine, one more broadly directed at consumers, or a specialty/trade publication, the key is approaching the editor in the right way at the most advantageous time.

Beginners usually write articles and send them in final form to magazine editors. This is like a father sewing a dress for his daughter without consulting her at all. It doesn't work! How much wiser to discuss it with her first, do some measuring, and share ideas about the style, length, and fabric. The same strategy applies to editors. You've got to find out what they want.

Remember: Amateurs write, then try to sell. Professionals do just the reverse. They sell the idea first, take the trip, gather precisely what they need on-site, then write an article to their editor's needs upon return. Well in advance of their excursion these writers send a one-page query letter to an editor that sells their travel story and themselves as a writer. An editor's positive response is usually specific: "Be sure to mention the bus system"; "Keep it very detailed: price and dates"; "Remember that our readers expect to spend $300 a day!" Or, by simply responding positively—"Let me see it," "Send it on spec," or "Sounds good, let me have a look"—but without further stipulations, the editor assumes that you know what the magazine uses and the size and style of its articles.

IT STARTS WITH A QUESTION

Query letters sent to a magazine editor are built around an inquiry, "Would you be interested in an article about...?" But to which editor do you write? Often the *Writer's Market* specifically states, "Send query letters to..." Or the editor of the section where the article would be used is named and titled, like Ms. Mary Jones, Articles Editor.

If it's not clear from the write-up, query the top person if it's a small to middle-sized publication; if it's on every supermarket checkout counter, query the managing editor.

Make your query letters positive, clear, and no longer than a full page. On that page bring the topic alive, demonstrating by your style how you will write the article. In addition, provide other necessary information: why readers would be interested, what your expertise is in the field (if necessary), what you've published of a similar nature, when you will take the trip (if in the future), when you can get the manuscript to the editor (three weeks after you return), and anything else that helps sell your idea.

Let me comment on the one-page stipulation. It's not rigid, but it is based on what most editors tell me: "If they can't sell me in one page, they sure can't do it in two." Yet when I spoke on a panel in New York City about querying for the American Society of Journalists and Authors, an editor of *Vogue*, also on the panel, said that she wanted two full pages to grasp the whole idea and to sample the person's writing. Another editor in the audience agreed. So the length is up to you. But one page has always worked best for me and those professional writers I know well. However long your letter, it should be neatly typed (or printed out with a computer) in a businesslike fashion on clean, business-sized paper, providing easy-to-read copy.

NEXT COMES A FEASIBILITY STUDY

Before you write a query letter you must process the idea through what I call a feasibility study, which is, in fact, two studies. The first asks whether it is feasible to write the article; the second, whether it is feasible to sell it.

A query letter asks if the editor would be interested in an article about... Should the editor reply positively, you must be certain that you can in fact write about the subject you've proposed. Therefore, as described earlier, you must conduct a limited amount of research before writing your query, to know with certainty that you could comply and also to gather enough information about the topic to write a solid, accurate, and exciting letter.

Given this, you don't want to spend *too* much time researching at the prequery stage. For one thing, editors don't respond favorably to every query. You would be wasting too much valuable time exploring to exhaustive depth what an hour or two could reveal. For another, all you really need to know is if the subject proposed can be written about in the style the letter suggests, and if so, where you can find the needed information after you receive the go-ahead.

"Is it feasible to sell?" requires a different kind of research, one best pursued through a three-step process: (1) Ask yourself "Who would be interested in reading about this topic?"; then list potential audiences from the most to the least interested. (2) Ask "What do they read?"; then next to each of your target audiences, list the magazines each might read. (3) Rank the magazines in that list by priority.

You can approach step one, finding the most likely readers, in three different ways. Using your imagination is the best. Close your eyes and think about the topic. Ask "Who cares at all about this?" Write down the types of people—professionals, students, hobbyists, homemakers, and so on—who might buy a magazine in order to read about your topic. Remember to include people in the travel trade. An article about a certain kind of hotel not only appeals to potential guests but also to those working at that hotel, other hotels, or in the travel business in general.

A second way is to look at the table of contents of the current *Writer's Market*, which lists well over one hundred publishing categories that, with some more imagination, can suggest even more kinds of readers.

Deduction is the third way. Check your topic in the *Reader's Guide* (found in your local library) to see where it has appeared in print before. By looking at the audience of the magazine in which it was previously published you can assume that it might work again for that audience, as well as for related audiences.

The question posed in step two, "What do they read?," is easier to answer. Check the current *Writer's Market* to see which magazines are listed. Then check other guides and library periodical holdings to see what else is published about your topic. Put all you find on a list.

Which brings us to step 3. If you could send a query to every magazine listed you wouldn't need to prioritize.

But you can't, mainly because each buys some form of exclusivity and you can't promise all rights to all people.

So you must put the best market first, from your perspective, then the second best, and so on. What do you use for criteria? When they pay, what they pay, how much freelance material they purchase, and how often they publish. Where do you find this information? In the current *Writer's Market* or, if the magazine isn't listed there, write directly to the magazine's editor (find the name and address in its masthead), asking whether they buy from freelancers, when they pay, the pay range, and other relevant questions. Also ask them to send a "guideline-for-writers" sheet, if they have one. This usually contains all the answers to your questions as well as provides you with information found in a typical *Writer's Market* write-up.

Magazines pay in one of two ways: on acceptance (their check may accompany their letter of acceptance of the manuscript or be sent on their next pay date, usually within 30 days), or on publication.

The latter is fraught with "if's"—they pay if they use it, if they remember, if they haven't folded, if you remind them that they forgot (*if* you can still find them!). So you may not want to query or send original work to a magazine that pays on publication.

Taking your prioritized list, draw a line to divide your markets into two parts. Put those that pay on acceptance above the line and query them in order of priority. Place those that pay on publication below the line and sell them reprints.

Reshuffle those above the line by how much they pay. It makes the most sense (and cents) to put the highest-paying publications first. The worst they can say to your query is no. Why talk yourself out of a top sale by not trying it first?

How much they pay, as well as how often the publication is issued and what percent is written by freelancers, should be explained in either the *Writer's Market* or the guideline-for-writers sheet.

If the payment is listed as a range, say $300–$550, rest assured that at the beginning you will be earning closer to the bottom than the top. The more they buy from you, the quicker you will move up. Some editors will include expenses after you're a valued member of the family. Photo payment is usually in addition to the base amount or range and can exceed it. But if the listing says they pay "for the package," that means copy and photos.

Finally, find out how often the magazine comes out and what percent of each issue is written by freelancers. A magazine buying 99% freelance is more desirable from a selling position than one buying 2%, as is a daily publication that uses three hundred times more copy than an annual. These features will cause you to move a magazine up or down on your list, all else being equal.

QUERY ONE PUBLICATION AT A TIME

Let's say that for one of the likely audiences you find five magazines, which you have prioritized. Your immediate inclination will be to write one query, modify it a bit for all five, and send a letter to each editor. But don't do this!

Why? If you query many magazines simultaneously and find that two or three want to see the article, you are in a tough spot. You can only send the manuscript to one, on the assumption (probably 99% accurate) that it will want to buy all or first rights. You must then ignore the other interested respondent(s) while you await a reply from the first editor. The editors who are ignored will simply not be interested in future queries from you— and you might not even sell your article to the first editor anyway! This is why you must query only one magazine at a time.

It makes no sense to lose editors through greed or impatience. There are few enough of them to start with! Try the first editor on your list. If he or she says no, try the second, and so on, until you have sold the item or exhausted your list of those who pay on acceptance.

That is not to say that you can't query others simultaneously about somewhat related topics. If you are writing about Brazil, don't query an all-you-ever-wanted-to-know article about Rio de Janeiro to several editors simultaneously. Use this query for one magazine, try another about Copacabana Beach, a third about Sugarloaf Mountain, a fourth about Maracanhã Stadium, a fifth about Tijuca Forest, and still another about the Imperial Palace. All share a Rio background yet each is distinctive. This allows you to write an article for every query that brings a positive reply.

Why not just pick out four or five ideas and write a sharp paragraph about each in the same letter, asking the editor to choose which article he or she would like you to submit? Some writers do that and it works for them. But they almost always have long, successful selling records and are known by the editors. I don't advise it early in the game for one simple reason: It's too hard to sell a full article to a paying editor by saying so little (one paragraph is not enough for little-known writers to demonstrate their ability).

In the beginning it makes much more sense to focus on your best idea, using the query letter to develop and sell it, and by extension sell yourself as a writer. This is not to say that in the same letter you can't spin off a second or even third angle based on your main idea. You might suggest a general article about Wales and then suggest later in the letter an alternative (or a sidebar), say, a highly focused piece on early Celtic castles in and near Cardiff. The postscript is ideal for this; make it a solid, selling paragraph.

When you have determined that it *is* feasible to write and to sell the article—when you have sufficient information about your topic and you've got a prioritized market list—it's time to write a query to the editor of the first magazine on your list. Before writing you may want to look at several issues of that magazine to learn its style, taboos, and expectations. This knowledge will help you write an effective query letter, tailored to the specific magazine.

SLANT AND CONTENT

A Sales Letter

The query letter is a sales letter. It should make the editor say, "My readers want to know more about that subject. I'd be a fool not to look at that article." The query must indicate what the editor can expect: a well-researched, sharply written manuscript done in a style appropriate to the topic. If the angle is humorous, the query must be written with the same degree of humor to show that you can do it. If serious, sobriety must prevail, but not to the detriment of the lively, vital exchange of information.

Since you will take the trip before you write the article, remember the three stipluations mentioned for the sales plan: You must indicate when you will be at the site, when you'll be back, and when you will have the final manuscript (with photos, if promised) in the editor's hands—usually within three weeks of the date of return. (If you have already taken the trip, simply deliver the manuscript within three weeks of receiving the go-ahead from the editor.)

THE REPLY

You can expect one of three results from your query: no reply at all, the answer no, or a qualified yes.

If you receive no reply within two months, send a copy of your query letter to the same editor, with a note attached. Your note might say (1) the query attached is a copy of a letter sent to you on such-and-such date; (2) perhaps it got lost in the mail; and (3) if the idea is still as exciting now as it was then, should we share it with your readers?

If the editor still hasn't replied a month later, the magazine has probably folded! Go to the next one on your list and write a new query to that editor.

How do you avoid the no-reply response? Keep your *Writer's Market* current by checking the "Markets" section each month in the new issue of *Writer's Digest Magazine* put out by the publisher of *Writer's Market*. Cross off all magazines that have folded, update current listings as necessary, and photocopy any new listings and append them to your book. (Keeping your *Writer's Market* current this way can help it last two years instead of only one.)

If the editor says no, thank God you didn't waste time writing a whole article for those pages! Blessed are editors who let you know quickly—and kindly. Simply go on to the next publication on your market list and query it.

The nicest reply is yes! Alas, it's almost always a qualified yes: "Let's see it," "Send it on spec(ulation)," or "Let me take a look." Not much wind for your sails, that tepid a reply. Yet in reality that's about as close to a sales commitment as you'll get, particularly when you're new to the editor.

When the editor sends even a qualified yes, your topic and name are written on the editor's calendar, probably for the issue that hits the stands two to three months after you promised to submit your manuscript. The editor wants you to submit top-grade material to adorn the magazine's pages. All that separates you from print and pay at this point is your writing.

YES? STUDY YOUR TARGET MARKET!

Top-grade submissions come from studying the target market closely after receiving an affirmative reply. Get the last three issues of the magazine and find at least one article in each as close as possible in subject, style, or tone to what you want to write about. From these articles deduce what the editor is seeking for those pages, and thus what you need to provide from the site to bring your manuscript alive and buyable.

Again, I'm going to borrow from my earlier book *How to Sell More Than 75% of Your Freelance Writing* (Prima, 1990, pp. 76–78). Called "How to Study a Printed Magazine Article," this 12-step process shows you how to analyze editors' needs and preferences by what they buy. (It works as well for newspaper travel articles.)

How to Study a Printed Magazine Article

1. Read the article closely, then ask yourself what basic or working question it answers. Write the question out. It may also answer secondary questions, so write those out too.

2. Now read the entry for that publication in the *Writer's Market* for the year of (or preceding) the article's appearance. Given the working question

in (1) and the indications in the *Writer's Market* of what that magazine was seeking, try to put yourself in the writer's shoes. How did the writer slant the subject to appeal to the magazine's readers? Why did the editor buy it? Study its length, illustrations, position in the magazine.

3. To see how the writer carries the main theme through the article, underline each word that relates directly to that theme, then outline the entire piece. Study the writer's use of facts, quotes, and anecdotes. What is the ratio between them? How is humor used? Is it spread and balanced to the same degree throughout? Do other articles in this issue use facts, quotes, anecdotes, and humor in roughly the same way and in the same proportion?

4. List every source used, including direct references and quotations. Where would the writer find the facts, opinions, and quotes that are not clearly identified by source in the article? If you are uncertain, indicate where you would find the material—or where you would go to find out.

5. Focus on the quotations. Why is each used? How does it carry the theme forward? Note how the source of the quotation is introduced, and how much the reader must know about the source to place the person and what is said into perspective.

6. Is the article written in first person (I), second (you), or third (he, she, or it)? How does that strengthen the article? Does the person change? Why or why not? Are most other articles in the same issue written in the same person?

7. Set the title aside and concentrate on the lead. How long is it, in words or sentences? How does it grab your interest? Does it make you want to

read more? Why? How does it compare with other leads in that issue?

8. Most articles begin with a short lead followed by a longer second or third paragraph that ties the lead to the body of the article. Called the transitional paragraph, it tells where you are going and how you will get there. It bridges the attention-grabbing elements of the lead to the expository elements of the body by setting direction, tone, and pace. Find the transitional paragraph and study it. Organizationally, after the lead it is the most important item in the article.

9. Now underline the first sentence in each paragraph. They should form a chain that will pull you through the piece. Note how the writer draws the paragraphs together with transitional words and phrases. Circle the words that perform this linking function. Often the same words or ideas will be repeated in the last sentence of one paragraph and the first sentence of the next.

10. Earlier you outlined the article. Now look at the transitional words and the underlined first sentences and see how the structure ties the theme together. Is the article structured chronologically, developmentally, by alternating examples, point by point? Or if the article was written to answer the working question you isolated in (1), did the answers to the secondary questions stemming from that working question provide the article's organizational structure?

11. How does the article end? Does it tie back to the lead? Does it repeat an opening phrase or idea? The conclusion should reinforce and strengthen the direction the article has taken. Does it? How?

12. Finally, look at the title. It may have been changed or rewritten by the editor. Nonetheless, does it correctly describe the article that follows? Does it tease, quote, pique one's curiosity, state facts? What technique does it use to make the reader want to read the article?

While you have the articles before you, check the editor's photographic needs as well. What kind of photos accompany the articles: b/w or color? Are they horizontal or vertical? Do they include people in every shot? Doing what? Were they taken by the editor? Do they use captions with each photo?

This isn't busywork. It tells you specifically the kinds of information you need to gather before the trip and at the site, as well as the type and quantity of photos you might need to provide. A careful study in advance can cut your working time on the trip by as much as 75%—and virtually assure you of a sale. Conversely, gathering material at random for some imaginary publication to be found later requires far more work and no assurance that it will even be enough or will result in a writable article for which a market can be found.

The chemical composition of a travel article is facts, quotes, and anecdotes, to which photography is a valuable addition.

As suggested earlier, the more you gather before the trip, the less risk you run of coming up short at the site. Read all you can about the destination: encyclopedias, books, recent articles in magazines and newspapers, travel brochures. Remember to ask yourself what earlier writers found sufficiently interesting to write about. Develop a grid as discussed in Chapter 2, creating your own "must see" list. See travelogues, live or on TV. Rent videotapes about the area. Record every fact that you think you might need for your articles, keeping track of the source of each. Put these facts on a legal pad or index cards to bring with you, so you can verify the most important at the site.

Don't rely on being able to find or use libraries for fact gathering on the trip, even if you can read the native language. You'll use your time far better if you gather the core of information before you go and save your working time on-site to observe, interview, and photograph.

While you're gathering facts also note, on a separate sheet, the name of every person quoted, plus anything about them mentioned. Editors almost always want live quotes; beginners rarely get them. The more informed and reliable the person quoted, the better. See who the professionals quoted earlier. Then if you can't find a knowledgeable person with whom you can speak when you arrive, you at least have a list of previously interviewed people you could seek out. Even if you can't find them, the locals are likely to direct you to others of similar stature or reliability.

Anecdotes bring articles alive, so write down any you find in your source materials. You will likely add more anecdotes acquired on-site, perhaps from your own activities.

Finally, see what others have photographed. It's a good idea to take more shots of the same thing but from different angles or in different contexts to fall back on should completely different photos be impossible or not come out as desired.

Remember, every hour you spend at home preparing the trip frees up that much precious time at the location. A well-researched base makes the days on-site less anxious, less harried, and just plain more fun. Isn't that really what your travel is about?

WHAT IF IT'S NO?

The answer no is not fatal, but it sure is depressing. You could quit writing, of course. Or send a foul retort by special delivery, guaranteeing that you'll never have to worry about appearing on those pages at all. Or you could read the rejection to see what the editor really meant.

Rejections come in all forms. The most discouraging appear to have been reproduced by the million on leaky, hand-cranked mimeograph machines, sliced into irregular forms, and piled up awaiting your self-addressed, stamped envelope. They say something like

> Thank you for your submission. It does not meet our present editorial needs. Good luck in placing it elsewhere. The editor.

In fact, that's precisely what they do mean. Your idea wasn't appropriate—and didn't excite the editor enough to generate a personal reply, which is what you would prefer (other than a booming acceptance!).

Sometimes the editor will return your query, or a copy, with *no* written across it in a firm hand. Not much to build on there, either.

Still, editors need good writers, and they can spot them through sharp, interesting queries. So even if the topic proposed doesn't work, you are really looking for two kinds of addenda to your rejection, typed or handwritten: "Not this time, but send another good query (or idea)" or "Can't use it now but try me again in (five) months."

The first says that you can write well enough, or so it seems from one query, but the topic missed. Find a better topic and query again, as well as you did or even better. Try to follow up on this immediately.

The second means that the editor just covered that

area or subject—they can only use so many articles about turtle racing in Tennessee—but in five months, or whenever indicated, it would be seriously considered again. If you can't sell the idea before that date, mark your calendar and send the query again. No editors ask to see a query twice if they aren't seriously interested. On the other hand, they are giving you a chance to sell it elsewhere, so their interest isn't rabid. And they have gotten it off their desk!

Before getting a positive response, beginners may write six, eight, or even ten queries, one after the other. Even hardened professionals, to whom queries are as familiar as their morning coffee, are pleased to sell to a third of the editors they query.

You must write each query fully intending to get a sale from it. I've seen at least 20 of my students hit pay dirt on their first try. Even if your query is rejected, learn from it and try again, and again. Successful querying comes from skill, tenacity, and sheer mathematics.

Unless you shouldn't have queried in the first place...

WHEN NOT TO QUERY

As I mentioned earlier, you submit the final draft for newspaper articles directly to the editor, no querying involved (more about this in Chapter 12).

Certain kinds of articles don't lend themselves to querying either. For instance: full-gusted humor. What would you say? "Would you like to read the funniest article ever written about the Cumberland Gap?" To which the editor would reply, "Send it to me and we'll see if it makes me laugh." Instead simply send the article. (But keep humor pieces short and spread the humor to the same degree throughout.)

How do you tell the difference between a *humor* article and one that is *humorous?* The "funniest ever written" is a straight humor piece, the purpose of which is to make you laugh, whatever the subject. Erma Bombeck or Woody Allen stuff. But humorous writing shares information humorously. The point is the information, the style is humorous. Therefore you *do* query— humorously, to the degree of humor in the article you're proposing. Humorous travel pieces sell well. You simply must not alter the truth, too much, to make it funny.

You also don't query for "fillers," those one-page-or-less items that contain less copy than a query itself would. These are often used as inserts, to fill up space. Simply write them and send them. The pay is low and slow, since editors usually pay for them when they're used.

A few magazines don't want to be queried ever, and they state so in the *Writer's Market* write-up. I usually ignore these publications, since researching and writing takes too much time to gamble on an editor's interest. Later I'll send these magazines rewrites of articles already sold.

Some highly subjective, first-person pieces are also hard to sell without being read, since their flavor can't be imparted in a query letter. I almost always send articles like these to newspapers.

EXAMPLE: QUERYING FOR THE BIG TRIP

Time for business! It all starts with a selling query, so I must get to work.

Is an article about the *Schloss* and Heidelberg feasible to sell? I ask myself, "Who would eagerly read several thousand words, enhanced by brilliant photos, about a magnificent castle overlooking a storybook city in romantic old Germany?" Romantic old Germans, of course, but they're hard to find in the United States. Anybody else with a speck of wanderlust, sense of adventure, or spark of curiosity would also be interested. And they're easier to find.

For the castle article I shoot straight for the larger travel magazines, using the current *Writer's Market* as my guide. I find seven likely magazines, six paying on acceptance, one on publication. I set the last aside now (I'll send reprints later). I list the remaining six in preferential order, with the highest payer first. These comprise my market list and I will query each in order. If one says yes before I hit the bottom, the rest will either get a different query about a different subject or a query with a rewrite angle after my return.

What do I know about the first: *BBB Magazine?* The *Writer's Market* description tells me who to query, the address, that it buys first rights and uses 70% freelance, that it's a monthly sent to 260,000 subscribers and sold on the newsstands, pays between $400 and $750, prefers articles of 1,600 to 2,000 words, seeks transparencies that add depth to the prose, and wants "the spirit of the site as well as the details."

Since I've read this magazine often I don't need to trot over to the library to see how it actually looks and reads. (I'll do that if I get the go-ahead so I'll know precisely what they want in their articles.) It's a first-rate glossy.

My slant? I'll let the *Schloss* and environs sell themselves as best I can on one page; then I'll do it even better in the article after I've seen Heidelberg in person. I must paint some mental pictures in the query.

I Send the Query Letter

Five or six paragraphs are all that separate me from gold and glitter. Will this be the query letter that pays, in part, for my German journey? (See Figure 5.)

Figure 5 Pretrip Query Letter

> P.O. Box 6405
> Santa Maria, CA 93456
> (805) 937-8711
> May 8, 1991
>
> Mrs. Linda Cammack
> Managing Editor, *BBB Magazine*
> 158 Lake St.
> San Francisco, CA 94118
>
> Dear Mrs. Cammack:
>
> *Das Schloss* looks so much like a giant fairytale castle it's em-
> barrassing. Its hodgepodge of Gothic spires, Ionic columns,
> half-fallen towers, see-through belfry, flowering gardens ter-
> raced in 1616, and three-story moat are thrust, a blushing red,
> against the green forest that overlooks Heidelberg.
>
> It's worse in the summer. One can almost hear the tenor
> strains of *The Student Prince* when the palace and the stone
> bridge over the Neckar River are lit up and fireworks explode
> from the majestic citadel, showering the narrow, cobbled
> streets and open-air beer gardens below.
>
> Nothing so defines Heidelberg and the Rhineland-Palatinate
> just 50 miles south of Frankfurt as the towering remnants of
> the electors' castle, begun in 1200 A.D. and shelled beyond use
> by Louis XIV in 1693. My article will focus there, a reliving of
> a morning's fun tour of the many buildings, the Great Terrace
> overlooking the city, the enormous 49,000-gallon wine vat,
> and the apothecary museum, tying in Mark Twain's com-
> ments and the architectural bonanza of styles that makes four
> or five hours just enough time to see and experience one of
> Germany's most-sought-out attractions.
>
> Added to that would be a trip up the winding stair path from
> *Marktplatz*, site of the farmer's market and central square, to
> the *Schloss*, and from there (by foot or cable railway) to lunch
> at the Molkenkur, a resort higher up the hill, and then across
> the valley fringed with pines to the top of the *Königstuhl*, the
> "King's seat," for a panoramic view two thousand feet down of
> the fertile vineyards, bustling river, and ancient university.

continued on page 96

I will be in Heidelberg in October before attending the Frankfurt Book Fair and could have the completed article to you on November 7, with 100 slides for your selection. The visit to the *Schloss*, the countryside, and Heidelberg will be tailored specifically to your readership, much as I've done in the one-thousand-plus articles I've put in print over the past 20 years. I could also add a fact sidebar on the city: how to reach it, local telephone numbers for info and lodging, temperature and weather, other key sites, calendar of events, much as you use on your pages, if interested.

Will you let me know soon?

Gordon Burgett

The Editor Replies

Off goes the query, to be read, sniffed, weighed, and mused over by the editor. "Soon," for the reply, is a loose term in the editorial world. It can mean instantly or whenever. So, much to my delight, two weeks to the day back comes a reply (Figure 6).

Figure 6 Reply to the Pretrip Query Letter

BBB Magazine
158 Lake St.
San Francisco, CA 94118
May 22, 1991

Mr. Gordon Burgett
P.O. Box 6405
Santa Maria, CA 93456

Dear Gordon,

Let me see your article about the castle and Heidelberg when you return. November 7 is fine. If I use it, it would be in the March (or April) issue.

Since this is our first contact, it must be on spec. Keep it to
2,000 words, even 1,500 is okay. Several paragraphs at least on
the rest of the charms of that city: the university and so on.
Eye-catching slides (we like Kodachrome best) increase your
chances. Long shot on a cover too (an extra $500), so send
some verticals. Captions required.

Expect about $450 if accepted, plus slides ($25 to $100 each).
Have a good time!

Best,

(Mrs.) Linda Cammack

Looks good! Chances of her buying the piece? Almost
100%, if it's as good as the other articles in her magazine,
if I capture those eye-catching photos, and if I bring
the place alive.

I'm already ahead financially since this will allow me
to deduct $450+ on my taxes, as long as I follow through
and submit the manuscript. It's a great "letter of intent."

Still, there's work to do now to get the actual cash
later. Off to the library to scour the last three issues
of *BBB Magazine*, listing everything I should gather on-
site. I zero in on at least one article in each issue closest
to what I'll write. I then analyze them to see how the
writers put together their articles to successfully appear
on the magazine's pages, so that I can do it too!

For example, I see that quotes are used less in these
articles than usual but that adjectives (word paintings)
are abundant. The articles supply precise costs, streets,
times. Lots of subheads break up the copy—one for every
three or four paragraphs. They quote tour guides; every
quote tied to full name and Mr./Mrs./Ms./Miss. Short
paragraphs (two to three sentences). The articles also
indicate how long things take: tours, meals to be served,
hikes. Very little humor.

This and everything else I find and need goes on my notepad, to be included later in my *Schloss*/Heidelberg– *BBB Magazine* file. Nothing is left to memory or chance. When I'm sitting in a beer hall on the *Hauptstrasse* laying out that day's attack on the castle I want every weapon on that list!

CHAPTER 6

Photos

How important is photography to selling travel articles?

If you are writing about the desolate northeastern backlands of Canudos, somewhere near the fringe of the known world, where the messianic madman Antônio Conselheiro held off the entire Brazilian Army in an epic battle 100 years ago, you'd better have a photo or two of the place, five is even better, to give credence to your words.

But if you're talking about Chicago's Loop or the Eiffel Tower, you don't need to take your own photos. You can obtain them for free if you need them at all (I'll tell you how later).

No form of writing is so interwoven with photography as travel. And nowhere can you so quickly double your income with a camera.

Photography gives your prose that extra dimension of immediacy. It adds a tangible fullness that lets vicarious travelers skim across thunderous waves on a surfboard or creep into the cavernous bowels of a mountain.

But is it absolutely mandatory? No. Word painters can survive on adjectives alone. But why not make use of the visual and prosper from it?

The danger with beginning travel writers and their cameras is that they too often overdo it. They forget that good copy is crucial, and good photos are an extra, though a valuable one. Never forget that the paycheck comes from the printed word, from the artful blend of facts, quotes, and anecdotes. If the copy sells, photos simply fatten the pot.

How much money can photography add to the kitty? A newspaper will pay between $10 to $25, sometimes more, for black-and-white (b/w) photos. A magazine will pay between $25 to $150 or more for slides; a slide used on the cover can bring between $200 to $800. Both *Writer's Market* and *Photographer's Market* explain a publication's wants, needs, and pay range.

What follows is not a step-by-step guide for professional photographers, nor will it tell you how to point the camera. To be honest, I'm still not quite sure what happens when I hear the shutter click, yet I've sold at least 400 photos with my articles! So if you're seeking the definitive word on f-stops, zoom lenses, and the kind of film for photographing rocket launches, this is the wrong book.

On the other hand, I can tell you how a true amateur can actually sell 400+ slides and b/w shots to magazines and newspapers, and how you might do the same (even if, like me, you wonder if the film is really going anywhere every time you crank the handle for a new roll). Nevertheless I can tell you how to submit and how to do the basics, profitably.

SOME GOOD ADVICE FOR THE AMATEUR

Nothing is more basic than the advice I got from a true professional after he reviewed some of my early photographic attempts. He told me in the firmest voice possible: "Take a lot, I mean a *lot* of pictures." On the remote possibility, I guess, that some of them might actually come out!

So that's my advice to you: Take lots of shots. A true pro might be pleased if 1 out of 100 was acceptable. My eye isn't nearly that discerning. I hope for 1 out of 15. It takes plenty of honest tries to get a dynamite picture to mate with good copy to create a super article.

Another comment I heard reinforces the many-shot philosophy: "It's a hell of a lot cheaper to take an extra roll than to fly back to Rome to get what you shoulda got!" Given this advice, what kind of photos do I usually take?

COLOR VERSUS BLACK-AND-WHITE

For magazines I always take color slides (although you will occasionally see color photos in newspapers, they're almost always from the travel editor's photo supply or from photo stock companies). For newspapers I usually take b/w's; occasionally a magazine will use these too, usually for the later pages.

Color shots can be either vertical or horizontal since the longer deadlines for magazines allow art editors the time to do fanciful cropping. I mix my slides up according to the subject itself, often shooting the same shot vertically *and* horizontally. I also try to get some reds and yellows in every slide, to complete the color spectrum, knowing that outdoor photos (the kind I generally shoot) already contain in abundance the browns, greens, and blues of nature. Where do I find red and yellow? Usually in the clothing of those I photograph. Color variety, however, is less important than clarity and brightness.

Newspapers prefer b/w verticals at about a ratio of 3 verticals to 1 horizontal. I usually submit an assortment of 16 shots, 12 verticals and 4 horizontals, so the editor has a choice. A newspaper's low-resolution print begs for high contrast and sharp, tight shots. Rather than a murky, global photo of the Grand Canyon, I shoot the mule train coming out of the Canyon, with the leader atop a mule, a second mule and rider at the edge of the shot, and the Canyon in the background.

If at all possible, get people in your photos. Preferably attractive people, unless you find a type who simply fits your copy to a tee. A grizzled, warty old varmint with gold pan in hand is what I want for a prospecting story. But, at the risk of being called sexist, I'd rather feature bikini-clad women in a piece about sunbathing in Santa Cruz—and I think that's what the travel editor and readers would like to see too.

Avoid obvious but unexplained (or inexplicable) contrasts, like midgets and giants casually strolling down the street together. Or bums and big-bucks sipping the same beer. The purpose of your picture somehow gets lost.

The people you're photographing should be doing something active related to the article, not simply staring at the camera or obviously posing for it. A mountain climbing piece calls for a person, or several, either climbing or fastening equipment or checking pitons or perhaps scouring a map, with a landmark mountain in the background.

CAMERA, FILM, AND FRAMESETTER

What size camera should you use? At least a 35mm camera, and later you'll find a larger one is even better. I carry two cameras with me at the same time, one for slides, the other for b/w's. Since one is an automatic and the other requires a light meter, I use the latter for b/w's, since they are generally harder to take well.

The standard camera lens size is 50mm or 55mm. If your model has a single-lens reflex, what you see through the viewfinder is roughly how the final shot will appear. You will probably want at least two more lenses: a wide-angle and a telephoto, for close-ups. Zoom lenses are particularly useful for outdoor or nature photography.

Take time buying what you need. A good, used 35mm camera from a reputable store is the place to start. Find a salesperson who knows cameras well and explain to them how you will use yours. Ask questions. Take two or three rolls and experiment before you travel. (I shot the entire first roll on my just-purchased 35mm camera with the lens cover doing what it does best!) Two key questions before you buy: Is the camera comfortable in your hands? Can you see clearly through the viewfinder, particularly if you wear glasses?

Don't buy a fancy camera case unless you plan to carry it with you 24 hours a day. A backpack or small, padded duffel bag works just as well and doesn't attract light-fingered attention. And remember to put your camera in the case, or at least keep the camera out of the sun or the subzero cold as much as possible. Dust, sand, salt water, and snow are its natural enemies. You can shoot in the rain but dry the camera off as quickly as possible, and always keep the lens dry.

At a minimum, per article, I take three rolls of 36-exposure b/w film and two rolls of color slides. But if I have a go-ahead from a magazine, my two-roll minimum quickly becomes five, eight, or even ten rolls. For color slides, Kodachrome 64 is my all-purpose favorite film. For black-and-white, Kodak Tri-X has a high enough ASA to include anything I shoot. Always bring more film with you than you think you can possibly use.

If I find a "framesetter," a photo that tells all in one picture, I might take a dozen shots of it each in color and b/w. For example, if in Holland I encounter a healthy, ruddy-cheeked lass dressed in Dutch costume, a bouquet of tulips in one arm, a giant piece of chocolate in the other, wooden shoes on her pink feet, a windmill behind her left shoulder, and a dike behind her right—it shouts "Holland"! I'll shoot her straight on, from the left and right, from low and high, and vary the background— then do it again with the other camera!

When you have that special shot, the one that tells all, "bracket" it. To do this, set your f-stop to the ideal shutter speed and lens opening, then shoot. Then move up one f-stop and shoot again; then down one and shoot once more. One of these will be perfect, one may be acceptable, and one won't be in focus. Great odds.

Still, most shots aren't this eye-catching. So you must ask yourself, What am I seeing that others would go out of their way to look at? If it adds to the substance of the article and can be captured photographically, fire away.

PHOTO RELEASES

Do you need a photo release of the people appearing in your shots? Rarely, unless they will be used as advertisements, appear on a cover, or feature in company or in-house publications, particularly if the publication includes the product in its title, like the *ABC Sausage Company Magazine*. (*Writer's Market* indicates which magazines require releases. These publications will provide a sample release, or you can copy the release from *Photographer's Market* and alter it for your own use.)

Except in the rare cases mentioned above, photos taken

in or from public places don't require releases or permission of any kind, nor do those used to communicate "news" or those of public figures.

On the other hand, it makes sense to get a release signed at the time when you focus on a specific model, or at least to get the person's name and address, in case you need a release later. This can be tricky, but let me show you how it might be done.

I was writing an article about the "Other Highway 1," from Marin County to Leggett, California, north of San Francisco. I needed a shot to symbolize the many pocket beaches along that route. But since the water is so cold there I figured I'd better start as far south as possible, at Muir Beach a bit north of the Golden Gate. Alas, when I showed up at 9:00 A.M. the beach was sunny but empty—and a beach shot without people isn't likely to be used.

I walked around looking for views I thought would best capture the scene, hoping that a person, attractive and beachlike (also dressed in red and yellow!) would appear. Even better, with a dog!

Up screeched a Volkswagen, out bounded a pooch that looked like it had just escaped from Orphan Annie, and shortly behind skipped a beautiful young blonde woman in a maroon sweatshirt and golden shorts. God listens! I approached her and said, "Hi, I'm Gordon Burgett. I'm writing an article for a newspaper on the East Coast and I was hoping to include some photos of people on the beach. Whatever you're planning on doing, would you mind if I took a few shots? I'll send you a copy of your picture and the article the moment it appears in print."

She agreed and I took several shots of her chasing the dog (toward me) down the beach. Then I asked if she would mind petting the dog at a spot I thought had the best chance of being used, a rock formation on the beach that allowed me to include the water, sand, and green mountains behind. I took most of the slides and b/w's there, explaining to her what I was doing and why.

When I finished I asked her name (I spelled it letter by letter so it was accurate) and address, so I could send her the photo and article. (Always do this afterward, when the person has a vested interest in sharing the information. Had I asked her first she might have sicked the dog on me and locked herself in the car!) Afterwards *always* send something to people who agree to pose: the actual photo in print, if used; a print and the article; or a slide, with a note thanking them again for their help.

After I've gotten a name and address I usually ask subjects for a bit more information for the caption (that line or two of type below photos, usually used in newspapers, that explains the picture), like their age, vocation, and why they are there. In this case, I also asked the dog's name. Even if your subjects are reticent to offer details, you already know enough for a simple caption: at least you know their names, the name of the site, and other circumstances.

Does this always work? Almost always, if you do it in a matter-of-fact, friendly way and keep professionally busy. Sometimes it works too well: The models want to stick with you for the rest of the day!

If you want to photograph people or groups, just ask. Seldom will they say no if they understand how the photos will be used and if you remain unobtrusive.

Many years back I was hiking through the narrow, copper-colored canyons at Turkey Run State Park, near Marshall, Indiana, when I encountered a group of Mennonite teenagers. Like the Amish, the boys wore hooked jeans (no buttons or zippers), the girls, flowing pastel dresses and bonnets. The color contrasts were striking, and lovely.

So I approached the oldest boy and told him what I was doing. Would they object if I simply followed along and took photos as they climbed and cavorted? The whole group drew together and talked about it, at length. Finally the spokesperson, another boy, came back, looked me hard in the eye, then smiled and shook my hand. He said that while they didn't read worldly magazines, if it made me happy I was invited to join them and use my camera. But please, he said in a lower voice, don't show it to our parents!

I didn't think I had a chance at all—but they cooperated and those photos were among the best I ever took or sold!

KEEPING TRACK AND PROVIDING CAPTIONS

How do I keep track of the photos taken and the people posed? On each can of film, I put a number (for b/w's) or a letter (for slides). In my camera case or back pocket I carry a small notepad. Then every time I take a batch of shots I indicate the number and/or letter of the can and record the information I want to use. Coordinating the shots and the caption data later is easy.

When I return from a trip, I have the slides developed and mounted in paper holders. To each I adhere a name-and-address tag. Later I will send the best of these slides to magazine editors in clear acetate insert holders, as we shall see in the example at the end of this chapter.

What do the caption sheets contain and how do they look? In a sentence or so you must explain what each slide shows, remembering that the editor has absolutely no notion of what he or she is looking at. To make things easier on the editor I put my slides in a loose narrative order, grouping those about the same site or topic together, and place them in the insert holder that way.

On the caption sheet I identify them by row and number and offer an explanation of each. I identify the article and myself on each caption sheet as well.

When a photo is particularly important or requires a more complete caption, err on the side of giving too much rather than too little information. Make certain that the writing is good and the facts are correct.

Sometimes the slides you submit are not ones you've taken. When this is the case indicate on the caption sheet those that need to be credited to another person or entity. In correspondence with the editor later, ask that those slides you want credited, either to you or to others, be included in the photo credit section of the publication.

It's wise to make a copy of each caption sheet. At least a dozen times an editor has asked for more information about a specific slide, row, and sheet, all the while keeping the original captions, so you'll need a copy for your own reference.

SUBMITTING TO NEWSPAPERS

The process of submitting photos to newspapers differs in detail from that just described for magazines. It's best seen in action, however, so I will refer you to the example in the chapter on newspapers (Chapter 12), where we follow the process step by step. At this point it's enough to say that newspaper shots must be clear (uncluttered) and person oriented.

MAILING YOUR PHOTOS

You can send most of your photos and slides by UPS or by regular first-class mail but not by registered mail.

I've never lost a photo in the mail nor failed to have one returned. But if I take once-in-a-lifetime b/w's (roughly that often), I have duplicate negatives made. And for extraordinary, irreplaceable slides, I make copies and send those for review. If they are selected, I *do* send the originals by registered mail, telling the editor in advance so the package won't be rejected by the publication. Remember to include a self-addressed, stamped envelope so that your slides are returned.

IF YOU HAVE NO PHOTOS

If you have no acceptable photos or no photos at all, somebody else probably has just what you need, and maybe for free!

See what the current *Photographer's Market* says about the availability of photos in the area of your concern. Also check the *Literary Market Place.*

If your topic touches businesses, organizations, or any group that would benefit from publicity, see if their public relations department can supply you with what you need, for free.

Nearly free are items from the U.S. or state governments. The U.S. Government Printing Office will tell you what's available, including items from the National Archives and the Library of Congress. In addition, tourist bureaus in the United States and abroad want to help you draw people their way, as do museums, historical archives, and places of diversion and amusement.

And don't forget your colleagues in the press. News services and newspapers have thousands of photos, used once and ready for reuse, usually for a token fee.

SOME FINAL THOUGHTS

Unless specifically stipulated, photos are sold on a one-time rights basis. To avoid misunderstanding, write on the caption sheet "All photos sold on a one-time rights basis." You can also add the copyright symbol, the date, and your name, which gives you some legal protection. If the photos will be used in a newspaper, most of which are not copyrighted, you can also request that they use the symbol and other information with every photo selected and printed.

Pray that some editor wants to buy all or some exclusive rights to your photos. That means much more money, if you want to sell them.

For magazines, even though I'm selling my shots for one-time use and I could use the same photo(s) anywhere else at any time, even simultaneously, I would probably not use them elsewhere until they'd seen print. Editors would probably get irate if a photo they had bought appeared on a competitor's pages before it appeared on theirs. For newspapers, keep it initially exclusive to the circulation or distribution area only, which for regional newspapers means about a 100-mile radius.

Two final questions, one at a time. What if you only took color prints rather than slides? Well, that's still a lot better than nothing. Some magazines might use them as is; others can convert them into slides, but quality will be compromised. Some newspapers might be interested if the prints are truly exceptional, but conversions for newspapers lose even more sharpness.

If you took color slides only, can they be converted into b/w prints? Yes, since color slides are positives (rather than negatives) they can be duplicated as either color or b/w prints. They won't be as sharp, though, and duplicating them isn't free. Some newspaper editors will absorb the trouble and cost, but most others probably won't.

If you have only one camera and can use only one format, take color slides. Your b/w's will never grow color (you hope!) and slides sell for a lot more money.

AND A FINAL OBSERVATION

Be careful and be prudent.

Once I decided to get a breathtaking shot of a creek plummeting hundreds of feet straight down onto a sandy riverbed in Ohio. I leaned over the edge of a jutting rock, where the water pushed me forward. I almost lost my camera and my footing—only a tough root and an alert passerby kept me from becoming a statistic.

Almost the same thing happened to me again, at Fôz de Iguaçú, the spectacular waterfalls where Argentina, Brazil, and Paraguay meet. Wading a fork of the Iguaçú River to take a shot at the edge, the current pushed faster than I could wade. Fortunately, a tree branch prevented me from being swept over the falls.

Prudence is required too. Walking through the major public park in Quito, Ecuador, I saw what looked to me to be a perfect Sunday afternoon scene. So I took a picture, unaware that a gambler was throwing dice a few feet ahead, which was illegal. Thinking I was the police he lunged for my camera rather than running away! So I ran, as fast as my camera bag would let me at 9,500 feet of altitude. We had a merry chase until it must have occurred to him that I wouldn't be running if I were a cop.

The moral here? Be aware when taking pictures of the physical dangers and perhaps of the social implications.

Don't get yourself killed just for a good shot—you won't be around to reap the rewards!

At this point I redirect you to books about travel photography or just plain old photography, which you can adapt to travel use. Also check local educational institutions to see if workshops or seminars about travel photography are being offered.

In the not-too-distant future almost all my advice and the advice in those books will probably be technologically out-of-date. The photographic process, the cameras, film development, and the process of submitting photos for publication could change. But one thing will remain the same: Somebody must point the camera (or whatever technological wonder) at a spectacular sunset with lovers walking hand-in-hand under the palms. And some editor will pay for that photo (or the result from the technological wonder). So it makes sense to learn to see, to judge, to point the camera, and take the picture. And be prepared for technological change.

EXAMPLE: PHOTOGRAPHING THE BIG TRIP

We're Heidelberg bound! I go to my closet and dust off my cameras, clean the lenses, make sure all the parts work (by moving them and taking some filmless shots), then carefully pack everything in my duffel bag.

Which lenses should I bring? The 50mm, of course, and the wide-angle. I'd rather use a zoom for much of the hiking and mountaineering photography, so I make a note to price them before I go. (I could also buy one in Germany.) And I throw in the telephoto, though I use it less than any other.

Then there's the issue of film. How much can I bring into Germany? Unlimited within reason, for the tourist,

I'm told by the consulate. If I plan to sell nine magazine pieces, minimum 2 rolls each of 36 exposures, that's 18, so I figure on 24, with more rolls readily available there. Black-and-whites? Eight newspaper articles times 3 rolls of 36 exposures each, 24. Make it 30 rolls. They won't fit in my lead wrapper (a lead-lined bag that protects film from X-rays) so I put in what I'm able, with the rest in a plastic bag in the duffel (to be passed by hand around every X-ray machine).

Crucial is my notepad. In the field I use two, one, carried in my back pocket, for photo data; the second, a stenographer's notebook, for interviewing and all other note taking. I put two of each in the duffel bag. Also a roll of adhesive tape and a colored pen, to number the cans of film when I get to my destination. And a couple of extra ballpoint pens. Finally, a half-dozen pleated sandwich bags, great on-site for hauling a dozen cans of film in another pocket, dry and available.

WHAT SHOULD I PHOTOGRAPH?

Every time I receive a positive response to a magazine query, I study the last three (or at least the most recent) issues, to see not only how other, similar articles were written but also how they were photographed.

I keep good notes on what the art editor buys: color or b/w photos, vertical or horizontal, what people in the pictures are doing, wide-angle or close-up, proximity to focal point, type of caption, and so on—all of which tells me the kind of things to seek out when I'm shooting for those pages. Though my assessment merely provides guidelines, I'll do well to follow them.

Studying my notes when I reach the *Schloss* reveals that the editor of the *BBB Magazine* wants eye-catchers in Kodachrome with captions; she also wants some photos of other sites in Heidelberg in addition to ones of the castle (I know this last because Mrs. Cammack, the editor, told me so in her query reply).

But I could have deduced as much from looking closely at the last few issues. The photos leap off the page and the colors jump.

Mrs. Cammack also suggested the possibility of $500 or more for a photo to be used on the cover. That's worth spending an additional hour at the site seeking verticals that will beg to be purchased. (I'll also take at least three rolls of black-and-white, since the castle will figure prominently in every newspaper article about Heidelberg; these photos might also find their way into some magazines.)

There are times when I have a definite photo plan. Usually I make such a plan when I know that I need a particular kind of shot or shots to show the readers back home what I am describing in words. In these (rare) cases I hunt out the visuals required and add whatever else looks interesting.

Otherwise, and especially if it's my first visit to the site, I let my eyes dictate what to shoot based on the most interesting thing that I plan to mention in the article. Whatever that is, it must be photographed, if possible, or something related to it must be. That is the core and I move out from there. I always hunt for the framesetter, the one shot that tells all. If I find it I take lots of photos.

And, as I said earlier, I always try to get people in photos, if possible, as long as the people don't undermine the point of the shot.

How Do I Submit Magazine Slides?

The process for submitting slides to magazines is fairly straightforward. In my query to *BBB* I promised 100+

photos, but the piece won't be thrown in the trash if I send only 85 or 96. Still, if I have 100+ that are usable— or even better, are extraordinary—off they will go.

That is, I'll take at least four or five rolls of Kodachrome at the *Schloss*, remembering to get lots of verticals for possible cover use. When I return I'll get them developed and mount them on paper.

When the slides are ready, I either put them on a lighted slide tray, or simply hold them up to the light, to select the good from the bad. I arrange the good slides in some sort of order, so that the descriptions on the caption sheet flow. I might place together those photos of the same subject, or I might arrange the photos to follow the path of the tour.

When I've selected my final group of, say, one hundred photos, I put a name tag on each slide and insert it, in order, into a 9 x 11″ acetate slide holder that has 20 pockets (see Figure 7). Thus I'll have five holders, totaling one hundred photos, to send to the editor with the manuscript.

Slides have no meaning without explanations, so with staples or tape I attach a caption sheet to the top of each slide holder. I put a title line at the top—"*Das Schloss*, Heidelberg (Page 1 of 5/Burgett)," changing the numbers for subsequent sheets—and type my full name, address, and phone on the bottom of each sheet. How might this first caption sheet of five look and read? See Figure 8.

Now I must wait for the editor's answer. If Mrs. Cammack buys the article, which is likely if I've delivered what I promised, then she will probably buy some slides as well.

If she buys she'll keep those slides she wants and send the rest back, usually with the letter of acceptance. She'll return the ones she used either before or as the article is printed, sometimes accompanying the first copy of the pertinent issue.

Figure 7 A Slide Holder Filled with Slides

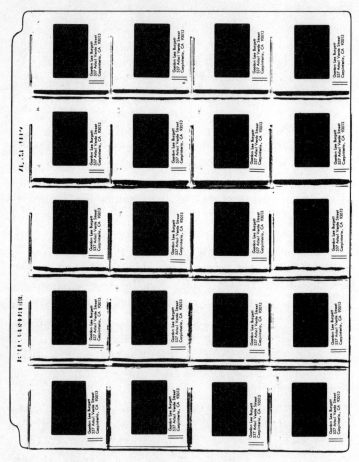

Figure 8 Caption Sheet for Slides

Das Schloss, Heidelberg (Page 1 of 5/Burgett)

Row 1: (1) The Hotel Ritter, seen in the foreground and built in 1592, sits in the Old Town section of Heidelberg, with the imposing *Schloss* towering in the distance. (2) A cable car waiting in the station near the *Kornmarkt* (a block from the site of the public baths, which date from 1265) will take tourists to the *Schloss*, to dine at the Molkenkur, or to the top of the peak at the *Königstuhl*. (3) A winding, picturesque path, the Kurzer Bucker, up the hill from Old Town to the castle grounds entrance. (4) A look at the massive fortifications from the entrance corner, with a popular snack bar and beer hall to the right. (5) A view of Heidelberg, below, from the Rondell, a promontory once occupied by a battery of guns; the Rhine Plain and the mountains of the Palatinate shine in the morning sun.

Row 2: (1) The "Elizabeth Gate," built, it's said, in one night for Frederick V's wife, Elizabeth Stuart, in 1615. Through the gate and across the moat you see the Library and the English Wing of the castle. (2) The same gate, with the Gate Tower, where the bridge crosses the moat, in the background. (3) The same as the previous slide, taken at night, with the Gate Tower illuminated. (4) A shot into the moat from the *Stuck Garten*, three stories deep, with a single-file line of young students quietly following their bearded teacher. (5) Another shot of the moat on the west side of the castle; the wall seems about to tumble into the dark waters below, exactly as it has for 400 years.

Row 3: All five shots in this row are of the gardens, which were first terraced between 1616 and 1619. (1) A long shot from the entrance to the grotto, the length of the southernmost grounds. (2) The same grotto from the Upper Terrace, across the Middle Terrace, toward the gardens and grotto. (3) A child playing in the fountain, with the Broken Tower and castle in the rear. (4) Massive walls holding the terraces in place, as a boy flies a kite. (5) From the grotto to the Scheffel-Terrace, with the retaining walls and the castle to the left.

Row 4: (1) Four-year-old Gregor Kruzel on his father's shoulders as they enter the castle grounds through the Gate Tower. (2) The clocks on the tower wall over the father and son. (3) Another shot at the moat and bridge structure between the gardens and the castle. (4) One of the most striking evidences of the battle in 1689, with the Broken Tower, built in the 1400s, sheared in the middle as seen from the bridge; note the curious tourist trying to figure out why it doesn't fall.

continued on page 118

(5) A look into the castle grounds, with the contrasting architectural styles of the walls to the rear. To the right a group queues up for a tour; to the left another is having a group photo taken.

Row 5: (1) Another distant look at the city, this from inside the castle, across the moat toward the Rondell and the Fat Tower, an empty shell that faces the Old Town on the castle's northwestern corner. (2) Three schoolgirls in Bavarian dress peer into the moat. (3) The Library, a Gothic building, totally intact with windows on all four sides, housed the princes' books, art objects, and treasure. (4) A family eating lunch by the Library. (5) A tour guide explaining the Library and the Women's Wing, next to it, to a group of Japanese businessmen, in English!

(All photos sold on a one-time rights basis.)

Gordon Burgett
P.O. Box 6405
Santa Maria CA 93456
(805) 937-8711

My job now is to put sharp photos in her hands, on schedule, and in a way that she can quickly grasp. The caption sheet and the acetate holders do just that.

PART THREE

During the Trip

CHAPTER 7

What to Do When You're There

Have fun!
But…if you're traveling halfway around the world just to make money, stay home! You can get paid for writing about the things you know well, right in your own backyard. And it's far less expensive to get there.

On the other hand, if you have a burning desire to experience the exotic, the foreign, the faraway, *and* make money, then get packing! You can travel wherever you want, write about it and get paid, deduct the writing costs from your taxes, and have fun all at once. Just don't forget the fun once you arrive.

The best way to do that is to plan and research thoroughly at home, gather enough query go-aheads to cover the basic costs before you leave, and stay well organized during the trip itself. You can get some of your organizing done before you depart or while en route.

For example, make a list of the three kinds of articles you might write as a result of your trip. The query go-aheads are the most important because they will justify (and, you hope, earn back) the costs. The post-trip queries are article possibilities you will explore on-site, querying about them when you return and then writing them up if the editors are interested. You will also do research and take photographs on-site for newspaper articles you'll write later.

Let's get the business chores out of the way first. We'll outline the above three approaches to time use. Then we'll loosen up for a moment to find those fun "extras" to write about when you're on-site. After that back again to business, showing you how to keep track of all your notes, interviews, and other paperwork.

PURSUE THE QUERY GO-AHEADS

The query go-aheads have top priority since you have promised to send editors copy when you return. Set aside approximately four hours a day (usually the first hours of the morning in my case) to work on go-aheads, until you have all the information, quotes, photos, and facts you need to provide solid, well-researched, balanced, and exciting pieces. Bring file folders or buy them there, designate one for each article, and write on the outside of each what you need to make the respective articles work. To keep track of your progress, check off each item as you gather it or its equivalent in copy value.

New writers never do enough interviewing, but editors virtually demand it in a final manuscript. Sharp, on-site quotes from people who are well informed bring almost any article alive and give it immediacy.

Either draw on the names from the list of quotations you prepared before you left (see Chapter 5 for "How to Study a Printed Magazine Article") or find locals in a position to know, then zero in on your topics. If there are people you must see in order to write a successful article, set an appointment time for the interview as soon as you arrive. Then you can plan the rest of your activities around those hours and days. (We'll discuss the interviewing process more fully in the next chapter.)

CHECK OUT POST-TRIP QUERIES

Your post-trip queries will come from three potential sources: topics you knew too little about to write an intelligent query letter before you left, topics you weren't certain you could cover while on-site, or topics you didn't know about until you arrived.

In the first case see if what you suspected would make a good article before leaving is as promising now that you are there. Who would buy the article? What do you need to write it? What kind of photos are necessary?

If it holds high promise, get to it, gather all the information you can find about it, take the shots, and hope you can sell it by query when you return. The problem with this approach is that you have no idea who will buy it and thus what slant you must take. To deal with this problem collect far more material than you do for a query go-ahead (where you've studied the publication before the trip and can tailor information gathering to the needs of the article).

You're in the same quandary with the topics you weren't sure you could cover. Usually your uncertainty comes from not knowing if a person needed for interview will be available or if a temporary condition, like a drought or political situation, will still prevail when you arrive. Now that you're on-site, you can see. If an article *is* possible; if you will be able to sell it for sufficient profit when you return; and if you have the time after working on your query go-aheads—write it up.

As for stories you discover at the site, they usually come from one of two activities. The first, from keeping your eyes open while touring and gathering other article information. The second, from asking what there is of particular interest locally that the tourists don't know about or don't see. We'll explore these more in "What to Do the Rest of the Day."

Sometimes new travel writers simply don't know what others want to read. So the last chapter in this book provides you with three hundred "starter" ideas, in the form of questions travel readers might ask, which you can apply to most areas or cultures.

If you gather what is needed to fully answer one or several particularly applicable ideas from Chapter 16, you could query about them when you return. If the response to your query is positive, you're 90% home to a sale! Or you might prepare an article from that material and sell it directly to newspapers (as we will see in Chapter 12). As you gain more experience, you will learn to work the material both ways, into two clearly distinct selling angles, one for magazines and one for newspapers.

DON'T FORGET NEWSPAPER ARTICLES

You'll write your newspaper articles after you return. There are several possible sources for these articles. They might come from material gathered for query go-aheads, though in final form the newspaper article must be markedly different and should not be sold until after the original magazine piece is in print. They might come from material gathered for post-trip query articles, as mentioned above. Or they might result from new items you find on-site.

To determine the angle I will use for my newspaper pieces I apply a reverse proportion tool: The more important the city, the smaller the focus can be. If your topic is Fortaleza, Brazil, your newspaper article covers the whole city, since very few U.S. readers know what or where it is. But if your topic is Montreal, London, or Mexico City, your newspaper article would likely focus on a well-preserved quaint corner or suburb, or a fun new activity at that locale, or even off-season bargains and special treatment when the crowds are gone. For well-known places you don't have to spend valuable copy space getting the reader's geographic sights in focus. They know where London is, they may even have been there, and they now want more detail.

While you're traveling fill your days and nights with activity. Some of that activity will be bacon earning: gathering information, impressions, and photos for the query go-aheads. Some will be gravy: any other material that will result in post-trip sales that earn above the basic trip costs. And some, just fat old nonwriting fun, which can range from lying immobile on a beach bathed in rays and soft breezes to dancing and hooting madly in clamorous abandon. (Often enough some of that nonwriting fun even sneaks its way into print!)

SET NO-NONSENSE WORKING HOURS

The temptation, once you're unshackled, far away, financially flush, and not due back for a week or two, is to treat yourself to 7 or 14 days of liquid, ribald madness, claim the flu or even more exotic malady, and dismiss travel writing as an impossibility invented to sell books (like this one). But if you succumb to this, you'll make some editors very unhappy—and you'll have to pay for your trip yourself!

I've found that about four hours of daily discipline creates the core of a dependable income and leaves at least eight more hours for dervish fancy. Or more income creation. Or some of both.

Why four hours? Because that's about what you will need to gather the essentials for the query go-aheads: the facts, interviews, photos, and observations.

Remember, you already know what you're writing about, have probably outlined the needed article, have noted what the editor uses and studied the kinds of photos that appear on those pages, and may have already scheduled the interviews before you left. What remains is connecting the dots and filling in the blanks. Crucial stuff, worthy of full attention and close double checking, but not overly time-consuming.

I plan six hours of field work per query go-ahead, so that's a day and a half per article of "hard time." An editor is waiting for solid, vibrant, informative copy. That's what I must gather in those six hours. A poor base for liquid, ribald madness, unless you do the hard work in the morning and play after lunch.

Of course some queried articles need more time to develop in the field, and some of the work will have to be done in the afternoon or evening. On the other hand, some articles are wrapped up and ready to go in just a few hours total. It gets down to the preparations you made before you left, your diligence during the working time, and a bit of luck.

Also, because you are working hard and pinching time doesn't mean that you must display a dour and rushed demeanor. A gentle humor and soft sincerity work best while gathering facts, interviewing, or just taking notes. Take your time, just make every minute results directed.

WHAT TO DO THE REST OF THE DAY

For a travel writer the rest of the day is in fact the whole day. It's what you do from the moment the rooster crows until your eyes refuse to see. It's every minute, every smell, every sound, every sense, everything heard or read, it's everything that enters your awareness from the moment you step off the plane or ship to the moment you step back on.

Plus everything in between your house and your ultimate or many destinations, for the act of traveling itself is also a prime subject for travel articles.

It's even the four hours of query go-ahead time. Some of my best articles were spin-offs from query go-aheads: different slants to the same queried topics, tied together with parts of interviews taken especially for those queried topics, plus bits of scattered facts and photos, plus other off-hours interviews or digging, all sewn into a new cloth and sold through a post-trip query.

It's a storefront glanced into en route to a query go-ahead interview, then visited later for a newspaper short. It's wondering why everybody keeps their refrigerator on the front porch as I walk to gather some other fact for a queried piece, then finding out that same afternoon and writing about it months later. (How do I find out? By research! Which means I simply ask people in a friendly way, "Why do people keep...?")

People confront new cities differently, so let me share my approach. I suggest that you create your own, using whatever you wish of mine.

I like to get a map and start near the center. The cathedral, the city hall, the park. I head first toward the oldest part of town, on foot. If it's a metropolis, I might go by bus or tram or "tube," anything that keeps me among the city's inhabitants. I like to hear what they say, see them interact, watch them laugh.

My notepad is out of sight until I see something I definitely want to revisit, which I write down: its name, what it is, its address, and how I got there. I might note general observations every hour or so, sitting on a park bench or in a cafe. At that point I make my notes as complete as possible: exact routes, actual costs, distances, times, precise attire, color of hair, the weather. Sometimes I unleash my camera and take a picture. Usually I try to remain as unobtrusive as possible, soaking up all I can.

A waste of time? Not a moment of it. I've captured the key items in my notepad; that night some of these will find their way into my synthesis notes (which I type up), as ideas for articles or as background information for articles already in motion.

When I'm touring a town I dress as similarly as possible to the locals. My notepad and camera aren't readily visible. I usually carry a local paper. I'm not the focal point. And I prefer to tour on foot. (I use taxis as a last resort, to reach appointments on time or for last-minute reconnoitering.)

Most days I run. When I'm on tour I do the same (except that I wear my glasses while trotting about, since I'm not on familiar turf and I want to be able to see the new sights in order to record them). Before I leave the hotel I have memorized a route or at least chosen a direction. I also write the hotel name and its address on a piece of paper and put it in my pocket. At my age when I stop running to look at something, it's considered sane and doesn't attract undue attention. If I get lost, I just ask and folks invariably point me in the right direction. Sometimes other runners join in or walkers stop me to talk. Some of my most interesting stories have come from simply doing elsewhere what I enjoy doing at home.

But you must think twice. In Edinburgh, Scotland, New Year's Eve is a particularly special night, and the following morning the streets are cold and empty. On one such New Year's morning I decided to run through the main downtown park and back, past Robert Louis Stevenson's childhood home. When I found that a key gate through a castle yard was locked, seemingly inadvertently, I scaled a sturdy statue and flipped over a high picket fence. No sooner had I begun to lower myself from the statue's metallic foot than a police officer with rifle pointed asked, "And where is it that you're thinking of going?" When I explained he blinked twice and suggested I return, promptly, the way I had come. I later discovered that the treasury and the crown jewels were in the building directly in front of me—and I was, plain to see, dropping in!

How does this wandering or running around convert itself into paying articles? In this case, immediately, into a visit the next day to see the crown jewels.

But in a larger sense, I ask myself, What are locals doing that American readers would like to know more about? If I see a score of surfers at a beach, I think of a surfing-in-somewhere-exotic article.

If I see a small funeral procession moving slowly down a street and a huge cross on a peak above a massive church nearby, I wonder whether these folks make regular religious pilgrimages to the top of that mountain. When? Can Americans join them? Another article.

Everything I see provokes questions. With whom do U.S. stamp collectors speak at the post office to buy special issues? What craft items are made locally and where can they be bought? When can you hear native music actually played by natives? How can a visitor see the countryside inexpensively? What is the single most impressive sight in the city? The best museum? How can visitors find out about university concerts and activities?

Some of these potential articles pop up on their own. Others must be dug for by asking local folks who know: hotel personnel, cab drivers, Americans living locally, students, or Peace Corps volunteers familiar with the local scene. Even by reading the local newspaper that I make a point to carry.

A Hawaiian busboy gave me solid advice decades ago: Ask the waitress, the busboy, or the concierge, in that order. Then tip them if the advice is good.

One question that has consistently brought me solid story material is, simply, "What's really worth doing here that the tourists don't know about?"

The "drunk boat," I was told in Manaus, one thousand miles up the Brazilian Amazon. This river craft ascended the Rio Negro, cut through a canal, and descended the Solimões River, dropping off revelers and picking up milk for the morning market. It left after the 3:00 A.M. rain and would return in about five hours, for the sum of $3.

What a spectacular way to see the howling jungle before dawn, man-sized *pirarucú* fish harpooned from canoes, darting parrots, thousands of iridescent-blue *morpho* butterflies, freshwater dolphins, and hundreds of Brazilians awakening to a new day. I called the resulting article "The Milk Boat" and sold it widely. (I did *not* title it "The Drunk Boat" because editors would object to that as being offensive.)

The point is that the more you see and absorb, the more likely you are to find the one peculiar item or the felicitous combination of many that a travel editor would love to put in print. It can be as obvious as a statue of Buddha or the Portuguese ship ballast that is now the stone mosaic of Rio's historic streets. Or as rare as attire from Tierra del Fuego or the baby teeth sold in Chinese apothecary shops.

The newspaper travel articles that I enjoy most take me by the hand and lead me into a fun adventure, describing, painting, and sharing what I want to know through the local participants' words. At the same time enough details are given for me to do it again in person. So that's usually how I write for the newspapers.

Your own tastes are usually a reliable guide for others. If something particularly interests you, pursue it fully, then sell it when you get back.

SHOULD YOU WRITE NEGATIVE TRAVEL ARTICLES?

In a perfect world with a free press and a fully tolerant readership, the question wouldn't make sense. But travel pages are supported by travel ads and the amount of positive copy far outweighs the negative. That says something.

Of course you can't be dishonest. But you can stress the positive, look to the bright side of travel, and let the negatives, occasionally, fall where they may.

Rather than saying "never go Big Joe's Restaurant" and then elaborating at bilious length, I'm more likely to say: "Rather than going to an earlier favorite, Big Joe's Restaurant, I'd try..." Or simply not mention it at all. Balance the good with the bad, if there's much of the latter.

Actually the problem seldom arises because I enjoy writing about places, activities, and travel events that are already positive and fun. Most of my solution comes from my selection of subject.

And if I do have a real stinker to share? Like traveling third class by wood burner to Majagual? Those become my humor pieces—so bad you couldn't help but bite your tongue, endure, and laugh. Heavy criticism is usable if put humorously.

KEEP TRACK OF YOUR PROGRESS

Keeping track of your progress and of the information gathered can help put each element of the trip in clearer perspective. There are several ways to do this.

The Master Chart

Some prefer a master chart drawn up at home or en route, then added to on the trip. That would include every pretrip query, the possible post-trip queries you want to explore on-site, potential newspaper articles to be researched and written later, and open space for new items to be developed at your destination. At the top of the chart are those "must-do" interviews, to be scheduled before you leave or as soon as you arrive.

A master chart helps you see where articles overlap and where one set of photos or an interview can be expanded to meet two or several needs. You can also quickly check off items, leaving the things to do in clear view.

File Folders

As suggested earlier, file folders can provide the same sort of visual progress sheet, with the steps to be taken and people to see noted on the front and crossed off as done.

Notes

Since articles must be accurate and interviews a careful reiteration of what was said, I find it helpful to put notes in usable prose at least once daily. For me the most convenient time is before I go to bed. (Others, dedicated partiers, prefer to do it the next morning.) For each article I worked on that day I slip a fresh sheet of paper in the typewriter, write out what I've gathered, and indicate the source of the material.

I note where interviews took place, with whom, others present (if any), and the time and date. Then I repeat the questions asked and the responses given. When finished, I slip the sheet(s) into the respective article files and cross off the corresponding items on the "to-do" list on the front of the file or on the master chart. When an interview can be used for more than one article I slip a note in the other file(s) telling where the original is and how it might be used for that article.

For the other assorted material that isn't tied to a specific preplanned article, I list ways it might be used or the slants I could take with it and see if it will provide support material for another piece.

Backup Documentation

One more thing remains to be accounted for: the backup documentation. There are two methods to choose from.

You can use tape recorders for interviews or to make comments and observations instead of, or in addition to, a notepad.

For interviews use two different ways to clearly note each person spoken to on the tape: record the information orally on the tape itself and in writing on the tape label. Number each tape and record the number in your nightly typed transcript. You will later want to keep that tape on file should there be any question of accuracy. A strong case can be made for keeping each interview on a separate tape.

Other interviewers prefer a notepad to a tape recorder (I use a stenographer's notebook). Since the comments will be in your own shorthand, make sure that you give the interview a clearly written title saying who is being interviewed, when, and where. Ultimately you'll remove this material from the notepad, staple it and file it appropriately as evidence that the interview took place and as a document of what was said (the latter will be approximate except for actual quotes, which must be accurate; more about this in Chapter 8).

Two final thoughts: You too might confine your four-hour fact gathering and photographing for query go-aheads to a particular portion of the day. As I said, mine is prenoon. That way traveling companions can plan their personal activities to coincide with your working period. (But you must be flexible too. Some people cannot be interviewed during your assigned hours, and some articles will keep you hustling from dawn to dusk, with the next day totally free.) Set up an ideal schedule and be prepared to adjust it.

Keep in mind that while gathering impressions, photos, or facts during other hours, you might get your companion(s) to join in the fun. Let them be the photographer for these off-hours articles (and give them the earnings later). Or let them talk with others while you are interviewing, to gather even more information. Use their senses. Ask them to describe places and moods to you, ask them what they think other Americans would most (or least) enjoy about the site. Give them a true sense of involvement and you will benefit from their wisdom, vision, and presence.

And finally, as I said at the outset, have fun. Set aside nonwriting time, putting away your notepad and camera, and become a total tourist (or pseudonative) for at least a while. Isn't a bit of freedom one of the reasons you took the trip in the first place?

EXAMPLE: WORKING AND PLAYING ON-SITE

I put Heidelberg first on my schedule for two reasons: First, I've got three articles' worth of research to squeeze into three days' time. Fortunately, I'll be particularly eager to get to it after the long cross-Atlantic flight to Frankfurt and the short drive south.

And second, if I don't get it done in these three days and a later destination proves disappointing in terms of article material, I can reschedule the latter parts of my trip and return to Heidelberg. (I could even do so in the afternoons or evenings while at the Book Fair, if absolutely necessary, since Heidelberg is nearby.)

Although I allow some flexibility in case I need more time in Heidelberg, I plan to complete the basics there in the scheduled time, which is from October 2 (after noon, since the flight arrives at 9:00 A.M. and it will take that long to clear customs, get the rental car, and drive into the city), until dawn on October 6, when I will head back north to cover the book fair at Frankfurt's sprawling convention center. Then, should something merit my return and it seems possible, I could come back.

Coordinating the Preplanning

In the months prior to my trip I did research on Germany and Heidelberg and from that drew up a list of things I think that readers (and I) would like to know more about.

Some of those were so promising and provided enough material already in print that I queried editors before leaving. Based on their positive replies I know that I need two articles: (1) an in-depth article about the castle and its environs, as we read earlier in the query reply from the *BBB Magazine*, and (2) an article about Heidelberg and the Rhine Valley that follows in Mark Twain's footsteps as reported in *A Tramp Abroad*.

A third idea ("Student Princeville") queried (and rejected) three times is out for a fourth, so I have no target market to guide my research. But I'll pursue it anyway, focusing on the university, student life, and a tie-in with the Romberg operetta. I'll fit the facts I gather into any subsequent go-ahead that I might receive after I return. Or I will write the article for newspapers. Or for both, as clearly different pieces.

I also plan to extract some information about the city for a pocket-trip story sent as a post-trip query, plus some information about the Heidelberg castle to incorporate into a larger article about German castles. And it occurs to me, an inveterate hiker, that there must be areas for hiking in the surrounding Palatinate Mountains as well as in the city itself, which I could add to my material for a magazine rewrite later.

Newspapers? A destination, "all-you-ever-wanted-to-know" piece on this tourist mecca, pulled together from all the items above, with special emphasis on the Old Town, castle, and university.

To make all these magazine and newspaper articles particularly salable? A ton of breathtaking photos, both color and black-and-white.

All of what I have gathered and thought about for each of these potential articles exists in files that I bring with me. In Chapter 3 I made a rough outline of what I'd have to do at each major stop based on the potential sales by region and city. I also figured out the time needed for the trip and the expenses I might incur. So I have that list too. What I must do now is create my master chart.

Creating a Master Chart

The term "master chart" sounds formal, but mine is simply a rough timetable of what I must do in each city (or region, as with the Rhine River trip). I write it in my notebook and check off each item as it is done.

For Heidelberg I really need to see three things in depth: the castle, the university and student haunts, and the Old Town section. Plus I should visit as many of the other key spots (museums, mainly) as possible and check out two good hiking trails, if they exist and I have time. That will cover my needs for the go-aheads and other projected articles and give me a solid base to build on for other, spontaneous articles.

It should also leave a night or two free!

I divide a page of my notebook into quarters, put the appropriate date at the top of each section (October 2 through 5), and list in each what I plan to do that day. See Figure 9 for my page.

Then Do It!

A master chart, or any to-do list, is one thing. Doing it is quite another. Sometimes a giant "other," because you're bushed, it's raining, nothing is as pretty or as exciting as you thought, or you're just plain petrified.

You can kick back, open up a paperback safely snuggled in your room, and forget about it. Or you can kick yourself in the pants and get moving. It's really up to you.

If you're bushed get to bed early the first night, or take a nap (anywhere will do), or lessen the stress by breaking the schedule into even smaller parts and do each bit at a time, much like the marathoners (at least

Figure 9 Sample Page from the Master Chart

Oct. 2	Oct. 3

arrive in Frankfurt, 9 a.m.
customs
rent car
drive to Heidelberg
find residence in Old Town (check tourist info at railroad station)
walk up to castle, late afternoon photo castle, outside, in late sun, dusk walk through Old Town at night
(sleep off jet lag)
	early interview, Convention and Visitor Bureau
	get cable car ticket
	spend rest of morning at castle
	  take tour of all sections
	  photo
	  find good source material in English
	check Molkenkur—lunch? p.m. snack?
	take cable car to Königstuhl
	time to hike farther? back to castle?
	free night
	(still sleep off jet lag?)

Oct. 4	Oct. 5
take 10 a.m. guided bus tour (1.5 hrs) go to university, lunch there see student jail photo Old Town in sun student haunts in center? visit museums 7 p.m., Kornmarkt, folk melodies by Town Hall Glockenspiel; photos? outdoor beer halls? student pubs at night? photo students in groups on street?	dawn, up to castle for early photos same of Old Town, bridge, Neckar River take hike up Philosopher's Walk to highest point hike other paths possible to hike directly from there to castle? finish hike at Königstuhl, if worth time river trip worthwhile? castles nearby? last chance to gather info/ photos

my kind) who finish by running from power pole to power pole or block to block as they near the end.

Rain you can't control (although you can plan your visit during the dry season). I could easily switch days on my schedule above. If it rained on October 3 when I planned to see the castle (mostly outdoors) and to hike to or from the nearby peak, I'd just follow my October 4 schedule instead, after the early morning interview. I'd do my October 3 schedule the next day, weather permitting.

Or I could break the day into pieces, doing outside things when it's dry and the rest, if possible (like seeing museums and conducting interviews), while the sky unloads.

As for things never being quite as they were billed, it happens. Adjust your expectations, find what is worth pursuing, and zero in there. Half the time it's your attitude that is sour, not the site itself. So nap, eat, hike, do something you enjoy, and then get back at it.

Petrified is how many travel writers feel the first time they tackle a big trip. Which is why small trips close to home with clearly defined objectives are the way to prevent or at least greatly reduce the fear.

Petrified of what? That you won't sell a word when you return? Not likely if you've queried, received positive replies, and can gather good information and photos.

That nobody will talk to you? People love to talk. All you must do is guide conversations so they're useful in print later.

That you'll lose every dollar you've invested in the trip? But at least you'll have a fun trip to show for it. And you can't lose, unless you simply do nothing and prepare no copy.

The cure is work: notes, interviews, photos, and plenty of the good old common sense that drove you to think that others would want to know about the places you visit. They do. They want you to succeed. They want you to travel for them, report back, and share the joy and excitement and honest appraisal of places and people and events they can't see in person.

I'm sharing these thoughts because I've had every one of them. Early on I would hibernate for hours on end, letting lunch drag into a long afternoon. I was full of doubts that anybody cared a whit about London at Christmas or Praia Branca (a fair distance from Rio). And other places, gleaming in the travelogues, were truly awful. Luckily my curiosity would somehow be piqued so that I would dig around and, surprisingly, always find something interesting to report. Almost all my fears were self-created. The worst thing I could do was nothing (and the same will be true for you).

Putting any doubts aside and with my master chart in hand, I've got to go to it! But there's one last thing. I don't *sprechen Sie Deutsch*.

But I Don't Speak German!

It's not for want of trying! I decided to put myself through a crash course three weeks before I left. Hell, I'd already learned Portuguese and Spanish, how hard could German be? I bought a couple of phrase books, a text, and put myself to it.

I discovered that *some* German is easy. Several hundred words are almost English, which is quite considerate. But about five million more all look like *schweisselflügelhopf*, or worse.

I'd do fine if all I needed was "*Bitte*" or "*Es ist Winter*" but I'd starve to death just trying to order schnitzels.

I will simply have to ask people if they speak English (if they don't understand that, then they don't!), take the tour of the castle given in my own tongue, and arrange interviews in advance with folks who speak what I speak. I'll also carry a phrase book and tiny dictionary in my other back pocket (or camera bag) just in case.

Do I have problems in Heidelberg? Nothing unexpected. Most of the people understand simple English, if spoken slowly and with a smile. The tour is excellent, the interview is as good, finding a place to stay is easy. Only in the restaurants do I have much of a problem. What reaches the table doesn't resemble what I expect, but I don't complain and, as my mother said, I clean my plate. Fortunately the waiters have more culinary sense than I have linguistic skill: even things that defy description and seem to have too many eyes taste good!

What would I have done had the language been an absolute barrier? Hired a student to translate for me. Where would I have found one? At the university, in the English or English literature department.

I've arrived safely, found food and lodging, and have my plan of work laid out. Now I must get to it, and interviewing is next on my agenda.

CHAPTER 8

Interviewing

Facts are the bones of travel articles, the basic structure to which all else adheres. But quotes, whether live or secondhand, bring people into the equation, and readers love to read what others think, say, or suggest.

Editors also want quotations, the actual words, in your articles. These make the piece relevant, keep the focus human, and let the publication's pages talk to its readers.

Well-chosen quotes are a godsend to writers. One sharp interview can make an otherwise humdrum article leap from the page, add depth, or inject humor. The words of others help you express your own feelings yet keep your copy in the third person—and they provide a welcome respite from the endless adjectives otherwise needed to create word pictures.

But you can't just buy interviews in the market like fish. Occasionally you'll find ready-to-use quotes in research material, from a reliable, maybe even a famous, source. Othertimes the person sitting next to you on a bus begins speaking in perfect English expressing the very thing your article needs said. And sometimes fish do fall from the sky. Just don't count on it.

Usually, to get the kind of quotable copy you want, you'll have to set up interviews on-site. Good interviews almost always take planning, time, tact, a recorded trail, and follow-through. We'll discuss each element in this chapter. For further details, I like Michael Schumacher's *The Writer's Complete Guide to Conducting Interviews.* Also check your library for earlier books about this process.

A final thought here. Just because somebody will speak with you doesn't mean that they know much, or anything at all, or that what they think they know is accurate. Or that they aren't trying to lure travelers into their brother-in-law's lamb house by bleating its charms. Or, the worst, that they aren't jokers trying to pull two legs at once. All interviewees aren't equal.

Having said that, getting good, live interviews is far easier than you imagine, but it requires some sleuthing and some preparation on your part.

WHOM DO YOU INTERVIEW?

First you must know why you want the interview. If you're writing about a rugged backpacking adventure from Mt. Whitney to Yosemite's El Capitan, you'll want to interview veteran survivors of that trek, rangers in charge of the parks you will pass through, and others in the know.

If your article is about glassblowing along the Ohio River, a glassblower or two, a plant manager perhaps, and maybe an expert on quality buying will add some depth to the local handout material on the subject and area.

Determine what people want to know about the topic and find articulate spokespeople with knowledge or appropriate credentials. If you're discussing the historical Yuma Federal Prison, don't interview other tourists baking in the desert sun. Find a historical ranger. Find quotes in print from Yuma's prisoners. Make every word speak with authority or unique flavor.

The easiest way to find names for interviews is to see to whom other writers have spoken when writing about the same or a similar subject. If a person they interviewed is the expert, that person, or someone nearly equivalent, should be on your list. If those interviewed came from a larger source group, go to others within that group. For example, if you are writing about RVs and exploring the unpaved backlands of Arkansas, go directly to the RV manufacturers to see what they say. Then to the RVers themselves.

Sometimes the article takes both sides of an issue: mountain bikers versus no-bike hikers on narrow, backwoods trails, for example. Let's say that you know the name of the spokesperson for the mountain bikers but not that of the opposition. To find it out ask the mountain biker spokesperson! He or she will know, better than anybody else, and 90% of the time will share the name with you.

Other times you'll have a super subject but simply no idea where to begin. Find the travel industry or association most closely related to your topic (do this by identifying the products or services involved) and ask them for names.

Other writers can also be very helpful. Travel or sports editors at nearby newspapers who have rubbed elbows with every kind of creature can usually point you to the right cage. Your local reference librarian frequently can offer solid suggestions as well.

ARRANGING THE INTERVIEW

Interviews are held in person or by telephone, the latter usually for interviews before or after your trip.

Sometimes the articles are on-the-spot occurrences, and you'll scurry about for the most qualified or appropriate person or two on-site to give your article "live words."

But usually you will have an idea of who you want to interview well in advance of arriving at your destination. If you're certain of your arrival dates and times, it is best to make an appointment in advance, setting aside anywhere from 15 to 60 minutes for the interview itself. Even if you don't know whom you want to see until after you've arrived, it's still best to call first, before showing up on their doorstep.

Once you have the key interview, or two, you can fill in with other, instant interviews at the site.

Most of my interviews at home have been by phone. Some after-the-fact travel articles have been enlarged and improved by a call or two after I've returned from my travels.

However, even when interviewing by phone I call to arrange a telephone appointment later, which I almost always limit to 15 minutes. But be ready to interview during this first call. At least 20 times I've heard, "Well, why don't we do it right now?"

Which is best, by phone or in person? You can look the person in the eye when interviewing in the flesh, and it's usually a bit more spontaneous, after the first nervous moments. Since so much humor is visual, you gain a lot by meeting in person. But you do have to take the time to get dressed up, get there, and get away.

The phone is far quicker and sometimes much more to the point. If I need sharp answers, no dallying, I choose the phone. But I sense more suspicion on the phone too. Your interviewees can't see you and aren't quite sure the whole thing is legitimate and positive. I've found that women are sometimes less inhibited on the phone and thus more expansive. It's the other way around for men.

No time for an appointment because you need the information yesterday? Call or show up anyway, beg forgiveness, explain the circumstances, and see what happens. No interview and no attempt results in nothing at all.

If the interviewee is savvy, he or she will want to know which publication you are writing for and what specifically you are writing about. The latter is easy; the first is tough, particularly if you are just taking your chances in the hope that some editor will buy your article. All you can say is "I don't know."

As bad is the reply that you are a freelancer or, God forbid, a journalism student completing a class assignment. (The more professional your interviewee, the less likely he or she will have time for an interview that's not assured of publication.)

The best reply is that you are on assignment from *X Magazine* or *Z Newspaper*, if true. The least you should have at hand, or tongue, is the name of a publication that would likely use your piece—and hope your interviewee doesn't probe too deeply. You queried *LMN Magazine*? I open up the conversation with "I'm preparing a magazine article for *LMN Magazine* and ..." It's true. They might even buy it!

WHY WOULD THEY SPEAK WITH YOU?

In the travel world most of the people you interview benefit from seeing their name in print. You are doing them a favor.

Some are owners or managers of profit-based firms, so by having their ski chalet or ferryboat mentioned, they profit. Others are experts. Being in print continues to validate their expertise and by extension sometimes gets them the perks that expertise brings: free equipment, meals, clients, consulting. Still others are in public relations and speak for their customers.

There are also those who don't directly benefit. Often they're just flattered to be asked. Or they believe strongly in something and want to share the good news with your readers. Still others simply want to see their name in print.

Don't worry about why they would speak to you. If they are the right person for your article, simply ask.

Beginning writers often wilt at the thought of talking to "big names" or "famous people." True, some folks with fame are hard to reach or to get to agree to an interview. The hardest, I've found, are academics, who are extremely suspicious of whatever you are doing, and lower-echelon business executives who are afraid to say hello for fear it's a trade secret and will put their jobs in jeopardy.

Yet most people if approached correctly will gladly speak with you for a few minutes, and some for longer.

I've spoken with presidents in South America, ambassadors, U.S. politicians of all stripes, movie stars, sports personalities, academics, businessfolk, and plenty of people just like us and hardly a one said no or failed to give me enough to significantly add to my article. Ask. The worst they can say is no. If you don't ask, the result is the same.

SHOULD YOU PAY FOR INTERVIEWS?

I don't pay for interviews. Sometimes you're asked by a potential interviewee, "What does this pay?" To which I smile and say, "Eternal fame, I guess. A chance to help others. Something to show to your grandchildrens' grand-children." And smile again and tell them why I think the subject is important and how I'd like the article to contain the most accurate information, and that's why I chose them to interview. "But if it's a problem..."

Rock stars, I hear, want cash on the line or no interviews. But in the travel world I've never been turned down yet.

Having said that, since I have to eat on the road and prefer good company at mealtime, as often as not I'll pop for lunch or supper, sometimes a libation, during which time I conduct the interview. So I guess that's payment, of the tax deductible variety.

Be warned, though, that interviewing while eating or drinking is much harder to do. You must still get to the heart of the interview, between ordering, sniffing, small talk, and other interruptions and distractions.

PLANNING THE INTERVIEW

Since by this time you already know whom you want to interview and roughly the kind of information you need, you must research both elements before actually speaking with the person.

You must know enough about your interviewee so that you don't spend precious talking minutes seeking the biographical facts that you should have already gathered.

For example, you must know how to spell and pronounce their name, the current position they hold, why they are qualified to answer your questions, and if applicable, how their position concerning an issue relates to others' positions. Finally, you must know how to get in touch with them after the interview, should you need to.

Where do you find all this information? Much of it comes from previous, published interviews with these people, from their affiliations with groups whose position or stand you are familiar with, or from their writings or speeches.

If they work for a company or an institution, see if that group has a public relations office that will send you biographical and other material. If they are entertainers or such, contact their agents. If they appear in *Current Biography, Who's Who,* or have been the subject of an article in a major newspaper or magazine, look there also.

When a person is only known locally, check with the town newspaper to see what it can offer. Some papers will let you see their clippings or morgue material. At others the editor is the entire filing system, and he or she may give you a "few fingers" of prose about the person in question, plus often a name or two of other locals who might provide more information.

Ask yourself before calling: If I could get only one thing from this person, what do I most want to know? Is it information, a strong quote, anecdotes, their expertise? Put that first on your list, then do the same for subsequent items, up to about five.

THE ACTUAL INTERVIEW

You have a limited amount of time and a specific need. The success of your interview will be determined by (1) whether you can actually get the interview, (2) whether you get the information you need, (3) whether you can do the interview without abusing the interviewee's time constraints, and (4) whether you establish a bond sufficiently strong that you can contact the person again with follow-up questions or clarifications.

Think in terms of the basic 15-minute interview, which will probably go longer if you do your part right. Then order your needs in a logical fashion, convert each into a question, and make the one thing you absolutely need to know your *second* question (I'll tell you why in a moment).

Let's say that you are interviewing Bill Denneen, a retired biologist and highly regarded Sierra Club tour leader in the region between Santa Maria and San Luis Obispo. You want to talk with him about the rigorous hike in the mountains and sand dunes along Pt. Sal Beach. What might you ask him and how might you say it?

Sample Interview Question List

1. "The hike is described as rigorous, Bill. What does that mean? Would you describe the terrain to me? Who shouldn't participate?"
2. "I've heard that the experience is really unforgettable. Why? What's there that's so special?"
3. "They tell me that you've led this trip hundreds of times. Why do you keep going back?"
4. "Have you had any odd or particularly funny things happen since you've been leading this tour? Have there ever been any serious accidents?"
5. "I'm sure that most hikers bring their cameras. What do they usually photograph?"

I put the five questions above in the order I want to ask them. Although question (2)—"What's so special there?"—is the one that interests me most, I put it in second place for two reasons.

First, I want to put the interviewee at ease. Question (1) gets Bill talking, lets him paint a picture for me and share some of his expertise. (If for some reason I don't find out, say, who shouldn't participate, I can always ask him later, or last.) Question (1) is also a fairly logical segue to question (2), because Bill can move from describing the terrain to revealing what is unforgettable about the trip.

The second reason I place my most important question in second place is that I definitely need an answer to it—it will give me the information I must have for my article. Since I need this answer, I want to place the question early (but not first). If, as sometimes happens when the interviewing process becomes more comfortable, the interviewee answers the question well and then begins to ramble (and eat up interview time), I still have gotten the answer I need.

The third question is really an extension of the second. It allows Bill to further explore why this hiking trip is special.

The fourth lets him tell some war stories, the funny and odd things that will liven up the article. And the fifth lets me focus on the visual highlights. Since I'll likely take the trip myself, it also lets me know what others think is worth recording photographically. But if I don't get to question (5), it's not fatal, because when I go there I can see for myself.

If Bill wants to talk longer, I've opened up five avenues that I can continue to explore with questions. Or I can just let him talk and see where that takes the interview. By the end of the fifth question I have plenty of information to use. I've gotten the answer to my core question, and the rest is pure bonus.

Do I ask the questions exactly as I have written them? Almost never. I memorize the first two questions and get the gist of the rest. I'll ask the first, let Bill talk, and then use the other questions, rephrasing to fit the conversational flow, as prods to get the information I seek. For me the best interview is one that flows smoothly from one point to another, with the interviewee doing the talking.

I think of the first question as getting the cattle moving in the direction of the second, and every other question as a gentle prodding into a slightly different but related pasture.

Why not just read the questions as written? Sometimes I have, particularly if the speaker was hostile and resented the whole experience. Reading keeps attention focused on the mechanical aspects of the interview process and helps to defuse some of the hostility, so that I can get the information I need. But 95% of the time I don't really want the person to know precisely what the question is, for a very good reason.

Veteran interviewees learn to spot the key questions and develop pat answers to them, answers that sound good but don't say much. Politicians are masters at it. So I try to have the questions flow from the context, as if they are simply expansions of points already being made. This doesn't trigger the automatic responses, at least not as often as set questions do. It leads to much more spontaneity and openness, and far better articles.

What if the interviewees want the questions submitted in advance? The rarest of requests in travel writing, but common enough in the political realm. Send them— in clearly understandable, straightforward English (don't use slang).

How do I keep notes during the interview? I seldom use a tape recorder, since they inhibit most people (and afterwards I have to transcribe the whole thing onto paper). Usually I write the key comments in partial sentences, using mostly verbs and nouns, on my stenographer's notepad. I simply add the question number when we address it.

You will probably want to directly quote one or two important comments. If you can't keep up with the speaker, ask, "Would you phrase that another way so the readers will better understand it?" As the speaker is saying it another way, continue writing the original comment down. Listen to the second and capture as much of it as you can too.

You don't need to write whole sentences to repeat what was said later. Just pay attention, ask questions when you don't understand, and capture the essence on paper, recording the key words, precise verbs, and memorable adjectives. Then sit down and transcribe these key elements that night or shortly after the interview. You'll find it coming back, as much by context as memory.

What if you don't get the quotation word for word? Of course you've got to try, but a close approximation is usually acceptable. Just don't change the meaning or the spirit of what was said.

Be sure to listen for asides as the person talks, little throwaway comments. Often they change the meaning dramatically. "He was as honest as you'll find...usually." Note these comments and raise questions on the spot or later. Ask, "When isn't he honest? In what way?"

Sometimes you can get even more information by purposely misunderstanding. I recall a person telling me that an admission cost was increasing to $35 per person in the near future. That seemed very high to me, so I said "$65? Isn't that a lot of money?" When he corrected me it gave me a chance to ask why, what response did they expect, and from there we moved into the whole area of cost and profit, which the speaker had artfully avoided until then.

The biggest problem new travel writers have is keeping quiet. They want to tell the interviewee about themselves. Or they are so nervous they feel they must talk. Smile, relax, be pleasant, ask questions, laugh or groan or do what an honest response requires, and just let the other person speak. Silence isn't toxic; the speaker will fill it. If the silence is prolonged ask, "Could you explain that more?" Or go to the next question.

Avoid yes/no questions and those with one-word replies (for instance, "What's the address, date, title?"). If an interviewee simply gives you a yes or no, ask why. Or why not? Dig for information.

What do you do if the person simply doesn't know the information you hoped to learn from them? Ask them if they have any idea who might. Sometimes they can even provide addresses or phone numbers.

What do you do if one of your questions is likely to be considered offensive and will end the interview? Ask it last! And preface it by saying, "I don't mean this to be offensive but I'm sure our readers would like to know if...Could you shed some light on that?"

I have a standard closing question that has been passed down from writer to writer: "Is there anything else I should have asked?" Sometimes they have something they want to say: a message. I dutifully write it down and thank them very much. That seldom sees print. But at other times interviewees have volunteered absolutely vital information I had no idea they knew. And kept me interviewing another 40 minutes.

Anyway, it's a sensible way to thank them and get away before the whole interviewing process becomes tedious and unpleasant.

But before you actually leave, one last bit of business remains. Would they mind you contacting them if a question comes up or a point needs clarifying while you're writing the final article? Most agree. Get their phone number if you don't have it. Check it with them if you do: "Should I call (the number)?"

KEEPING TRACK OF WHAT IS SAID

How long do you have before the magic words turn to mush?

In my case my memory is good for about a day for details, specific comments, and impressions. If I pay close attention during the interview, capture the key points on my notepad, and catch word for word the one or two most important comments as they were said (even at the time repeating the quote back to the person, when appropriate, to be doubly certain I have it right), I can then duplicate almost all the rest on the typewriter, if I do it that same day. My notes are the maps that bring back the actual terrain.

Most people have blind spots in their memory. Mine is what a person looks like and what they wear, whereas numbers stick like glue. So when I interview a person whose physical appearance and attire are important, I write that down either before we speak or immediately after, while they are still in sight. If I don't, people with blonde hair become redheaded, those without glasses acquire spectacles, and God knows what they covered their bodies with—if they *were* covered (if not, I probably *would* recall that!).

FOLLOWING UP

What do I do when interviewees want to preview the article while I'm writing it? I say, "Sorry, that's against the magazine's policy." It may be, but it's also against mine. My obligation is twofold: to tell the truth as they gave it to me and to write an honest, selling article. I won't alter what they said to make it salable. But I also don't want them to interfere with my writing. I've never had a person complain. Guess it's too hard to buck magazine policy.

After the interview, a thank-you note is due, and expected. Later I always send a copy of the article plus another note thanking them again for their help in making it possible.

There's more than courtesy involved in sending the thank-you note and article. Nearly half the time I'm able to interview the same person again for another piece, the second time more likely by phone.

Once in a 20-minute call I gathered information for five articles about gray whales from the same expert ocean-ographer. I explained who I was and what I wanted, then named the publications. "Let's get to it—I'll be famous!" he said, laughing. I agreed and suggested an easy format: I'd ask about the specific details I needed to know for each publication in that order. Like shooting fish...oops.

I later sent that scientist a copy of each article, plus a letter to his department chair noting his much appreciated and very professional assistance, to be added to his personnel, or promotion, file. The point: If inter-viewees are particularly helpful, let their superiors know. But ask the speaker first before you do it—and get the correct names, titles, and addresses. Sometimes I even ask how the letter might be phrased for maximum help.

If you keep the lines of communication open, are courteous, and show true concern for the speaker, from the first to last step, you'll create good articles and make repeat interviews possible.

EXAMPLE: INTERVIEWING ON THE BIG TRIP

I plan on getting two interviews about the *Schloss* and will probably speak to five or six more people whose comments I'll also include somewhere in my articles about it. Plus I'll get some quotes from written sources, like Mark Twain and Goethe, either in my pretrip research or after I return home.

Although my first interview will be at the Convention and Visitors Bureau in Heidelberg the morning of October 3, I don't yet know with whom. So when I arrive after noon on October 2, I call for an appointment, explaining that I'm a professional travel writer from the United States, I have commitments to write two magazine articles about Heidelberg, and I would like to spend about 45 minutes as early the next morning as possible with a knowledgeable, English-speaking person from the bureau to best organize the task.

Easy enough. A win-win situation, with the hour the only thing really to be decided.

I appear promptly at 9:00 A.M. the next morning with my master chart, notebook, query go-ahead replies (should they ask for some verification, which they almost never do), cameras in clear view, and a pleasant smile.

This will be less an interview than a probe. I explain what I have in mind, the three key things I must explore, the time schedule I've set up, and ask, first, Am I going about it sensibly? Should I be able to do what I wish in that time? And what would they suggest I do differently?

Then go over each day in detail.

Today (October 3) I plan to take the cable car to the top of the peak. Can I stop, then reboard at the castle, and again at the Molkenkur, and get to the *Königstuhl*? Is the Molkenkur worth seeing? Is the *Königstuhl* worth the ascent? Why? Can I hike back down? How long does it take? Is the path marked? What does the sign say in German, so I don't inadvertently hike to Berlin? Should I get a one-way ticket? Is that possible?

Let's stop for a second here. It's very likely that at this point I will be given some free tickets—the cable car, bus, tours, and so on. I never ask, but if there are no strings attached (I hope there *are* strings on the cable car!), I thank them and accept.

Up to now I've been asking logistics questions. How to get from here to there. The answers will save me a lot of time, and I'll usually get at least a good local map as a result.

But I have other questions too. Which tours are worth taking at the castle? Are there English-speaking guides? Is any guide particularly good, since what I hear will be widely repeated? When does he or she lead a tour? Is it possible to be included in that tour? Are there people working at the castle who are trained to answer additional questions I will have, in English?

Also, though I'm here in early October, I need to know of special events that take place in or around or related to the castle during the rest of the year. Can you give me details? Are slides or prints available of these events that I could also submit with my photos?

What printed material in English do they have about the things I've discussed? Can I take a copy of each now? Do they have a comprehensive map or brochure about greater Heidelberg? Also, what books are particularly accurate and comprehensive that I could buy to use as a backup source when I return? With whom could I speak, by phone, once I'm back in the United States should specific questions arise? Phone number? The hours they work?

And more. Sometimes a person in the visitor's center is in fact an expert on some facet of the city. Or knows one. Or will accompany you on part of the trip. A probing interview of this kind often unearths much of value you would never learn about in any other way, and certainly not as quickly. That's why I've scheduled it before I dig in.

The purpose is to get all the needed and readily available information possible about the key topics. I will cover the next two days in much the same way, zeroing in on the university and the Old Town section.

Interviewing the Tour Guide

My second interview is with the tour guide showing me around the *Schloss*. Often such an interview is nothing more than standing on the fringe, taking down the key points in my notebook, writing in the margin places to return to photo later, and occasionally asking a question if I'm uncertain or need another fact. I read the guide's name tag to get the correct spelling, shake hands afterward, express my thanks for an (excellent, very informative, humorous—you supply the adjectives) tour. I then mention that I'm writing an article for *BBB Magazine* about the castle, I'd like to send them a copy when it appears in print in several months, and they wouldn't object to my using their comments, would they?

About 95% of the time guides are flattered and want to know more about me! In those cases I ask them where I should send the article, which normally gets me their address. I double-check the name spelling at that time, sometimes adding the first name and even Mr., Ms., or Mrs. If they are particularly open, I ask whether they would mind if I called them should I have a stray question begging an answer once I return. If they are agreeable I need to get their number and the best time to reach them.

The other 5%? Smile, leave, and use what you heard anyway. Just don't tie their name to it. "The tour guide..."

Incidentally, sometimes I do use a tape recorder for just these purposes. If they speak loudly enough and they don't mind being taped (I ask), I turn it up full, stand near the guide, and take other notes—what the place looks like, comments others make outside the recorder's range, thoughts about other information or photos needed, and the like.

When you interview people, do you need their permission to use what they say? Nope. You must report it accurately, that's all. I simply try to keep the conversation alive and get access to them if I need even more.

One last note: If others are tipping the tour guide, which is common in many places, be sure to tip too (a bit generously is even better).

Interviewing Other Tourists

I mentioned earlier that I expect to include comments from five or six others at some point in my articles, other than tour guides and experts or people directly related to the focal topics.

I will do a lot of mixing with people while taking notes and photos of the castle (and anything else). Frequently I'll ask questions, just to get them talking. "What kind of architecture do you suppose that is?" "I wonder if this moat ever had water in it?" "I just got here. What's the prettiest or most outstanding thing to photograph?"

Some will look at me as if I just dropped in from Pluto, particularly if they only speak their own rare tongue. But most people are friendly, clever, and humorous. And occasionally I encounter a real expert who can give yards of depth in a few inches of prose. I never know unless I ask. And there are other people I don't even have to ask, I just need to listen.

I will drop some of these comments into my articles without attribution. "A father said to his son..." But others—ones of substance that provide valuable information—will require a source. I make sure to introduce myself to the person responsible and ask if I can use their remarks in my article. I then get their name and affiliation, job, or background.

And Later That Night...

I put in an hour or so of true drudgery, typing up what I captured in my notebook or even the gist of what's on the tape recorder, then separating it (or creating cross-referenced notes) for the respective files. The last things I do are to check off the work done that day, take a quick look at what I have to do tomorrow, suffer bodily and dental ablutions, and sleep like the dead.

More interviews tomorrow.

PART FOUR

After the Trip

CHAPTER 9

The Trip Back and the Critical Three Weeks That Follow

The work you do in the three weeks after your trip is critical. You've got to get the promised articles and their photos to the editors in that time. These articles have priority. Next in priority are, respectively, post-trip queries, newspaper articles, and resales or any other sales you can squeeze out of those golden days and nights on the road.

As soon as you get back you should have your slides and black-and-whites (b/w's) developed (remember to have proof sheets made of the b/w's). But you can't wait for your photos to be ready before you begin writing your articles.

Between the fact gathering and the submission of the final manuscript, most articles go through three development stages: blocking, roughing and editing.

BLOCKING

Unless you're too exhausted from the fun and hustle of your trip, an ideal time to pull your material together and block it is on your way home.

Blocking isn't the actual writing. That will come later. To block you simply take a sheet of paper and list the article's components in the order in which they'd best be used. The purpose is to create a road map that will make the actual writing faster and more purposeful.

Sometimes articles are most easily broken into segments that will use subheads. Other times they come together best by just organizing the components.

If a quote would make a good lead, note it first. If a short transitional paragraph should come second, followed by a fact, then an anecdote, add them to the list. Keep this up, sketching out the article or outlining it in detail from the material you have on hand. If something is missing, note that too so you can find and insert it later.

Start a new page for each article you block. When you're through place the page(s) in the appropriate folder.

Blocking helps you develop a logical plan or design that carries the text forward and puts all the support material where you need it. You turn an organizational eye to what you have to work with and how it can be molded into a selling piece.

Incidentally, seasoned writers sometimes block articles before they take the trip, after closely studying other pieces in the targeted magazine and seeing the formats most preferred by the editor. Then they work to fill in the gaps on-site, leaving some flexibility for new, compelling material to be added or to fill the gaps they couldn't otherwise fill.

You might say that blocking really begins with the work you did pretrip. You began to create the article then, when you discovered what the editor and readers expected from your writing. During the trip you modified these expectations by what you actually found on-site. Now you put it all on paper, in block form.

Once home, the bags unpacked and the pets fed, open each pretrip query article folder and take out the blocking sheet(s). You're now ready for the roughing stage of writing your articles.

ROUGHING

Rough all the pretrip queries first, then edit (or rewrite) them one at a time.

Professional writers learn one thing early: It's far easier to rewrite than to do the original writing. So they get their first drafts down without delay or fanfare. They simply dust off their typewriter, pull out the blocking sheet(s), spread out their facts, interviews, and other elements from the trip, and dig in, converting the rough data and words into organized text as outlined in the blocking, without much regard for spelling, punctuation, or grammar. That's why it's called "roughing."

When they finish with one article, they move to the next. Roughing may take an hour, perhaps two, per article. The only editing professionals do at this phase is the occasional V mark indicating where new or unavailable material might later be inserted. They also might add a handwritten note to the typescript about unused items or additional thoughts, to be considered later when editing. Time is of essence here: Get it down and move on to the next piece.

EDITING

When all the pretrip query articles have been roughed, get to the more time-consuming task of editing. This is when you turn a crude stone into a polished gem. Editing usually takes you two to three times longer per article than roughing does (we'll cover writing and editing in more detail in Chapter 10).

At this point you take another hard look at the target magazine. Review what you think the editor wants, the stylistic and content parameters, the taboos, the kinds of people who read those pages, and what the write-up in the latest *Writer's Market* calls for.

Does the roughed article meet those desires and demands? Does it make sense as composed? Is it interesting? Do the sections flow well? Do you have enough authoritative quotes? Is there a proper blend of fact, quote, and anecdote? If humor is used, is it spread to the same degree throughout the text? Can your text be comprehended quickly, without the benefit of inside knowledge? What is missing? What would make this text even better?

When you are satisfied that the general order and contents work, focus on the words themselves. Is the tone consistent? Is everything clear, concise, and topic directed? Are the words you use the ones that the readers would best understand? Is the text visual? Does it infuse the reader with a full sense of the place or theme? Can they see, smell, hear, feel, taste it? Do the quotes sound real? Is it grammatically correct? Are the words properly spelled? Does the article read as well as or better than other articles in the magazine?

Look at the adverbs. Why aren't you using stronger or better verbs or nouns instead? The same with the adjectives. Can you paint a cleaner picture with fewer words? Is it obvious what every pronoun refers to?

When you're satisfied on all points set the piece aside and start on the next one. Let the edited manuscript sit for a day or two, before going back and reading it again, first to yourself and then aloud. Where does the piece bog down? Where does the energy ebb? What points could be made clearer? Make the changes, then read it aloud again. When it is as good as you can make it, prepare the final draft in manuscript form (a double-spaced typescript on 8½ x 11" paper; more about this in Chapter 10), print it out, put your name tags on each page, and get the manila envelope ready for mailing.

CHOOSING PHOTOGRAPHS

All that remains is to select the photographs and get this Pulitzer shoe-in on its way. Since the article is for a magazine, review the appropriate slides. Set aside all that are fuzzy or otherwise unusable. If you have duplications or near-duplications, choose only the best. Label each slide mount with your address tag, insert it into a clear slide holder, prepare a caption sheet for each holder, put an address label on the caption sheet and make a copy, and add the slide holders and caption sheets to the manuscript (see Chapter 6 for details).

If the magazine editor wants b/w's, send proof sheets (uncut) with the manuscript (and slides) and ask which shots are preferred, so that when you get the proof sheet back you can send either the negatives or prints. Be sure to ask what print size you should send. (You will see in Chapter 12 that this process for b/w's differs for newspaper submissions.)

SENDING IT IN

The last step is a quick cover note reminding the editor that enclosed is the article about such-and-such place requested in their query reply of such-and-such date, with illustrations, and that you are looking forward to a response at their earliest possible convenience. Should they have any questions or if you can help them further in any way, please contact you at (your phone number). Place the cover letter on top, the article next, and the illustrations last, with perhaps some cardboard behind the illustrations for protection. Remember to enclose a self-addressed, stamped envelope with enough postage to get the whole package back, God forbid.

No time to brood or muse. You've got another article to edit!

EXAMPLE: PREPARING THE CASTLE ARTICLE

Blocking the Article

Sometimes I do my blocking while still on the trip, to see if I have holes that need filling. That's a good idea if you're new at the game because it's one hundred times less expensive and easier to grab that last fact or quote while on-site than to try to get it later, an ocean and many time zones away.

Usually, though, I do my blocking in the airplane. I pull my files out of my carry-on and silence my traveling companion with a loving nod (unless I'm sitting next to a stranger, then a courteous reply to a conversational foray in another language is all I need make). I proceed to go through the articles one at a time.

What does blocking mean to me? Determining before I write the text where its building blocks go. Positioning what I want to share so it best meets the readers' needs.

What does the reader of *BBB Magazine* want to know about *Das Schloss* and Heidelberg? And how do they want to know it? They want to know what it is and why it's worth seeing; they want a visit painted in words reinforced with photos for those who will never get the opportunity to go there—all done with verve and excitement, completely honest.

What does the editor want? According to my notes on similar articles in *BBB Magazine*, Mrs. Cammack wants a punchy lead, short paragraphs, lots of subheads, not too many quotes, plenty of adjectives, and a mellow conclusion.

To block this article I take the information and impressions I've accumulated and begin their conversion into smooth, readable text. Rereading my notes I close my eyes and picture the readers of *BBB Magazine*. Then I try to formulate what I'll say to them to grab and keep their attention.

Of course I'll speak to them in paragraphs, and for a 2,000-word article at about 12 words a sentence and three sentences a paragraph, I'll need 55 paragraphs. With a subhead every, say, 5 paragraphs, I'll need about eleven segments for the article.

Sometimes a leads jumps out at me while I'm blocking, but that's an exception. I used to spend hours mulling over leads. No longer. Now I just get writing, and when I've got the piece headed in the right direction with the parts in approximately the right places, I go back and find or create a lead that shows where the whole article is going.

So to get writing now means I must create the eleven or so segments first.

What I initially put down is this:

Preliminary Blocking

Lead

Size/massive presence of *Schloss*, description

Totally accessible, grounds open, illuminated

History, 1693 destruction, de Graimberg stopped the ruins from being used as stone quarry, current regulations about preservation

What remains of earlier days: architectural styles, inside rooms/halls, terraced garden, moat, towers, drawbridge

Best way to grasp full impact, through tours: types, hours, in English, cost, best guides, other items available (books, mementos)

Hidden treasures: Great Vat, Sprung Tower; comments by Mark Twain, tour leader

What's best seen alone: gardens, moat, Great Terrace; best times of year to see it

Imagine life inside those walls 350 years ago

Still close to nature: cable car or hike through pines up to *Königstuhl,* can stop for lunch or supper at Molkenkur on way; see view of Rhine Valley, Neckar River, Heidelberg below

Return to *Kornmarkt* at foot of castle, hear Town Hall *glockenspiel* play, explore historic Old Town, sup and sing in open-air beer hall with *Schloss* fireworks exploding overhead...

To complete the blocking I must subdivide the segments. That is, insert the facts, quotes, and other material I will use in each section. I might take one of the segments above and expand on it this way:

Expanded Blocking Segment

Hidden treasures: Great Vat, Sprung Tower; comments by Mark Twain, tour leader

biggest surprise, Great Vat; describe, walk on staircase around and over it, size (use tour guide quote)

statue of Perkeo, tie into wine room, open to public

Mark Twain comment about castle, quote about learning one word in German, *bier*

Sprung tower, stand at its base, feel force of 400 years of leaning

In other words, I break the article into segments (in this case, the material between subheads), then I write in what I have available for that copy. And then it's on to blocking the next article.

Roughing the Article

I'm now back home, rested after a hectic flight and the great bag grab at the airport (this time I got mine first!). The film has been sent for development, my computer sits where I left it, and it's time to turn my fun abroad into financial freedom at home.

I take the blocking page for the *BBB Magazine* piece and scatter around my desk the interviews, notes, quotes, map, travel guides, and even some photos to help refresh my memory. Looking at all this starts me writing, and I get the words down from first to last.

Successful writers don't compose final copy at one sitting any more than sculptors create final forms in one blow. It takes a concept, adding words, refining, reading aloud, moving text, checking the thesaurus, reading again, and then again. Even after all this you may want to change a word or two. You move from hammer to chisel to file to sandpaper to the touch of your hand.

Let's follow one paragraph, the lead, through this process. Atypically I have something in mind for this particular lead that will immediately tie this overpowering castle into the American scene: Disneyland and Hollywood. What first occurs to me?

Roughing Copy

When it comes to giant, breathtaking castles, Walt

Disney couldn't improve on Heidelberg's *Schloss*. Its verdant terraces, cannonball-pocked towers, and lonely, see-through belfry rise above the city into the pine mountains behind. Even Hollywood would fall short of the reality.

From here I would talk about the fairyland setting of Heidelberg, *The Student Prince* and the country's oldest university, open-air beer gardens, narrow streets through blocks of museumlike buildings, all magically alive on summer nights with the bridge and castle illuminated and fireworks exploding over the most romantic of all Germany cities. And so on, following the outline of the blocking.

I know that every line I write needs work. That doesn't bother me at the roughing stage. The idea is to let the words flow, get them down, and later find the precise terms, the best images, and the most harmonious combinations of sound and meaning. For now, getting it on paper is the first and toughest step. The rest, the editing and polishing, takes longer but for me is much more fun.

Do I rough all the pending articles one after the other, or do I edit each the moment that the roughing is done? It depends on how close I am to the deadline. Since I have several weeks I'll go ahead and rough the article about Mark Twain and Heidelberg, while letting the rough of the castle article age for a few days. Then I'll come back to it with a fresh perspective.

Editing the Article

I'm back! A few days have passed and it is now time to go through the roughed version of the castle article with a lot more attention. I figure that since I spent two hours roughing, and since the editing and final manuscript preparation can run three times that long, I might be looking at six more hours of work. Although sometimes editing zips right along...

The lead needs work. I'll go over each sentence and indicate the kinds of thoughts that come to mind. I'll create the final lead later.

When it comes to giant, breathtaking castles, Walt Disney couldn't improve on Heidelberg's Schloss. Sounds too wordy. I want the first sentence in the lead to be punchy, if possible. "Giant, breathtaking" is flabby. Maybe massive. I'll play around with this after I look at the other sentences. I like the idea, though. Every American knows Walt Disney.

Its verdant terraces, cannonball-pocked towers, and lonely, see-through belfry rise above the city into the pine mountains behind. Wordier yet. Verdant? Green? The pine mountains are also green. Maybe tiered, since that's what makes them castlelike. Cannonball-pocked doesn't sound too good. Ruined? How would they stand? Half-ruined. They are. You *can* see through the belfry (it has nothing inside) if you're standing on the terraces level with it, but surely nobody could see through it from miles away. Old? No. Ancient? And "rise above the city"? Need something better. Pine mountains? Mountains made of pine? They're pine forests. Not much of a mountain anyway, only 2,000 feet high.

Even Hollywood would fall short of the reality. Not very well focused, mixing Disney and Hollywood. Also draws away from the castle, which is the mental vision I want to create. When people think of castles they think of kings and courts and other regal paraphernalia. I could say, "All that's missing is the king." Sounds too short (even if the king is tall!). They were called electors, anyway, though some were called kings too. I'll use the word king here and explain "electors" later, in the historical part. Let me play with this sentence...

I continue to mull over these ideas, trying to come up with the best version. Even after I do I might come back to it repeatedly, to adjust it to something I say later in another section or to insert something to complete the picture I want to share. I finally create a great lead:

Edited Copy

When it comes to castles, Walt Disney couldn't improve on Heidelberg's massive *Schloss*. Its tiered terraces, half-ruined towers, and ancient belfry soar above the city into the pine-forested mountains behind. All that's missing are plumed trumpeters, the troops, and the King.

Every paragraph gets the same close treatment. When I have what I think is a well-balanced piece, I again visualize my readers and ask, Will this help them? Will they understand it? Will it grab and keep their attention? Is it 100% accurate? I read it and reread it; I set it down again to read a day or two later; then I review it once more, paragraph by paragraph.

When the editing is done, I proudly type up my newest creation in acceptable manuscript form. But before I send it to Mrs. Cammack I've got to assemble the appropriate photos.

Selecting the Photographs for The Article

From my many slides I must choose the one hundred or so I will mail with the manuscript.

First I throw the totally useless slides away, then I sort the rest by *site*. If I mention a particular site or feature in the article I try to find one, two, or many slides that best show it from different angles, times of day,

or focal points. Then I choose other, super shots that
are related to the article.

I have plenty of photos of almost every aspect of the
castle. To these I add several of the castle taken from
the Old Town section, one from the footpath, several
from the *Königstuhl*, perhaps another from across the
Neckar River. Plus one shot each of other key sites in
the city, should the art editor want to balance the
presentation that way.

I group the photos by logic and geography both in
the acetate holders and on the caption sheets (see
Chapter 6).

I must remember to keep some sharp slides aside for
the other articles I will write. Thank goodness I took lots
of photos whenever I found a particularly exciting view.

Sending a Cover Letter

Do I need a cover letter with this submission? Many
months have passed since I queried, so I probably do.
In fact, I always send one with articles that come from
pretrip queries. But seldom if I send queries after the
trip. I include one that is brief and positive (Figure 10).

Figure 10 Cover Letter for Submitting a Manuscript to a Magazine

P.O. Box 6405
Santa Maria, CA 93456
(805) 937-8711
November 5, 1991

Mrs. Linda Cammack
Managing Editor, *BBB Magazine*
158 Lake St.
San Francisco, CA 94118

Dear Mrs. Cammack:

I'm back from Germany, bursting with enthusiasm about the
trip, and am particularly pleased with the information and

continued on page 178

photos I got at the *Schloss* for the article, enclosed, that you asked to see in your query reply of May 22.

One hundred Kodachrome slides are included, most about the castle, of course, but twenty more of other places of interest in Heidelberg, as you suggested. I took as many good verticals as I could, hoping that one might qualify as a cover selection.

I can also send this copy by disk, prepared on an MS-DOS IBM-XT, with Sprint software. If you tell me what you use, if IBM-compatible, I can translate it through Sprint into that program. If you have any other questions or I can be of any help, please write or call.

Would you let me know about the article and photos at your earliest convenience?

Respectfully,

Gordon Burgett

CHAPTER 10

Putting the Words on Paper

If I could really tell you how to write—what words to put precisely where—I could perform miracles. This is not the case. Too much of writing is in your creative juices, in that mind-to-ear part of the soul, to ever successfully codify and put into a never-fail formula.

Yet I can suggest what seems to work best, what is usually done in travel articles that sell, and some thought patterns that might make the writing process easier. Actually, it's simpler to tell you what not to say or do.

STYLE

Articles share information. They are paths to knowledge. The fastest paths are the straightest and least adorned with obstacles or distractions. Most readers don't want tedious hurdles between what they want to know and what you have to say. They don't mind you lining the path with flowers, for purposeful adornment, or lightening up the journey with a bit of anecdotal or analogous variety, but they mainly want you to get the message home.

This usually translates into nouns and verbs conventionally arranged in relatively short sentences. Adjectives used as needed, pronouns with clear antecedents (exactly who "it" is), and adverbs employed only when absolutely necessary—don't "speak softly," whisper; don't "run quickly," dash or sprint. Avoid the word very as much as you avoid packing your piece with superlatives. In truth, how much restaurant food is "absolutely scrumptious"? None is "very, very scrumptious," or none that any self-respecting travel editors would share with their readers.

Voice

Articles are written in first person (I), second person (you), or third person (he, she, it, or "Mrs. Smith"). You must pick one and stick with it.

Beginners are enamored with first person, on the conviction that everybody would just love to relive every second of a hike the writer took eons ago as a child, up a trail to some half-dry reservoir. This predilection of first-time writers is the very reason that travel editors plead no "me-and-Joe" stories please! Diaries should be adored, and kept, at home.

There are times, however, when first-person articles are called for: when the action described as singular or hard to repeat (high adventure falls into that category), when it absolutely requires personal comments or observations ("I was trapped overnight in King Tut's tomb!"), or when the subject is highly subjective or intimate (third-person love stories lose something).

Second person—you would enjoy this, do that—isn't as commonly used as one might imagine, in part because it's hard to find a perfect "you" to whom it might universally apply. It can also sound too bossy or preachy. Still, many newspaper items take this tone, and personal accounts in magazines sometimes also take the voice that one uses in a family letter, the unstated "you."

To the suprise of newcomers most articles are written in the objective third person, impersonal, one step removed. This is how newspaper copy is written. When in doubt, employ the third person.

I recommend a simple rule of thumb for deciding which voice to use: Read the publication where you want your article to appear and use what it uses. My articles on travel in the Midwest for *Better Homes and Gardens* were in the third person because that's what the magazine always used. My high adventure pieces, mainly gold hunting on the Upper Amazon, were sent to publications that only used first-person hair-raisers. My newspaper advice items ("Ten Fun Things to Do in Quito, Ecuador") were second person since newspaper travel normally accepts all three voices and advice works best with a me-to-you attitude.

Punctuation

Several marks of punctuation cause problems for new writers. One is the semicolon. Use it sparingly and always correctly. A high school grammar text tells you how. Also use dashes appropriately and indicate them correctly in your copy (a dash on your typewriter or computer is two hyphens, with a space before and after the dash). Type hyphens singular, with no space before and after. Never end a typeset or printed line with a hyphen, even if it looks odd to carry the whole hyphenated composite over to the next line. Carry it over, with the typesetter and editor's blessing.

Then there is the question of how to punctuate items in a series. Choose the series comma: "Bill, Betty, and Babs" (the series comma is the one before "and").

CONTENT

The Lead

Every article has a lead, which consists of the first paragraph or occasionally the first two paragraphs. No combination of words that follow are as important.

Editors call these openers "hook leads" because when properly done, they pull the reader in. If the first few words don't create interest or curiosity, if you don't entice the reader to look through the door, you will never get them in the room.

Keep your lead short. A sentence or two is fine, three is probably too many, and four is a funeral oration.

You needn't write your lead first. Just write your copy and worry about the lead later. Better yet, write five or ten leads before or after the rough body of the text is completed. Then pick the best and bring the rest of the text in line. It takes only a few verb changes, a new transition, and off you go.

When I taught journalism my students learned the seven most frequently used types of leads the hard way: I had them take home their shiny new article, just written for class (some, I suspect, written moments before), so they could write seven different openings for the next class session.

Not all worked equally well, of course, but by knowing the various types they could select the best one in the future. (We used Daniel Williamson's excellent *Feature Writing for Newspapers* as the guide for the leads.)

What are the seven types of leads?

The Seven Most-used Types of Leads

1. The summary lead. For hard news, the most common. This approach lets a strong and interesting

subject sell itself by getting straight to it: "Ricky Larf was captain of the basketball team, a straight-A student, and father of three sons, all by different teenage girls, when he disappeared from the face of the earth."

2. The *narrative* lead. Hard to do, but very effective. Put your readers in the story by making them identify with or become the protagonist. Used often for travel adventure: "Larry Danton's sinewy 6'7" frame, shiny new rifle, and razor-sharp fillet knife were as useless as an ice cube on the Amazon as he stared into the blow gun nervously pressed to the Auca Indian's mouth."

3. The *descriptive* lead. A favorite in travel because, through adjectives, you bring the subject or site into instant focus: "Tex Bennett's face was a Technicolor diary: his right cheek a ruin from an Apache bullet, his nose a red beacon from back-creek moonshine, his last tooth a bright yellow stump."

4. The *quotation* lead. The quote must be sharp, short, and directly related to the article that follows: " 'Thar she blows!' shouted the skipper to scores of camera-pointing landlubbers hugging the side deck as a spout of water shot 20 feet into the air."

5. The *question* lead. Editors don't like these because they're too easy and too often misleading. But precise questions can work well in travel: "Why spend more than $100 to tour the Galápagos Islands for two weeks?"

6. The *direct-address* lead. Uses the word *you*, thus pulling the reader immediately into the text. This approach only works in second-person articles and is hard to do well. "It happens. You're carefully brushing back the hard-packed sand at a Turkish dig and you see the bones of a child's hand..."

7. The *trick* or *teaser* lead. Any gimmick that will get readers' attention, to tease or trick them into reading the lead. Usually funny, always to the point. I started an article about Mason City, Iowa, which was "River City, USA" in Meredith Willson's *Music Man*, with lyrics:

> You got trouble, friend,
> Right here, I say,
> Trouble right here in River City!

The Transitional Paragraph

The first hook is really the title, followed by the second hook, the lead. These are the eye-catchers. Their function is to attract readers' attention and then lure them into your article. Most of what follows is the body, the information you want to share. But strategically hiding between the hooks and the body is a paragraph or two, sometimes three, that is a verbal map explaining where the article is going and how it will get there.

Many readers don't know this. They aren't aware of transitional paragraph(s). Nor are some writers, but these paragraphs play a vital role. Following the lead, they explain the theme, indicate the article's destination and method of arrival, and establish the tone of the article.

Most frequently, transitional paragraph(s) tell whether the article will be structured chronologically, geographically (often by section, city, region, or country), or developmentally (fill in the passport application, have photos taken, pay the fee, etc.).

Journalists usually call these paragraphs the "bridge" because they carry the reader from the lead into the body text. Although some articles don't have bridges, most do. Study these paragraphs closely. They are pathfinders for readers. They also help keep your words from spinning off into nowhere.

Paragraph Length

If the lead seems too short, so will the paragraphs, which might also be a sentence long, usually two, sometimes three, and rarely four.

But paragraph length differs by type of publication. The lengths above apply to newspaper copy. Magazines are looser and some allow paragraphs of six or even eight sentences. As a rule, the more academic the publication, the longer (and often duller) its paragraphs will be.

Books run the gamut, with novels at times having full-page sentences. With fiction, all rules are off!

Simply study the publication (or one similar) that you want to write for and fashion your paragraphs to the length it prefers. The more commercial the publication, the more it will avoid large blocks of copy because it impedes reading flow and intimidates the reader.

Write your copy like the copy in the publication in which you want to appear. Forget the old school rules that said paragraphs ended when the subject (or the writer) expired! After a couple of sentences (or six typeset lines for newspapers) it's time for a new paragraph! Write for speed and clarity.

And seek variety. Break up your page with quotes and anecdotes, keeping your descriptions visual, tight, and short.

Sidebars

Sidebars (also called boxes) are commonly used with travel articles, allowing you to offer additional information in a different context and to add more depth and range to your copy.

Most of us are familiar with *Time* and *Newsweek*, both of which use sidebars extensively. A political story in

Time might discuss, say, a crisis in the Middle East in the main article and provide a separate, adjacent box of information (often shaded a different color) that zeros in on a smaller-focus item, like how this situation affects one family or whether life at an isolated oasis has changed.

There are three kinds of sidebars. If the article is global (or macro), the sidebar zooms in on a micro topic. Or else the reverse (micro topic with global sidebar). The third type of sidebar is simply factual material that enhances the larger piece.

Here are two examples, both linked to whale-watching articles. The first appeared in a newspaper article in which I showed how individuals or families could board ships at the piers in southern California from December to March and venture a few miles oceanward to see migrating grays. The sidebar listed the piers from San Diego to Santa Barbara, with the names of the ships, the days and times they sailed, the cost, and specific stipulations, if any.

The second occurred in an article called "Whale Watch" in *Dynamic Years*, a publication for seniors. A few days after I sent the article to the editor I happened to sit next to a weathered fellow on an airplane. Turns out he had been the captain of the ship that had captured Gigi, the first gray in captivity, caught for scientific purposes for Sea World. I got out my notepad, interviewed Frank Mason, and called the editor the next morning, suggesting this as a good sidebar. He agreed and I sent if off, earning myself an extra $150 and providing an interesting sidelight that greatly personalized the main article.

Incidentally, this is one of the rare situations when I contact editors by phone. I sensed that the magazine was about to set the article in type and lay out the issue, so mailing the inquiry might have taken too long (those were pre-FAX days).

Always think of possible sidebars when you send your magazine query, focusing on the main theme in the letter but suggesting that, if interested, you could also provide a sidebar about *X* or *Y*, which you explain to the editor in a sentence or two.

If you're writing about a winter solstice trip to a Navajo religious site, describe what else can be seen and done on the reservation. If this information doesn't blend comfortably into the text, create a sidebar. If you write about spending the Fourth of July on Cape Cod, let the readers know what else takes place there during the month of July. Another sidebar. If you're showing how Portugal is the best bargain in Europe, create a box comparing the buying power of the escudo with, say, the franc, deutsche mark, peseta, lira, and pound.

Should you discover valuable sidebar information at the site, gather the information you need and, when you submit the go-ahead article, ask the magazine editor whether he or she wants the sidebar as well. Make this cover letter a short query, enclosing a self-addressed, stamped envelope (SASE) for reply.

For newspapers, submit both the article and the sidebar at the same time, noting in capital letters at the top, "SIDEBAR."

The Conclusion

All newspaper and magazine articles must come to a close, and how you write the conclusion is important.

These articles are not short stories with surprise endings. And although news articles simply stop when the news ends, travel articles (in both newspapers and magazines) must have conclusions that reinforce what their leads promise. If you're talking about saving money while touring Nepal, the conclusion should return to the money-saving theme. If nostalgia is your theme, your ending should leave a lump in the throat when the last word is read.

Let me share a well-used technique for ending articles that don't lend themselves to an obvious conclusion: Look for a word or phrase from the lead that can be comfortably returned to and repeated in the final paragraph. That gives the reader the sense of having gone full circle, of a journey fully taken. Don't force it, though, and avoid using something from the title (because often the editor rewrites or completely changes it, so that a reference to the title in the conclusion would no longer make any sense).

The Title

When you write travel for a newspaper don't worry about a title, unless the piece is clearly humorous. Just call it "Bodie, California" or "Railroad Bike Path, Sparta, Wisconsin."

But when you write for magazines, think of the title as the first lead. Although it's only a few words long, it should make readers want to see more, it should pull them into the actual lead (the first or first two paragraphs), which in turn pulls them into the rest of the piece. Once there, studies show, readers will finish the article if it sustains their interest and doesn't obstruct their easy comprehension by making them wade through large blocks of copy.

A title is your article's headline: It seduces readers by telling them what the article is about. If it's humorous, write the title with the same kind and amount of humor as the article. If it's witty and full of wordplay, the title should be too. If it's so funny readers will have trouble holding on to the paper, the title should virtually laugh out loud. Editors rarely change humor titles, even in newspapers, so attention is vital here. Look for humor titles, in the text itself, not in the lead (it's best to write humor titles after you've written your copy). And don't include inside jokes in the title. Since your readers haven't read the inside yet, they won't get the joke— and probably won't bother to read the article.

Stated in reverse: Don't write an article to match a title. That's like starting with a punch line, then trying to invent a joke for it! By starting with the title you set artificial limits for yourself before you have done the research or structuring. Write the article, then write a title that reflects its content.

In the sections here on style and content we've examined the characteristics that all good articles possess. Of course the best guide to how you should write is already in print, right there on the pages where you want your words to appear. Read the publication and write that way, only better.

We're now ready to look at the physical form you should give your manuscript in order to submit it (and have it looked upon favorably).

FORM

There is no absolutely "correct" form for manuscripts. As an editor I have seen them submitted in all shapes and colors, bound or looseleaf and out of order; once I got a manuscript with a shopping list on the back, and another time I received an article in the wrong language (I think).

In fact, between the writing and the actual form of the manuscript, editors are far more tolerant about how the words arrive than what they say or how they say it.

Still, editors do have preferences in form. And there are some editors who simply will not read copy that isn't submitted in the "conventional" style.

Some things will get your manuscript sent back about
as fast as it's seen: handwritten copy, unreadable text,
obvious and frequent misspellings, and English that
clearly isn't. An editor's life is hard enough without
working with writers who make it harder.

Still, super writing is hard for any editor to reject,
however it is submitted. As the *Writer's Market* write-
up for the "Sunday Journal Magazine" of the *Providence
Journal* used to say, after offering the standard
submission advice, "But if your stuff is really good, we'll
buy it if it comes in by Pony Express." (A truly safe
offer since the Pony Express never came east of St. Joseph,
Missouri!)

The magic words here are *really good*. Electric,
fetching prose will always overrule lousy packaging. Yet
copy from new writers, and even from foot-weary
professionals on lesser days, is more likely "good" than
"really good." So poor presentation is a hurdle you cannot
afford.

There's another reason why sticking with the conventional style makes sense, at least early on. New writers
pose as professionals while they grow into the suit,
hoping the editor won't ask too many questions about
their track record. It's easier to make the pose believable
by doing what most professionals do: offer clean copy,
proper spacing and numbering, on-time delivery, names
and labels where necessary, and so on. (Yes, some professionals are slobs. Emulate them, if you must, after you've
sold your five-hundredth article.)

So here are some general guidelines about a manuscript form that seems to be widely acceptable.

Manuscript Specifics

Type your manuscript on standard (8½ x 11") white
paper, one side only. Use elite or pica type, not script.

The ribbon should be reasonably new and black. Clean the keys if they are clogged with ink—the c, e, and o should be clear (these keys are good cleaning guides).

If you're using a computer, make sure the print is easy to read. Most editors balk at the old dot matrix printer where you practically have to connect the dots to decipher the letters and where there are no descenders (the y, for example, doesn't descend below the line, and all letters are equal in height). Most writers now use laser, letter quality, or good near-letter quality printers, all of which can provide legible print. Some editors prefer articles on disk, so you might ask once you've received a positive reply from your query (or you might suggest its availability to newspaper editors when you submit the hard copy).

Few editors accept faxed manuscripts yet but you might ask about that too, once the manuscript has received the nod.

In addition to providing legible copy, remember to provide plenty of white space. Don't cover the entire page with text. Leave ample margins in every direction. Fifteen spaces for the left margin leaves the editor enough room to write in the typesetting instructions. Leave about the same amount of space, unjustified, on the right.

Start copy halfway down your first page. In the center of that empty top half write the title in CAPITAL LETTERS. Don't <u>underline</u> it or put "quotation marks" around it (unless they are needed to indicate a nickname or other special designation).

About three lines below the title, also centered, write "by (your name)." This is your byline. Always insert one, even if the publication doesn't use bylines—this shows the editor who should be paid!

In the upper righthand corner write the approximate word count, rounded off to the closest 25. You can write this number in by hand, since it's wisest (most accurate) to count words after the manuscript is typed or printed. (Every word counts. Even little words.)

At the top of each subsequent page, about six lines down from the top and six lines above the copy, flush left in line with the margin, write the title (whole or abbreviated) in CAPITAL LETTERS, followed by a comma, your name (in regular type), another comma, and then the page number.

Indent each paragraph five spaces, double-space between the lines, and triple-space between paragraphs, if you wish. If you want the article set with white (blank) space between sections of your copy, skip about five lines and type the space symbol (#) in the center of that white space.

Don't leave "widows" (single lines, alone, on the bottom or the top of a page, "widowed" and left to fend for themselves). These bedevil editors because typesetters frequently miss them, leaving senseless holes in the middle of your article. Newspaper editors particularly loathe them—and most magazine editors started in the newspaper world.

If you want to use italics in your article, don't type or print in an *italic* font. Instead underline all italics. Likewise with **bold face**, underline with a wavy line and write "BF" in large letters in the closest margin with a line leading to the copy you want in bold.

Put your name and address on every page. A quick way is to buy those 1,000-for-$1.50 return-address stickers and put one in the lower righthand corner of each page. (For pieces submitted simultaneously to different newspapers, put the stickers on the master and they will reproduce on the copies.)

On the last page of your manuscript, a few lines below the last words, center the word *end* or write its symbol (#####). The old newspaper tradition was to put, lower right, "Page (number) of (number)" on each page, with the first number increasing from page to page. Example: "Page 1 of 4," "Page 2 of 4," and so on. You can do this on the manuscripts you submit to newspapers, if you wish.

Onionskin paper makes editors weep. It curls up and turns yellow. Likewise avoid erasable paper. The minute a thumb touches it the typed words are lost, to that thumb. Plain white 20-pound or mimeo paper is fine. The idea is that the copy should be permanent, legible, and flat. To keep it flat you can mail the manuscript unfolded in a full-sized manila envelope or folded once in a half-sized manila, enclosing an SASE (for submission to U.S. publications).

Those are the usual specifics, with a few extras thrown in. Feel free to worry about content and style, but don't worry about form. Simply present your copy as indicated above and improvise where the guidelines don't apply. Common sense and the editor's weak eyesight rule.

#####

CHAPTER 11

Post-Trip Querying

What if you know about a potential article before you leave on a trip but can't, won't, or don't have time to query before you depart?

Or you discover a super subject you want to share in print once you are there?

Or one or several of your query go-aheads branch off into exciting directions that provide unique and clearly different article themes of their own?

In each case, if you fully researched the new article topics on-site, after your trip is the time to see which editors are eager to put your stories on their magazine pages!

When you've written your pretrip query articles, matched them with photos, and sent them off, you can get their post-trip counterparts off, to begin the mystical life that only query letters beget.

Then, in the weeks (or months) that editors take to reply, you can write and send the newspaper articles.

Post-trip queries differ in only one way from those plotted and mailed before the trip: You've been to the site. Instead of promising a future date of departure, return, and three weeks to write gilded prose, now all you need is the three weeks, or until the editor wants the article.

Having been at the site makes the query composition much easier. You needn't rely on others' impressions and facts from which to postulate a likely article. You have a kit bag of your own true data and memories from which you can craft a tight, image-creating query to wrest an eager affirmative.

You know precisely what you can promise because you know what you have gathered and what photos you have taken. That, in turn, makes the hunt for the best markets easier.

In fact, feasibility studies for post-trip queries are fast and precise. Is it feasible to write? Of course. You know what information you have and from which angles it can be approached. Is it feasible to sell? Preparing your market list couldn't be easier. Which magazine's readers would be interested in the angles you can offer? Put them in order and start querying from the top!

What's left? Doing it! Get a query about each potential article in the mail. Follow through on each reply. If rejected, write another query to the next publication on the list. If the editor wants more, study the publication and write a top-grade article about what you promised in the query. Match the photos to the prose and get that breadwinner en route!

EXAMPLE: POST-TRIP QUERIES FOR THE BIG TRIP

I've taken the trip, written my query go-ahead articles, and sent all the appropriate slides. Now I'm ready to write the post-trip queries to other magazine editors, getting these potential articles in motion so I can turn to the newspaper articles while awaiting a reply.

Before I left I made notes of various on-site topics to research and query editors about when I returned.

I also left open the likelihood that other ideas would suggest themselves on-site.

One of those ideas pans out—to present "pocket-trip stories about excursions" in and near Frankfurt for visitors with a few extra days to spend in that huge but drab city. A better idea after the fact than before, so first I do some thinking, then some checking to find the best markets for this piece.

Who would those people most likely be? Probably not tourists. They go to places of their own choice. Not the average U.S. reader, who thinks you put mustard on a Frankfurt on the Fourth of July. Businessfolk, that's who. At least those who are Europe-bound, many of whom pass through Frankfurt, like it or not.

So I head to the library to see which magazines the international or well-heeled business types are most likely to read. Between the magazines on the racks and those listed in *Writer's Market* and *Business Index*, I find five (my selection is subjective, of course). I study their needs as best I can and put them in a marketing order. *CCC Magazine* is first.

Now I must write a query letter that piques the interest of Ms. Beatrice LaMer, the articles editor, as well as convinces her that what I promise must be bought for her pages (see Figure 11).

Comments About the Post-Trip Query Letter

CCC Magazine is written specifically to business executives who frequently travel abroad, so I tie that into my theme in the first paragraph.

Dead days in Frankfurt are a common enough lament, so I build on that in the first and second paragraphs, suggesting that there is much more the magazine's readers would like to do in and near the city if they had specific details. Thus paragraph three.

Figure 11 Post-Trip Query Letter

P.O. Box 6405
Santa Maria, CA 93456
(805) 937-8711
November 10, 1991

Ms. Beatrice LaMer
Articles Editor, *CCC Magazine*
456 Spring Street
Chenoa, Illinois 61726

Dear Ms. LaMer:

Since your magazine is widely read by business executives
who regularly venture to Europe, let's bring them some fun
choices of what to do after or between their labors. Let's help
them turn those dead days in Frankfurt into exciting
memories.

Once you've walked through downtown Frankfurt, you've
seen it all. It's back to the hotel, a good beer hall, a movie
(probably in German), or the cavernous airport.

So let's give your readers headed that way a how-to article
with every needed detail about four different, inexpensive
one- or two-day "pocket trips" they can take within about 75
miles of that city: what they do, where they go, the cost, but
most of all, why they'd enjoy each of the excursions.

The easiest is right in town. Few visitors realize that Frankfurt
is one of Europe's top art centers, with three buildings to
match: the *Städelsches Kunstinstitut* (the major art museum,
with works by Rubens, Rembrandt, van Eyck, Botticelli, Monet,
and Picasso), The *Liebighaus* (with its world-class collection
of sculpture), and the *Museum für Kunsthandwerk* (full of
eye-popping decorative arts).

Another is an hour away on the city tram, through the open
countryside to Wiesbaden, on the Rhine River, to see the ancient but still-enjoyed baths, the famed casino, and the dis-
tinctly Germanic charms of that city. Directly across the river
is Mainz; although less charming than Wiesbaden, it's the site
of the Gutenberg Museum, of movable-type and Bible (1455)
fame.

From Wiesbaden begins the most historic of the Rhine River cruises (and the third pocket trip), to Rüdesheim, Lorch, and Koblenz, past castles, monasteries, and Riesling vineyards, through the land of Lohengrin, narrow streets, and wee museums.

The fourth is 50 miles in the other direction, by train or bus, to Heidelberg, setting for *The Student Prince*, site of Germany's oldest university (1386), its most spectacular castle, and a plethora of open-air markets and beer gardens. Visitors can hike (or cable car ride) through the pine forest at the edge of the city to *Königstuhl*, go to museums, or take boat rides up and down the sparkling Neckar River.

I just returned from this area, having attended the Frankfurt Book Fair, and heard the laments of other businessfolk unaware of the riches almost at hand. I can have this article to you, in manuscript or IBM disk form, three weeks after you give me the go-ahead. I can also provide approximately one hundred sharp slides, to illustrate each of the pocket trips suggested, plus sidebars about any specific facet, if interested. Finally, I'll tailor this piece to your readers, as I've done more than one thousand times before for other articles in print over the past 20 years.

Are you game? Shall we "save" those stranded souls? Just let me know.

Gordon Burgett

Note that the trips are short, only a day or two, and nearby. They are also inexpensive, since the travelers will likely pay with their own money (rather than expense-account dollars).

I must now sell Ms. LaMer on the four "fun" places that are the heart of the proposed article. I focus on what visitors would see at the locations, one trip per paragraph. These could be longer but I like to limit queries to one tight, typed page. It's enough to give the editor the substance and direction of the article.

How do I know that travelers would be interested (maybe even desperate) for such diversions? Because I just returned and heard of the laments firsthand. Did I? Well, secondhand, but I'd heard of Frankfurt being a dead stop often enough to know that the comment, from an American businessperson's perspective, was accurate.

The clincher: more than one hundred sharp slides, sidebars if wanted, and a tailor-made gem for the nod. Plus a delivery date in about three weeks. I like to end with a question or two to encourage the editor's response. "Just let me know" means *fax me instantly*. Or at least write. Soon.

I'll wait for a reply before contacting the next of the four magazines on my market list, just as I would do with a pretrip query list.

But let's say Ms. LaMer does buy this article, what do I do with the other four markets thus being deprived of my intoxicating prose? I can either remold my idea into a clearly unique article, I can combine it with other topics I found in Germany to form a different article, or I can try a completely distinct theme and send off queries, one at a time or one each on the different articles. Or I can sell the article as a report after it appears on *CCC*'s pages.

My inclination? Purely pecuniary. Since these magazines pay on acceptance—why else would I query them?—they probably won't buy reprints. And they'll pay much more for articles handcrafted for their own readers. I'd query each of them, until I ran out of markets or ideas. Tenacity pays when you have the right stuff for good copy and sharp slides.

CHAPTER 12

Newspapers: A Strategic Bombardment

The larger newspapers don't buy much copy from freelancers—except for travel, where they find it far less expensive to pay you for your words about a trip recently completed than to send a perk-paid reporter around the world for a few thousand adjectives!

The requirements are simple enough: scintillating copy that is current, accurate, more objective than fawningly biased, an appropriate length, and flat out interesting to the reader. Also, if you are describing something unimaginable to the average mortal, photos are appreciated.

First question, who buys? Almost every major newspaper buys at one time or another, though perhaps 20% are "off the market" at any one time—because of a glutted market, empty coffers, using syndicated pieces only, between editors, or other, less tangible reasons succinctly defined in the word *no*.

How do you find the major newspapers? You can use the *Gale Directory of Publications and Broadcast Media*, the *Working Press of the Nation*, or other reference works your library might suggest.

I created my own list, complete with addresses and ZIP codes, by copying the "newspapers" section of *Literary Market Place*. I then crossed out the name and title of the book editor and replaced it with the words *Travel Editor*. This provided me with a list to work from, on the safe assumption that if a newspaper has a book editor it also has a travel editor.

Another way to get a list is to buy the "100 Best Travel Newspaper Markets" released every September 1, for $7 complete (available from Communication Unlimited, listed in "Sources for Travel Writers" at the end of this book). Following a discussion of how to sell to newspapers is a three-page list, which you could simply take to a copy shop for reproduction on Avery labels.

TWO KINDS OF NEWSPAPERS

It isn't financially wise to sell to every newspaper. To determine where to sell your writing you must realize that newspapers fall into two camps: national and regional.

A national publication wants exclusive national rights. So you can't sell to more than one of them, or to any of them and to regional newspapers at the same time.

Regionals, on the other hand, don't want to see the same article in their own area, in either a national or a nearby regional newspaper. This means that within a 100-mile radius you cannot submit an article simultaneously to another regional newspaper or to a national newspaper at all.

Which further means that through regional sales you can easily send the same article to Chicago, Los Angeles, New York, Minneapolis, New Orleans, Seattle, Miami, Toronto, and Denver all at the same time—plus one hundred other cities in between.

To make things simple, I exclude the nationals. The *New York Times* is a fine newspaper but it must do without my travel musings. The same for the *Christian Science Monitor*, the *Wall Street Journal*, and *USA Today*. Somehow they continue muddling on without my words or thoughts...

Which means that when I have a travel piece of interest nationwide I get out my map, draw imaginary circles, and send clear copies of one master to many editors simultaneously.

SIMULTANEOUS SUBMISSIONS

A good way to create an ongoing and comprehensive market list for newspapers is to write a solid article with nationwide appeal, identify those cities that are sufficiently far apart from each other, and send your piece to as many of them as you can at the same time.

If there are three potential newspapers in the same area—say, from Chicago, Milwaukee, and South Bend—try one, if it says no, try another, and so on until you've made a sale or run out of markets!

When you receive your responses, put those that buy at the top of your new market list. Complete it with those that don't buy but that do send you a standard (or even spectacular) rejection. They *are* buying, although not that particular piece.

An estimated 20% will reject with a notation that they aren't currently buying freelance material. Put them on a special list to try next year. Most return to the fold eventually, buying from the public.

The regionals pay from $85 to about $220 per article, averaging about $125 each, always on publication (the nationals usually pay more). About half the papers that buy my copy also buy my photos (99% black-and-whites [b/w's]); about half of those buy multiple photos. Black-and-whites bring $10 to $15; slides (bought from free-lancers almost as frequently as exposes written in Esperanto!) pay two to three times as much.

The beauty is that when you have an article of buying quality, usually three or four editors indulge. If four do buy the same article, you earn at least $500, plus another $50 or so for photos.

How many articles a year do newspapers buy from freelancers? Some pick up as few as six, if they're buying at all. Others, literally hundreds. Your competition is other freelancers, other travel editors, and staffers from that paper sent on assignment with the directive to also "get a travel piece while you're there."

Freelancers aren't very competitive for a newspaper's key articles, which often run about 2,500 words. Given a choice between your manuscript, however sparkling, and the editor's own humble words, humility wins. Or the humble words of fellow travel editors.

You will generally sell at the second-article level. Fortunately, most of the larger periodicals use three or four "seconds" per travel issue. These usually include from 1,000 to 1,600 words, but I have found 1,200 to 1,350 words to be just about right, with b/w's bought and used to stretch the prose where it falls short. Given the pay ranges cited, second articles pay from 40 to 50 cents a word (including the word *it* and prepositions).

Send a Note-sized Cover Letter with Your Article

To submit an article simultaneously to various newspapers, make a clear master and send collated copies of it to each travel editor, with a special cover note attached, and either a self-addressed, stamped envelope (SASE) or postcard enclosed.

The cover note contains six key elements: (1) At the top is your name, address, ZIP, and phone number, all centered. (2) Your salutation is either to "Travel Editor" or, after you develop a selling relationship, to the editor by name. (3) Your first paragraph sells the article attached. (4) The second discusses photos. (5) The third is a closing directive. (6) Your signed name comes last.

Make yourself accessible to the editor. In addition to your address tell how you can be reached by phone. Rarely will editors rush to the telephone, but I can't remember a time when a phone call from an editor didn't result in a sale.

Conversely, I never call them. They buy copy and want to see it first, so the submission process as described seems to work best. Nor do I know of any editor who wants newspaper submissions sent by FAX. It could happen but it's far more likely after you have a selling record with that editor. Let the editor suggest it, or ask after a few sales.

A salutation of "Dear Travel Editor" is fine when you're sending articles to editors you haven't submitted to before. They don't know you, you don't know them. But after you've connected or when you are sending to specific editors regularly, use their name and spell it correctly. Travel editors are just like other humans: They respond favorably to being called by name. And dislike being called by another's, particularly a travel editor who hasn't been on staff for a decade.

Attach the note to the front of the first page of your manuscript. Since travel editors are busy they'd rather read a succinct note than the whole manuscript. If it grabs their attention, they will then read the submission and likely buy it. If it doesn't, they'll immediately toss it in the rejection pile.

That's why the first paragraph of your cover note is crucial. It must tell what your article is about, convey the flavor of the text, and make the editor want to read more—all in a few sentences. Ideally in two concise sentences since almost all newspaper paragraphs are two sentences or less. You can stretch it a bit here because so much must be done in so little space. The editor can quickly confirm that the article itself adheres to that two-sentence paragraph length by glancing at the first page of the manuscript.

In the second paragraph you indicate whether you have b/w photos (or, less desired, slides) to illustrate the article, how you can submit them, and that you'd be happy to do so, if the editor is interested.

If a photo is the most important part of the submission, elaborate on it in detail. You might even consider switching the second and first paragraphs! For instance, if I'm submitting an article about whale watching from canoes in Scammon's Lagoon and I have a shot of a watcher actually petting a docile cetacean, that would be the highlight of my cover note! (But I'd still not send the actual photo until requested.)

In the third paragraph you simply ask the editor not to return the manuscript but rather send the verdict in either the SASE or on the postcard enclosed. What good is a crumpled manuscript, often decorated with doodles? And why pay additional postage to get it back when a single stamp for a small envelope or postcard will do?

Note that you must send something stamped with your manuscript submission to get a reply. If you send an SASE, you often get your note torn off and returned in it, with comments on the back. Postcards work just as well (see Figure 12), with boxes to check and space for comments on the back, your name and address on the front, and (for best results) an actual stamp in the upper right-hand corner.

**Figure 12 Sample Postcard for Reply to Newspaper
Simultaneous Submission**

Regarding the article titled _____

submitted on _____ by Gordon Burgett

☐ I am holding it for future use and will either let you know
   soon or will pay upon publication.

☐ Not for us now, but thanks for sending it.

☐ Let's see your photos: _____

☐ Comments:

Name _____ Newspaper_____

You must fill in the article title and the submission
date. (You can do this by hand as long as it's readable.)

All you must do now is sign your name to the cover
letter (it's okay if this is illegible since your name appears
typewritten elsewhere: on the byline, on the SASE or
postcard, and at the top of the cover note itself, above
the address). Just so the editor knows how it should be
spelled on the check.

What length should the cover note be? Short enough
to let the editor read it quickly and long enough to do
its job. But another factor enters in. Even though the
best place to put this note is on top of the first page
of the manuscript, stapled in the upper lefthand corner,
I want to avoid covering any copy. I make my note short
enough so that my lead paragraph is visible.

The first page of my manuscript has the title and byline
in the top half, plus the word count in the upper righthand
corner, with the rest of the space left open so the editor
can write in typesetting instructions. I cover only the
top half with my note leaving the lead and the rest of
the first-page copy readable on the bottom half. And

I usually include the title, plus my name, in the note itself.

I want editors to become so intrigued by the cover note that their eyes involuntarily drop to the actual article lead; there they become enraptured, continue to the second paragraph, remain enchanted, slide to the third paragraph and turn the page...Ideally, after reading the entire article the editor will return to the note, finish it, and let me know immediately that the manuscript is being kept and the photos are wanted *now*!

The beauty of the cover note? It simplifies everybody's job and increases your selling ratio and response time considerably. Newspaper travel editors are too busy for the kinds of queries that magazines accept. Although they must see the actual copy, the note gives them a thumbnail sketch to read first. Done right, that note piques their curiosity, gets them to read the text quickly, and closes—or loses—the sale. But a loss is better than no-reply limbo. Widespread, multiple submissions deftly done are the key to success when writing newspaper travel.

Don't Dally!

When you return, after sending out the pretrip query go-ahead articles and the post-trip query letters, get your newspaper articles written and sent. Prepare the manuscripts, a cover note for each, a return SASE or postcard, and send the package either flat in a full-sized manila envelope or with a single fold in a half-sized manila envelope.

Don't wait too long. Situations change. East Germany wasn't the same place a day after the Berlin Wall came tumbling down. The oldest buildings eventually crumble, seas pollute, resorts close their doors, and restaurants change chefs. Get your copy in print quickly, before the topics become inaccurate, obsolete, dangerous, or uninteresting.

What if you have a hot item, say, Oktoberfest in October? Change the order of your work. Write and send your hot item first, while the photos or slides are being quickly developed. But if you think one of your steady clients might be interested, call and offer to send your article by modem, FAX, or overnight delivery while the photos are still on the roll. You can get to the photos immediately afterward.

(As I said, I almost never call editors, and especially not with a query. But sometimes, very rarely, an instant opportunity is best handled this way. Alas, 99% of the time it's not that urgent, and the editor isn't that receptive.)

Two more points. What shouldn't newspaper travel articles say? And how do you avoid glutting the market?

Obviously some things should not be found in your manuscript: vulgarity, sexual innuendo, racial or religious slurs, and anything else you normally don't find in public print, or wince at when you do.

I'd also avoid much negativity, as I mentioned earlier. Travel sections contain travel ads. And even though newspaper editors champion the division between the freedom of the press and the business of selling advertising, you'll notice a dearth of articles that talk down what the adjacent advertisement talk up. The mere existence of a travel section promotes travel. If you blatantly discourage it, you will quickly find yourself without a printed platform.

And finally, if you've just returned from Moravia or Easter Island overflowing with material for at least seven different, super newspaper articles, how do you best get those into print? By not flooding the market all at once.

The public's reading appetite for Moravia or Easter Island is quickly sated. If you simultaneously send all seven articles to one editor, you will get six or seven rejections. It's a simple supply and demand problem. The demand is low; you're bursting with supply.

So write the seven articles while they're fresh. Pick the most newsworthy—changes, new facts, unknown circumstances—and send it out first. Then send one article at a time at measured intervals thereafter. For England, Germany, Japan, and perhaps Mexico, a new piece every two weeks. For most larger countries, maybe once a month. For places like Moravia and Easter Island, maybe every six months.

EXAMPLE: SUBMITTING YOUR ARTICLES AND PHOTOS TO NEWSPAPERS

Submitting Newspaper Travel Articles

Time to hit the newspapers nationwide! My pretrip go-aheads are long gone, the post-trip queries are in the mail, and now it's the newspapers' chance to taste my verbal delicacies. Alas, a meal this good ain't free.

So I check my list of potential newspaper article topics, written before I left and added to during the trip, to see which articles have the best chance of being bought. From those I pick the most urgent or the most newsworthy to write first.

If travel restrictions were just lifted on the site I visited, I move that item up. If it's a ski piece and the snow has only one month left, I write about that first. Then I write the less urgent items.

Heidelberg is always fetching, so I draw from my query go-ahead research on the *Schloss*, add the observations and quotes I gathered there, look through the printed matter I picked up locally, and write a 1,300-word manuscript about the larger city. Then I write an appealing cover letter, a half-page long, to send to each of the ten (or one hundred) newspaper editors that I think might buy this topic (see Figure 13). I staple each cover letter to the front of a complete manuscript.

Figure 13 Cover Letter for Newspaper Simultaneous Submission

GORDON BURGETT
P.O. Box 6405
Santa Maria, CA 93456
(805) 937-8711

1300 words

Dear Mr. Johnson:

Heidelberg is romantic Germany all in one: *The Student Prince* and the nation's oldest university (1386); its most spectacular castle overlooking the open-air market and beer gardens below; the six-hundred-thousand year-old jawbone of one of its earliest citizens, the "Heidelberg Man," at the Palatinate Museum; boat rides up and down the Neckar River, linking the vertical vineyards along its banks with the Rhine; a cable car trip through pine woods to *Königstuhl*, for a panoramic view at 2,000 feet, beer halls and wiener schnitzel and arm-linked bands of students singing on the streets... Is it any wonder that Americans deplane in Frankfurt and head 50 miles south at double-time?

Let me send you my 16 sharpest b/w's to select from, if interested—or I can pick out the five best. (I also have slides of Heidelberg should you want color.)

Please don't return the ms, just your verdict in the SASE. Thanks.

Gordon Burgett

ROMANTIC OLD HEIDELBERG
by Gordon Lee Burgett

The only thing that's missing is Mario Lanza and the dueling swords of *The Student Prince*!

Otherwise, Heidelberg is a step back into history, with students arm-in-arm still singing (or chanting) as they walk the narrow streets to or from the beer halls, while a massive, haunted castle watches from the wooded hills overhead.

Germany's oldest university (begun in 1386) retains its feisty intrigue—and its Student Prison. Add to that the sparkling Neckar River (a few miles short of joining the Rhine), street after street of festively preserved ancient buildings, open-air markets, beer gardens, a cable car to the top of the towering *Königstuhl*, wiener schnitzel, and a six-hundred-thousand-year-old jaw from the "Heidelberg Man," and is it any wonder that Americans deplaning in Frankfurt head 50 miles south at double-time to join in?

Comments About the Cover Letter

Newspaper travel editors aren't going to spend hours laboring over what I want them to buy. They'll read a manuscript, if they have to. But a cover letter—really, a cover note—is much better, since it gets right to the point, offers a tasty writing sample, and talks about black-and-whites all at once.

A mixed blessing because if I write a lousy note, the gem of a manuscript attached probably gets thrown out with the note.

This note is directed to Mr. Johnson at the *DDD Newspaper*. The first paragraph says it all: Heidelberg is one great place to visit, I can bring it alive, and your readers will run 50 miles at double-time to read it! Well, not exactly, nor would I boast about my writing in this note. But if my note doesn't have vigor my article probably isn't going to be bought.

Mr. Johnson may have been to Heidelberg so I must remember not to overdo the adjectives and make unfounded claims. Just keep it honest, upbeat, and descriptive in the same tone as the manuscript attached.

The first paragraph of this cover letter is inevitably different from that of the manuscript. I must say more and I must say it faster in the cover letter. The purposes differ.

In the second paragraph I tell what I can provide in the way of b/w's. I even mention slides here since Heidelberg is so photogenic he just might use them.

And my third paragraph specifies that I don't want to pay the postage to get back this full manuscript. Just send the verdict to me in the small (#9) SASE enclosed.

How does this submission actually look? See Figure 13 for the first page of the manuscript (of course I send *all* the pages!) with the cover letter stapled in the upper lefthand corner.

Then I wait. Since I sent basically the same cover letter and manuscript to many travel editors, some will reject it—but others will want it, some with photos, and some will just use the words without illustrations. All pay upon publication, and 90% will send me a copy of the piece in print. I've never yet failed to get back a negative from a travel editor, so they too will be back in due order.

What do I hear from Mr. Johnson? Good news! He'll use the article and wants to see all 16 b/w's (see Figure 14). Which means he'll use 1, 2, perhaps even 4 or 5 of them. (When editors ask to see your photos it's almost certain they will buy at least one.)

Submitting Newspaper Travel Photos

Fortunately in Heidelberg I took six rolls of 36-exposure b/w's, so I have no trouble finding 16 different shots for Johnson, even after sending two other sets of 16 and a set of 5 to other travel editors who asked before him.

Figure 14 Reply to Newspaper Manuscript Submission

DDD Newspaper
1234 Main Street
St. Almo, Nebraska

Gordon,

I'm holding your article about Heidelberg. Good job! Hoping to use it next month, or may not slot it until March when we talk about summer trips to Europe. Let's see all 16 b/w's.

Len Johnson
Travel/Entertainment Editor

I like to send at least 12 verticals out of the 16 photos (or 3 of the 5) since newspapers prefer them. So I look through the proof sheets of shots not sent elsewhere (since none are back yet from earlier submissions) and select the best (see Figure 15 for an example of a proof sheet).

To create a photo choice sheet, on an 8½ x 11" sheet of paper I adhere the little prints from the proof sheet in rows, four across and four deep. I number each row and each photo in that row. I also put a title line at the top of the page virtually identical to that on the caption sheet that will accompany it. See Figure 16 for the b/w choice page for the Heidelberg article.

I must provide an explanation of each shot on the photo choice page; in other words I must supply a caption sheet (similar to the one for slides in Chapter 6). So I refer to my notes and research sources in order to prepare a clear description of each print. These descriptions correspond by row and number to the prints on the b/w photo choice page. I include a title line at the top and my address on the bottom. I then make a copy of this sheet (for the very rare occasion when a travel editor wants even more information from me but hasn't returned the caption sheet; I keep a copy so I know what he or she is talking about!). See Figure 17 for the Heidelberg caption sheet that will accompany the b/w photo choice page.

The complete photo response includes the b/w photo choice sheet, the caption sheet, a #10 SASE, and a short cover note (as in Figure 18).

Mr. Johnson now has the manuscript and the cover letter that accompanied it. In addition, since he replied requesting 16 b/w's, I sent 16 for his selection, plus a caption sheet, cover note, and another SASE to get the b/w photo choice sheet back with his selection.

About a week later I received the sheet with five prints circled and these words written in the corner: "Gordon,

Figure 15 Proof Sheet (example only; not of Heidelberg)

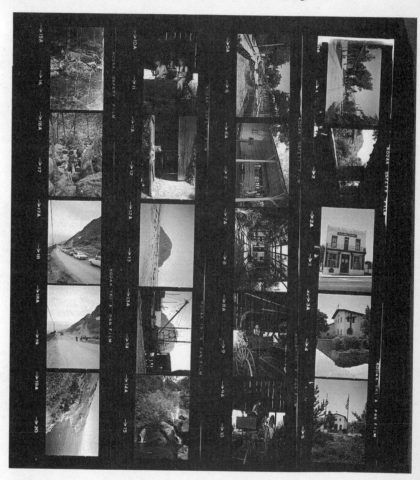

Note: The figures in this chapter explain the process to follow when sending articles and photos to newspapers. The photos in Figures 15, 16, and 19 show how to submit b/w photos to newspapers. Many of these photos appear courtesy of the German National Tourist Office.

Figure 16 Black-and-White Photo Choice Page

Heidelberg, b/w pix; 1 of 1 / Burgett

ROW 1

(1)   (2)   (3)   (4)

ROW 2

(1)   (2)   (3)   (4)

ROW 3

(1)   (2)   (3)   (4)

ROW 4

(1)   (2)   (3)   (4)

Figure 17 Caption Sheet for Black-and-White Photos

Heidelberg (Captions of b/w pix; 1 of 1/Burgett)

Row 1: (1) From June to September *The Student Prince* is performed with the castle ruins as a backdrop, as part of the Heidelberg Dance Festival. (2) With the *Schloss* in the distance, spectacular fireworks are displayed on June and September evenings, best seen aboard a Neckar River passenger boat. (3) View of Heidelberg and the cable car that links the city to the top of the pine-crested, 2000-foot *Königstuhl*. (4) Spectacular view of the *Schloss* and the Neckar River, the latter soon to join the Rhine.

Row 2: (1) Hikers, singly or in groups, climb the many rolling hills and gentle peaks in the Neckar Valley. Many trails begin in Heidelberg. (2) Abundant forests and hiking trails dot the mountains surrounding Heidelberg, much of it directly accessible by foot or cable car. (3) Many of the boat trips from Heidelberg traverse the loveliest valleys of the Neckar and Rhine Rivers, to Koblenz, St. Goar, and Rüdesheim. (4) Downtown Heidelberg seen from the *Schloss,* including the Church of the Holy Ghost (built in 1339-1441), the Ritter Hotel (1592), and the famed, ancient university.

Row 3: (1) Another view of Heidelberg as seen from the *Schloss,* with its gables, narrow streets, and open-air markets and beer halls. (2) A favorite boat trip from Heidelberg, down the Neckar and Rhine Rivers, is to Rüdesheim, with its castle hotel overlooking the town, vineyards, and taverns. (3) Visitors to Heidelberg can rent a car and tour the Castle Road through the Neckar Valley to see the many castles in Neckarsteinach, Dilsberg, and Hirschorn. (4) Other local castles and a monastery can be visited in one day by crossing the bridge from "Old Heidelberg" and hiking upward into the mountains.

Row 4: (1) The Tourist Office, near the railroad station, has an abundance of hiking maps to visit the woods, overviews, and wild gardens in and near Heidelberg. (2) Tours by boat leave hourly from downtown Heidelberg, day or night, to "castle-watch" on the Neckar and Rhine Rivers. (3) Another boating favorite heads north of the Neckar to see the vineyards and castles that hug the shoreline. (4) The twin towers and the portcullis of the Bridge Gate, the fifth bridge over the Neckar River since medieval times. The *Schloss* oversees!

(All photos sold on a one-time rights basis.)

Gordon Burgett
P.O. Box 6405
Santa Maria, CA 93456
(805) 937-8711

Figure 18 Cover Letter for Newspaper Photo Submission

> P.O. Box 6405
> Santa Maria, CA 93456
> (805) 937-8711
>
> Dear Mr. Johnson:
>
> Here are the 16 best from my proof sheets. Let me know
> which of the negatives to send and if you need more info than
> appears in the respective captions. Would you please return
> these proofs with your reply, in the SASE? Thanks.
>
> Gordon Burgett

I like five. Send me the negs and we'll see how many
I can use. Best wishes, Len Johnson."

I get the negatives out of their protective envelopes,
match each print to its negative, and very carefully cut
each negative out of its strip. I put individual negatives
into their own small envelopes (which I bought at the
photo supply store). Then I place all five in a larger,
thicker envelope on which I've written my name and
return address. I place this inside two small cardboard
sheets, taped shut on all four sides. On the outside of
the cardboard I attach a copy of the note Mr. Johnson
sent me. I then send this package in a manila envelope,
on which I write: "Photo Negatives Inside—Please Handle
With Care!" And off it goes!

But What If the Editor Wants My "Five Best"?

Sometimes editors ask for only a small number of photos.
Stranger things happen. Johnson might be a gambler,
or he may need to get my material immediately. (Later,
when you are known by the travel editor and your photos

are consistently usable, sending five will become the usual procedure.)

So, instead of the more elaborate, two-step process just described, I put everything needed on one sheet: my five-best b/w proof pictures (probably three verticals or more) and the captions for each shot (see Figure 19 for an example).

I cut out the negatives for those five photos, prepare an SASE, and include a note to the editor, something like that in Figure 20.

I bundle up my five-best package and zip it back to the editor, again noting on the outside of the envelope: "Photo Negatives Inside—Please Handle with Care!"

Whether the editor wants 5 shots or 16, all I can do now is wait. Wait to see my article in print, wait for a check in the mail, wait for my negatives to be returned. All this takes is patience.

Incidentally, when your negatives and proof sheet prints are returned, you can put the prints in circulation again. You are free to offer them to other newspaper editors in the future, because photos are bought for one-time use unless specifically stipulated.

There's another bonus to this system. Because the pay is so low for newspaper photos, you send the negatives to the editor, who has them reproduced as the 8 x 10" prints they need for cropping and page composition. Some editors actually send these giant prints to you after the piece has been used! Because of this I've occasionally been able to offer these prints to subsequent editors, to speed up the process. (But usually I just keep them as a reward, though for what I'm not sure.)

In this chapter I've provided you with an example of simultaneous submissions to newspapers. In short, my submission plan is to sell many different articles, each to as many regional newspapers as will use them. But

Figure 19 "Five-Best" Newspaper Photo Submission

(1)   (2)   (3)

(4)   (5)

Photo 1: The twin towers and the portcullis of the Bridge Gate, the fifth bridge over the Neckar River since medieval times, seen from the side of the river facing the older city and castle.

Photo 2: View of Heidelberg and the cable car that links the city to the top of the pine-crested, 2000-foot *Königstuhl.*

Photo 3: Spectacular view of the *Schloss* and the Neckar River, the latter soon to join the Rhine.

Photo 4: Abundant forests and hiking trails dot the mountains surrounding Heidelberg, much of it directly accessible by foot or cable car.

Photo 5: Downtown Heidelberg seen from the *Schloss,* including the Church of the Holy Ghost (built in 1339–1441), the Ritter Hotel (1592), and the famed, ancient university.

(All photos sold on a one-time rights basis.)

Gordon Burgett
P.O. Box 6405
Santa Maria, CA 93456
(805) 937-8711

Figure 20 Cover Letter for "Five-Best" Newspaper Photo Submission

Gordon Burgett
P.O. Box 6405
Santa Maria, CA 93456
(805) 937-8711

Dear Mr. Johnson,

Here are the five best from my proof sheets, with their negatives and captions. Please let me know if you need more extensive captions. After they are used, would you please return
these negatives and proofs in the SASE? Thanks.

Gordon Burgett

since the focus of all these articles is a well-known place,
Germany, I must scatter the submissions, writing the
various articles while the subjects are fresh in mind,
then submitting one article at a time with a cover letter
to many markets at intervals of three weeks to a month.

CHAPTER 13

Selling Your Copy and Photos Again and Again

Since you've lathered yourself into a froth writing a super article and illustrating it with unforgettable photos, why sell them only once?

With your newspaper pieces you've already followed the multiple sales route, offering both the copy and a choice of black-and-whites (b/w's) to as many regional newspapers as you wished or that didn't overlap each others' circulation area. Now you can do the same with your magazine pieces and their corresponding slides or b/w's.

RESELLING MAGAZINE ARTICLES

You can resell your magazine articles and photos, unless you sold all rights to the manuscript or sold the photos on an exclusive basis. Both are unlikely, but if either is the case then that particular article or photo has come to the end of its short but lucrative life. The buyer bought those words in that order, forever. Or that image captured on that slide or print, forever.

But all is not lost. You can sell a similar photo. Or a rewritten manuscript. You didn't sell the subject to the buyers, just a particular, singular treatment of it. Anything else you sell must be clearly different. To rewrite an article, change the title, lead, conclusion, and order. Better yet, approach the topic from a new angle or slant, so that everything else naturally changes. You can even use some of the original quotes, if they are in a sufficiently different setting. But for a photo sold on an all rights basis? Use a different shot, period.

Almost all magazine travel editors buy first rights to the copy and buy the photography on a one-time rights basis. Therefore, once an article or photo has actually appeared in print in a magazine, you may sell those words and that photo again and again.

What if an editor buys and pays for your journalistic gem but it never reaches print? Limbo. This has happened to me three times. In each instance I waited a year, then wrote the editors asking them if they planned on using the article they had bought a year ago. If not would they please release the rights back to me? All three said yes, did so in response to my letter, and apologized (as much as editors apologize) for not using it, saying roughly the same thing: They had to restructure a certain issue at the last minute, planned to use my article later but it had since become dated, and now after a year they wouldn't be using it at all. The payment was mine. So were the copy and photos, to rework if possible into another first rights sale for some other publication. (I sold two but the third, about the bicentennial, was too dated after 1976 had passed.)

REWRITING THE ORIGINAL

The moment you convert an original pretrip query letter into an article and sell it, all you need do is rewrite it, albeit substantially, to sell it again. And again, rewritten. And again, rewritten.

You've collected a pool of usable information, quotes, anecdotes, and photos. Why use them only once?

Most article themes can be approached from many different angles. The house where Lincoln lived in Salem, Illinois, the store where he worked, Lincoln's life in the town (with Salem as the backdrop), what happened to the town since Lincoln's time, and so on. All using Salem as the primary focus or as a secondary one.

If you queried about one angle, you can query about any other angle, before or after visiting Salem. Just so each article is clearly distinct, each has its own life. Each is sold, probably, on a first rights basis. (And each can be sold again, as often as possible, as a reprint! More about this below.)

Rewrites exist only in my mind and on my desk. The editors receiving the queries don't know of the original query, nor should they. My rewrite query is of a different topic. It doesn't mention the other query, or if the original is in print, the article.

The query process has already been described: Write a query, send it—include a self-addressed, stamped envelope (SASE)—and if the response is positive, write what you promised and put it in the editor's hands in three weeks. For that reason you do most rewrites after your trip is completed, when you have a pool full of usable material at your disposal.

SELLING REPRINT (SECOND) RIGHTS

Let's assume that a magazine does buy the first rights to your article and photos and that these appear in print. The publication has used what it bought. But you can still sell the copy on a reprint (also called second rights) basis. (There are no third or subsequent rights.) You needn't contact the editor to whom you first sold the article. The rights are automatically yours.

You sold the photos on a one-time rights basis, unless otherwise stated, and you can continue to sell them on that basis, forever.

How do you sell your article and photos to other magazines? The process is simple.

Editors at every buying level normally send you a copy or two of the issue that includes your material. Take one of the copies of that first rights sale, cut out your material, reassemble it in consecutive fashion, and adhere it to standard 8½ x 11" paper. If it's not obvious, also write the name of the publication in which your article appeared, the date it appeared, and the words *first rights sale* on the master. Then make as many clear copies as you need.

Which publications do you query? Those that pay on publication are by far the most likely purchasers since few professionals do original work for them. These magazines buy the bulk of their copy this way. But don't forget magazines that pay on acceptance whose readership doesn't overlap much with the original buyer's. Sometimes these magazines are interested. Make a list of all the publications you think might buy the second rights and then query them. All it costs to find out is a copy of the original article now in print, a cover letter, and some postage.

There is one situation, though, in which you may not wish to simultaneously submit even though it is perfectly legal and ethical. That's when both publications are direct competitors. I used to sell to the PSA and Air California in-flight magazines when both airlines served the West Coast. They were tooth-and-nail competitors. I would send my article first to one, and if it said no, then to the other. Even though there was no exclusivity, had I sold the same article to both and both used it, each editor would have been hopping mad at me and probably wouldn't have bought in the future. In a similar situation, prudence and patience are better than a closed market.

Sometimes an article doesn't quite fit your new market. It uses examples of welders whereas the new publication sells to flower arrangers. In those cases I suggest modest changes to the editor. In the first three paragraphs of the cover letter I describe the article in print and how I could modify it for the editor's readers.

What kind of modification? Different quotes, or interviews with people of interest to the magazine's readers. If the original talks about the school system in Ceylon for the general reader and the second publication is for school teachers, I might suggest inserting special interview material from several Ceylonese teachers. Or I might simply restructure the facts of a piece to more closely match the reader's interests.

The only problem with offering extensive modifications is that you must have access to the information needed for the substitution. This can be difficult if the site is half way around the world!

The Cover Letter for Reprints

Once you've produced the clear copies of your article and photos as described above, compose a sharp cover letter, one for each potential buyer, to accompany the copies. These can be sent simultaneously, each with an SASE enclosed, to as many editors as you wish since second or reprint rights do not carry any exclusivity. The one-time rights for photos also convey no such guarantee or implication.

What do you say in the cover letter? Describe what you have to sell in the first two paragraphs. You can then state the publication history and rights information in the third paragraph, and perhaps explain what photos or slides you have available for sale in the fourth. You may wish to offer the manuscript in original double-spaced format for the typesetter's ease, so you can suggest that in the fifth paragraph. And a closing, if any, followed by your name.

The first paragraphs sell the manuscript, so they should carry the same excitement or punch that made the piece sell originally, written in the same style as the article itself. If humorous, they should contain humor to the same degree. If serious, a sober mien but lots of information so the piece has the proper feel of substance.

The third paragraph contains the legal necessities. In it you tell who bought the first rights, when the article first appeared in print, and what rights you are now selling. (This refers to the copy only. The editor will assume that the photos were and are currently being sold on a one-time rights basis.) I usually say something like "First rights to this article were sold to X publication and it appeared in print on Y date, as you can see by the copy enclosed. I am offering you reprint rights."

The first editor may have bought 3 slides and an inside b/w photo from a choice of 120 slides and 72 b/w's (in proof sheet form). But you will want to offer the editors of the second rights publications access to all the illustrations, those bought in the first sale and those not chosen then. The fourth paragraph is a good place to do this, describing what you have and how you can submit it, and encouraging the editor to request the photos (rather than having hundreds of slides and proof sheets cruising profitlessly through Uncle Sam's tentacular mailworld).

Incidentally, if you have some truly spectacular photos or slides, here is where you laud their value and availability. But don't send them until requested.

The last paragraph serves two functions. One, it tells editors that, if interested, you will gladly send the original manuscript for typesetting (so that they don't have to use the article clipping for that purpose). Two, it lets you know which editors are seriously considering using your article, since those who request the original usually end up publishing it.

Why is the latter important? Because some publications that pay when the item is used are very slow to send you a check, meaning you must prod them. So if you know which of the pay-on-publication magazines are sincerely interested (those that requested the original manuscript), you can keep an eye on subsequent issues. If your piece appears, wait a few weeks or a month for payment. If you don't receive it, write the publication. Though editors have failed to pay me only twice in far more than one thousand sales, I suspect that I picked up 25 or so foot-draggers by just letting them know that I was pleased with the appearance and use of the article but had still not received the payment. They knew that I knew, and payment followed.

How much do editors pay for second rights or reprints? The current *Writer's Market* will give the range, but rest assured that reprints will be near the bottom. Often only one-half or one-third of the top pay rate.

On the other hand, all it takes to get double or triple yardage out of one set of words and illustrations is some digging, some copying, writing a few letters (slightly adjusted from one working letter), the price of envelopes and stamps, and the energy to get all this in motion. Plus, of course, an original sale!

EXAMPLE: QUERYING FOR REWRITES AND REPRINTS

There are two main paths suggested above to turn your words over often and profitably. I plan to follow both with the copy I wrote about my German trip, because I think Germany offers enough new material for creating some marketable rewrites and generates enough interest to sell the original as a reprint. I'll divide the example into two parts, focus on each, and share the critical selling letter in both cases.

Rewrite of the Original

The pretrip query and the resulting article focus on the *Schloss*, and secondarily on Heidelberg. It would be easy to branch out from that base, gather more information about Heidelberg and other local attractions, and then match it to the needs of various magazines.

For example, hiking magazines seem to be fascinated with Germany, Switzerland, the Alps, and almost any place in Europe of particular hiking interest.

That's but one of many special interest magazines that could be queried in a similar way. Others might be magazines devoted to wine, medieval architecture, chocolate, alchemy, archaeology, ancient universities, student travel, or river cruises. All could focus to good advantage on Heidelberg.

The system of finding markets for rewrites is no different than it is for the original query, consisting of a two-part feasibility study: It is feasible to write and is it feasible to sell? If it is both, find markets in the *Writer's Market* or the academic discipline indexes, prioritize them, and get the queries moving.

For now, I'll focus on a hiking magazine. See Figure 21 for my rewrite query.

This query is no different in form from the original pretrip query, except that I've written it after I return and have the hiking information in hand.

The lead, or first paragraph, talks about an article on hiking and romantic old Heidelberg. The second expands

Figure 21 Query Letter for a Magazine Rewrite

P.O. Box 6405
Santa Maria, CA 93456
(805) 937-8711
December 1, 1991

Mr. Russell Frances
Editor, *EEE Magazine*
789 River Rd.
Oklahoma City, OK 73132

Dear Mr. Frances:

I'd like to write an article for your pages that I think most of
your hiking readers would find particularly exciting: three
hikes through and around one of Germany's most historic and
romantic sites, Heidelberg!

One of the hikes is more cultural and historical than arduous.
The other two are more demanding, through the thick pine
mountains on either side of the Neckar River, where the hikers
could either return to the city the same night or camp in the
wilderness. The article would give full details—the distance
of each hike, the time and equipment required, the altitude,
route, purpose, and the proper attire.

The city hike, about 10 miles long, would explore the core
and fringe of Old Heidelberg, stomping grounds of *The Student Prince*, the nation's oldest university (1386), four museums, open-air markets and beer gardens, street after narrow
street of festively preserved ancient buildings, and a magnificent mountain castle with miles of terraced gardens that
alone would take half a day to see well on foot.

A second hike passes the castle, crosses a valley, and scales
the 2,000-foot *Königstuhl* ("King's Seat"), from which the entire region can be seen. No less than 20 different foot trails
branch off from there, most into virgin forest long a favorite of
German backpackers.

The third hike heads in the opposite direction from the historic center of Heidelberg, across the bridge (built for the fifth
time in 1788), along the "Philosopher's Way," up the land-
scaped slope to the Bismarck Monument, and from there by

continued on page 232

other marked paths to the observation tower on *Heiligenberg*, past the remains of a Celtic fort to the ruins of ninth-century St. Michael's Basilica and monastery. Again, a half-dozen paths continue on into the woods...

I just returned from this area, having attended the Frankfurt Book Fair, and have taken all the trails I describe, plus spoken with dedicated local hikers to gather their comments and suggestions for the text. I also have about 75 sharp slides related to the locations described, if interested. Finally, I'll tailor this piece to your readers' needs, as I've done more than one thousand times before for articles sold in the past 20 years, and can have it in your hands three weeks after you give me the go-ahead.

It's hard to imagine a place where there's so much to see with nature still in sight or at hand. Should we share this with the readers of *EEE Magazine*? Just let me know.

Gordon Burgett

on the three hikes the article would describe, plus shows the kinds of details it would include.

Then each of the hikes is further developed in its own paragraph. The letter ends with why I am qualified to write the article (just back from the area and have hiked the trails), what I have in the way of illustrations, the date the copy will be delivered, and how I will tailor this for the editor's readers "as I've done more than one thousand times before..." I close with a question to elicit a response from the editor.

I may discover four hiking magazines that would be interested. Using the same criteria that I used for my pre-trip research, I'll determine the desirability of each magazine (from my standpoint) and then I'll prioritize them. I'll either send the same query to each magazine on my list, one at a time, or I'll send different queries (different hikes and settings) to each publication simultaneously.

The logic is straightforward: Keep a chunk of the original article (though rewritten to meet the new readers' needs), since the original has already proven successful and you have solid research on it. Then patch on other information to create an altogether different article. As much profit again for half the work. By the fifth rewrite it's almost a sin.

Reprint of the Original

In Chapters 9 and 10 we noted the progress of the original *Schloss* article for *BBB Magazine*. The article finally appeared in print on February 15.

Actually I received my copy on February 2, before it reached the stands. A few days later I went back to the file and reviewed the earlier markets I had planned to query, to see if there were any I hadn't queried or any that would be likely to buy a reprint of the original.

Since all the publications on my original market list paid on acceptance, which ones, if any, would even consider buying second or reprint rights? Only those that regularly use this kind of material, whose circulation is small, and where readers wouldn't likely have seen the original in print (usually because the two publications are in very different fields).

As it is, the only magazines left on my list I had either queried or they simply weren't good candidates for a reprint. So I returned to *Writer's Market* to compose a new list of travel-interested magazines that paid on publication. They are my target market for reprints!

First I prepare a pasteup of the article so that it reproduces clearly, and then I make as many copies (plus one for myself) as I will send out to potential buyers. In case my article gets separated from my cover letter, I put my name, address, and phone number on it. And, if it's not obvious, the name and date of the magazine it comes from.

Then I write an enticing cover letter that does what it must do: Sell the subject, state the conditions, offer the original text, and ask a question. See Figure 22 for that letter.

Figure 22 Cover Letter for a Magazine Reprint

P.O. Box 6405
Santa Maria, CA 93456
(805) 937-8711
February 25, 1992

Mr. Brandon Douglas
Editor, *FFF Magazine*
853 Mill Rd.
Spokane, WA 99218

Dear Mr. Douglas:

Das Schloss looks so much like a giant fairytale castle it's embarrassing, with its hodgepodge of spires and columns, half-fallen towers, see-through belfry, flowering gardens, and deep moats. And it's just the topping on Heidelberg's cake!

The city of *The Student Prince* sits below, the Neckar River in the background, the nation's oldest university (1386) in sight, and open-air markets and beer gardens within distant earshot. Yet it's the huge castle that keeps drawing the attention and the visitors venturing 50 miles south of Frankfurt, and that's what I'd like to share with your readers.

The article attached is currently appearing in *BBB Magazine*, which bought first rights. I am offering reprint rights and access to any photos you see in print, plus some 95 more slides that will bring the magnificent *Schloss* even more alive for your readers.

The castle housed the electors of the Rhineland Palatinate. Begun in 1200, it was shelled beyond use by Louis XIV in 1693. The article relives a morning tour of its many sections and gardens, its Great Terrace overlooking the city, and the largest wine vat in the world, still intact in the castle's bowels. Plus an afternoon hike or cable car ride up the pine-crested peak behind the *Schloss* for an unforgettable panoramic view of the entire valley.

I know it's hard to typeset against a magazine article, so I'll gladly send you the piece in its original manuscript form—or on disk, if my IBM is compatible. Should we share the *Schloss* with your readers now? Who knows what it will look like in another 700 years!

Gordon Burgett

This reprint cover letter looks suspiciously like the original query! And why shouldn't it? The first query worked, the article contents are the same, and these editors have never seen it before. All I need to do is change the address and salutation and this becomes a one-fits-all letter. Therefore it had better be good!

I've only trimmed the first two paragraphs a bit since I want it all on one page.

The third paragraph includes the three obligatory items: who bought first rights, when the article appeared, and what I am offering the editor (second, or reprint, rights). That done, I can simultaneously submit and am legally in the clear!

In this particular cover letter I included information about photos in the third paragraph as well. The form for this type of letter isn't rigid, though I don't think I'd lead with the legal business until I had softened the editor up with some alluring opening paragraphs. (A copy of the article accompanies the letter so the editor already knows you're hawking a reprint!)

Once I've addressed the legalities, I can get back to the article's contents in paragraph four. And the last paragraph is standard, though lately I'm offering to send the articles on IBM-based disks along with or instead of the original manuscript. In either case, if editors request an item, I know they are likely to use it—and I know to watch for payment! In this paragraph I also like to include my "should-we-share" to prompt the editor's response.

If an editor says no? All it cost you was a bit of time to run off the letter and address the envelope and the SASE, plus some postage. If an editor says yes? Bring on the gravy train! Well, maybe the gravy bowl.

CHAPTER 14

Other Ways to Sell Your Travel Writing Information and Skills

Many exciting things happen when you travel. You have fun, you explore new sites or revisit favorite places, you create new friendships or strengthen old ones, and you learn new things.

It's that knowledge that you share with others in your magazine and newspaper articles. Yet there's a funny thing about knowledge. It has the miraculous powers of Silly Putty. It can be recast, reshaped, or combined into myriad new forms, each of which can be sold under its new identity.

There's more. In developing skills to find and then share your travel information in print, you also develop skills that serve you well in related fields. So the question becomes: How can you sell that information and those skills other ways?

SELLING YOUR TRAVEL WRITING INFORMATION IN OTHER WAYS

You've already seen how magazine articles can be sold once, then resold as reprints without a whit of change. Or how the same information in an article can be approached from a different angle or slant and rewritten into an entirely different piece, which in turn can be resold as a reprint of a rewrite!

And how newspaper articles can be sold widely in their original form by offering them to readers sufficiently distant from each other.

But why couldn't your trip form the crux of a book? Or be the setting for a novel? Is there a need for one or a set of brochures about the region? Could you develop and sell a travelogue based on your adventures and photography? Could you sell your photos alone or through a stock agency? How else might you sell your core of information again and again?

Let's take a brief look at the possibilities, less to provide definitive how-to information than to suggest additional avenues worth your consideration and perhaps later your in-depth investigation.

Writing a Travel Book

On the one hand, there is always a need for new travel books. Current books go out of date quickly, local economies and skylines change, "in" activities fly out as fast as autumn leaves drop, and buyers look closely at travel book copyright dates.

On the other hand, the demand for such books is intimately related to the volume of Americans headed to a particular place. A guide to London always outsells a guide to Fernando de Noronha. And sales are the name of the game. Bookstores want books from publishers that will sell in volume and quickly, so publishers seek precisely the same from writers: books that people want to buy.

If you're interested in trying your hand at a travel book, consider two kinds. One, the all-you-need-to-know book, a compendium of encyclopedic knowledge, with illustrations. Two, a more tightly focused work that serves a more specific need.

Examples of the latter might be titled "Backroad Bicycling Trips Through...," "Pub Crawling in Downtown...," "Summer Fairs in...," or "The Complete Guide to Medieval Castles in..."

These books are easier to write than the encyclopedic books because their scope is more limited and may better fit your field(s) of interest or expertise. But often the markets are likewise smaller. Rather than approaching a major publishing house that sells full-spectrum books, you might best approach niche publishers whose clientele eagerly buy books about a specific field. Cycling book publishers, for example, for "Backroad Bicycling Trips Through..."

How necessary your photos are to a book's production will be decided by the publisher, but you're ahead of the game if you have a topic in mind before you take your trip. You can either begin the querying process well before leaving so you'll know whether you need to take photos and what kind. Or, at the least, while there you can take plenty of photos similar to or better than those in other books of the same kind.

Travel books often require two trips. During the first you survey the topic, take the basic photos, and gather as much working information as possible. From this compilation you write the query and prepare the supporting data. During your second trip you go to the heart of the research and take more and better photos.

Will publishers pay you to take those trips? Almost never. Ultimately you'll be paid from royalties—and (the more creative publishers might suggest) by God, later, for having made others' lives fuller on earth! (Try that one on your banker if your trip requires a loan!)

Can you use the same material for articles now and for a book later? You bet. Sell the information in article form to magazines and newspapers first, using the income to justify tax deductions and to pay for the initial trip. Then send an article or two with your book query and other attachments, both to show the interest that already exists in the topic and how you write about it. The article copy is yours. Others buy the rights to use it first in magazines and/or newspapers. If you don't sell all rights, the book rights are still eagerly waiting to be sold!

Querying for Book Sales

I can't go into details here regarding the querying process for selling an idea for a book. Basically, however, it is this: Send a two-page query letter accompanied by an outline or annotated table of contents, a synopsis (if needed), and a reference/resource sheet. You can vary this format somewhat depending upon what you have ready or what you think the particular publisher would like to see. If interested, the editor will request sample chapters, and of course, if you receive approval (Yes, we want to publish your book!), you'll send the complete manuscript. For further details of this process see my book *How to Sell More than 75% of Your Freelance Writing.*

Using Your Trip in Another Book

Sometimes the knowledge you gather on a trip will find its way into print indirectly. You might be writing a tome on tapestry, and while in Egypt you obtain valuable insights that add depth to your book.

Or you might be writing a thriller that requires your hero, thought by the authorities to be a machete-wielding lunatic, to hide away for a few weeks while he proves his innocence and catches the true villain. Where better than in Baños, Ecuador? So while there you compile notes about the setting, a *pensión* where the hero might hide, the weather, the difficulties, the dialogue. Later, your visit and those notes will imbue your work will pungent reality.

And you can convert that specific information into articles for magazines or newspapers. Or later you could devote an entire book to Egyptian tapestries or to life in Baños, using the information obtained on your trip to form the core of a query letter with attachments.

Can you deduct part or all your travel expenses for the initial trip if this information finds its way into print? Probably only part of the expenses, and only after the book is in print and earns you as much as the percentage allowable. In the first case the problem is that you didn't lay a foundation to prove you needed to take the trip to write the book. In the second case you can't deduct expenses for fiction until the book materializes, when the income equals the necessary expenses. But in both cases, keep records of the costs. And if they aren't already deductible through article sales, check with the IRS to see how these expenses might be deductible.

Preparing Travel Brochures

Travel brochures are hard to sell generally but might be worth serious consideration if you are already well positioned in a niche market.

Let's say that your specialty is backpacking. You already have written a book about the subject, are a member of several associations or groups, and perceive a need for specific booklets about trails, rules, and date ranges for particular countries, something small enough to fit in the pack yet durable and waterproof.

You design the product, prepare the maps and data, and produce the booklets (you become your own publisher). How do you sell them? By mail specifically to the backpackers belonging to backpacker associations, to subscribers to magazines read by backpackers, and to any others you have included on your own in-house mailing list. Plus to secondary markets through display ads in the appropriate publications, at selected sports stores (probably through a sales representative), even at a booth at a backpackers convention. My book *Self-Publishing to Tightly-Targeted Markets* should provide specific guidance here.

You might also be able to interest a larger publisher if you think your series of brochures could be anthologized into one volume.

Creating a Travelogue

When I was young, travelogues were the rage. People filled auditoriums straining to see movies and slides of the Belgian Congo and gaze upon bushy-haired explorers who had survived the wilds of southern Alberta.

Then television came along and made tapirs and Tangiers as everyday as soap and water. Out went the greatest hope held by travelers who weren't given to writing to convert thousands of dollars spent on travel into many thousands back, for years and years.

Nowadays if you have a travelogue in mind, you must explore television as the most receptive purchaser. For starters, that means identifying every program that features travel both primarily or secondarily, contacting the producers, and doing what they suggest, often on speculation.

Minitravelogues, the best of your video or slides plus exciting narration, are still in demand by church groups, schools, and senior centers. But your pay, if any, will most likely come as food and fame. Hard to convince the IRS on deduction day that those are the things upon which a profitable business can be built.

Selling Your Photos Again

Rohn Engh, in *Sell and Re-Sell Your Photos*, says that twenty thousand photos are sold every day in little-known, wide-open markets at fees of $20 to $100 for black-and-white (b/w) and often twice as much for color!

Give the editors who buy your magazines and newspaper articles first crack, of course. But why retire a fetching slide or a telling b/w without trying to turn it over, and over, and over?

The question is how much you wish to involve yourself in the photography. You can do it all: your own stock agency, full effort, maximum profit. Or you can dabble, using other agencies and personally zeroing in when a market seems obvious.

One thing is certain. The need for good photos is huge, the income can easily equal what you earn from writing, and the details can drive you nuts.

Read Engh's book: It is excellent, thorough, and very clear on the process one follows. Then do as much as you want to make travel photography a solid source of dependable income, to help offset the costs of the trip and bring in a fat profit.

SELLING YOUR TRAVEL WRITING SKILLS

Freelance travel writing is hard and economically insecure work. Planning tightly, pursuing diligently, and writing deftly, you might eke out a decent income and see much of the world. But as a steady diet most writers have other jobs around which they can write travel articles part-time. I did it for years while deaning and teaching Portuguese and history at the college level. Almost any vocation works. The four that seem the most compatible with travel writing might be:

As a Travel Editor

As the popularity of travel continues to grow, the travel market continues to seek more outlets for advertising. And advertisers want their ads placed in the midst of travel copy that will attract readers, who will then read the ads. The tail wags the dog. The desire for travel copy requires travel editors to solicit and manage it.

What's the chance that over time your stellar prose and scintillating insights will prompt the editor-in-chief of a newspaper to beg you to run the travel department?

About as likely as a live interview with Elvis. That's a plum spot often rewarded to a faithful in-house workhorse easing toward retirement, a journeyperson long on writing who can learn about travel on the job as editor. Your best hope would be to join a newspaper staff and work up to an assistant editorship, then cross your fingers.

Magazines, on the other hand, are more likely to hunt for a specialist with both journalistic and travel experience. Here your writing credits, travel mileage, and grasp of page composition and content requirements might put you in the running.

You can draw attention to your qualifications three ways. One, keep producing top-quality travel pieces over a sustained period of time. Two, join one or several associations of travel writers. And three, learn the other skills that editors need by becoming an editor at a small, nearby publication, even for minimal pay. After you have established a solid reputation as a travel writer and have proven you can perform as an editor, let magazine editors and association colleagues know that you are available for an associate or assistant editorship.

As a Photographer

By dividing your talents evenly between writing and travel photography you can quickly increase your overall income.

Most travel writers at best dabble with a camera, and some refuse flat out to look through a lens. But the two skills, each paying modestly, can be combined to sweeten the end product, raise its perceived value, distinguish its producer as uniquely twice talented, and open a future in both areas.

How do you do it? Read every book about writing and photography, take every needed course or workshop, then go into the field and work single-mindedly to create a rare, unforgettable blend of words and art.

As a Travel Agent or Tour Director

You might think that if you work in the travel industry you will get to travel at a reduced rate, can afford to venture farther or more often, will be in a position to write more, and between your employment and your freelance writing will live happily ever after.

Robert Scott Milne, now publisher of the highly respected *Travelwriter Marketletter*, has been a full-time freelancer for almost 20 years. In *Opportunities in Travel Careers* he says, "Examine your reasons for wanting to be a travel agent employee or owner. If the main attraction is personal travel, rethink the matter thoroughly.

Could you earn higher pay in another industry and travel just as much?"

The reasons he cites are known to everyone in the trade: the pay range is low, the work is too often seasonal, you are the first to get bumped when the plane fills, and the higher up you progress in the industry, the less time you have to travel at all.

On the other hand, because the pay is low, travel at a reduced rate is considered one of the perks, at least for the beginner.

Tour directors might be better positioned to turn their activities into copy, though often on-site responsibilities preclude much free time to pursue facts, quotes, and anecdotes.

If interested, TTT (transportation, travel, and tourism) courses are sprouting nationwide, usually at the junior or community college level. Or contact one of the related associations—ASTA, ARTA, ICTA, or CLIA—for information about travel agency careers or courses (see "Sources for Travel Writers" at the end of this book for addresses and phone numbers).

Through Public Relations

Public relations may well be the field most compatible with commercial travel writing, because in many cases it is the same bird with different feathers.

Most outsiders presume that the sole purpose of "p.r." people is to put their client before the public eye (or ear) as often as possible in as favorable a light as can be cast, truth be damned.

Favorable, almost always, but disregard for the truth is done at peril. Access to most media is closely guarded by editors seeking facts objectively framed. The common ground where public relations and media meet best is through information clearly and honestly shared, with the degree of objectivity a major determination of whether the information is reproduced.

Since print is the communications medium most used for public relations, somebody must prepare the press releases, brochures, reports, newsletters, and magazines. And when the client is travel based, who better than an experienced writer with an objective travel writing background?

In addition to writing and editing, photography and graphics skills are sought. Developing special events is a natural for a travel writer where the site or subject is travel related or involves different cultures and locations. And public speaking, another aspect of public relations, often requires the same degree of articulation that writing does.

The key single qualification sought by public relations departments? Experience in print journalism! A college degree is highly desirable, a master's degree in public relations is widely available (although rarely mandatory in this job market), and the field continues to grow as business and government expand. Best yet, the pay range is comfortable.

There is more to travel writing than just writing travel. Sell your information and your skills again and again. Knowledge and craft are the very best investment: They always pay compound dividends.

PART FIVE

Related Information

CHAPTER 15

Those Marvelous Freebies!

FANTASY

Newcomers to the travel profession envision a wide world of freebies—open tickets to anywhere any time from globe-girdling airlines, complimentary passes to showcase hotels, and nonstop banquets and booze from four-star chuck wagons. All the writer has to do on the way to the beach is fax copy and photos to enraptured editors, who of course will pay tomorrow!

Nice fantasy, but not quite accurate.

REALITY

Freebies exist—but not quite as you may imagine. Some foreign countries do transport planeloads of travel writers, wine them and dine them, and ply them with press releases and photo kits. All for free, or just about.

Occasionally resorts will pop for a few nights or a weekend, including drinks and food. Amusement parks give free all-ride passes. Restaurants feed those with a tap to publicity. In fact, almost any person or business that stands to win big by cultivating your good favor might cut you in on the freebie game.

The hardest touch, oddly, is the airlines, who let travel agents see the world on standby but invoke three hundred regulations when it comes to travel writers—except when the airlines are touting a new route!

Free?

Well no, nothing is free. And freebie givers aren't fools. They aren't interested in a would-be writer long on hope but short on clips (copies of earlier articles or items in print) or credits. In exchange for footing part or all of the bill, they expect, or at least are betting on, a favorable comment (or a raving, three-page review) in print for plenty of potential customers to read. The better your credentials and the broader the circulation of your magazine or newspaper, the more likely you are to get the nod.

But freebie takers can find themselves in a bit of a pickle. Beholden to the gift giver, they try to slip in a plug or positive comment without writing obvious public relations blather, all the while attempting to maintain a wider, professional perspective.

Putting Freebies in Perspective

There is a way out of the freebie dilemma. Make it known up front that, should some of your tab be paid or special favors extended, you are nevertheless an objective journalist and there can be no strings attached. You will give whatever it is that the business or organization sells an honest and straightforward look, nothing more, nothing less.

However, it's rare that a travel writing novice even gets tempted. The killing question is "Where have you been in print?" Later it becomes "Let me see your go-ahead letter." So you usually have to pay dues for months or years—getting your feet firmly planted, your writing skills honed, and wooing editors with sharp copy tailored to their readers and delivered on time. Once you've established your reputation as a travel writer, you will be approached for freebies, or you will know how and when to solicit them.

Joining one of the several travel writer's associations usually is a rite of passage to freebieville (see "Sources for Travel Writers" at the end of this book for names and addresses). Yet acceptance by these associations often requires a certain number of travel articles in print. A second set of dues to be paid. Once a member, your best benefit is your contact with true vets who can tell you precisely how freebies can reward you, the giver, and most important, the reader.

Be aware, though, that some of the major newspapers will not use your copy if any part of your travel was sponsored or subsidized (paid for). Some even go further: Sponsored once, you are a pariah forever. It's a quandary that every writer must resolve.

Some Advice for Beginners

My advice to beginners about freebies is simple: Pay your own way, 100%, in the beginning. Focus on the place and topic rather than on the "extras." Keep queries in circulation, organize well and research deep, pluck out winning prose from well-structured trips, and accumulate clips and credits. All kinds of rewards will result, including no-strings freebies that accrue to the successful.

Do I take freebies? Almost never. The best freebie I ever accepted was one I engineered myself: a trip to Canada in the winter, to show through vivid and fact-filled writing what there was to do up North rather than bask in the Bahamas sun. The Canadian government was as mystified as I was but nevertheless footed the bill for two of the coldest weeks I've ever spent, shunting me from Chicago to Edmonton, Winnipeg, Calgary, Banff-Jasper, Vancouver, and Victoria.

The result? Six articles, about snow castles, having to plug your car heater cable into the parking meter, skiing, the art center in Banff where Shakespeare was performed while starving wolves patrolled the edge of town, shirt-sleeve golfing on Saltspring Island in January, and Victoria, that wee bit of England, snow-free.

I got the credits and the cash and Canada got honest press exposure at a time when, to most people's way of thinking, it was best left to freeze. Probably never did get a convert from the Caribbean but it was the best kind of mutual aid, without a string to be seen.

Of course, I had been in print probably four hundred times before, mostly in travel, so the Canadians knew what I could do. This reinforces my point: Forget freebies until you've got a competitive edge, then you can decide for yourself whether to accept them.

It must be said again: Write for the reader and the gold will follow. Do it right—be honest, dig deep, make your words jump off the page—and the rewards will come your way.

CHAPTER 16

Computers and Copy Submission

Computers have become so commonplace in the writing world in the past ten years that for simple manuscript preparation and printing they have all but replaced the typewriter.

The editor's question isn't whether you have an IBM or a Macintosh, not even whether your printer is a dot matrix or the newest 600 dpi laser printer, but is the copy easy to read? In that sense, nothing has changed. Editors hated typed vowels filled with black by crummy typewriters; today they hate unreadable copy just as much. And the result is the same: manuscripts rejected, mostly unread.

The newest computer-related questions are:

1. Should you fax your query letter rather than mail it?

2. Are the editors linked to e-mail so you can send your query to them via modem. Will the editor respond the same way?

3. If your manuscript is accepted, should you send it on paper, by fax, by modem, or on a mailed disk?

4. If sent by modem or disk, doesn't the hardware/software issue enter in?

5. When submitting copy directly to newspapers, without a query, should it be sent on paper, by fax, via modem, or on disk? Again, does it matter which computer and software you are using?

Let me answer these one at a time, as best I can in this quickly changing world.

1. Should you fax your query letter rather than mail it?

Let the current *Writer's Market* (or its monthly "Markets" update in the *Writer's Digest Magazine*) be your guide. In 1993 editors weren't suggesting this approach. If that changes in subsequent years, the guides will show how the editors want to be queried at that time.

The value of a fax is its immediacy, yet magazines by their nature, most being monthlies, need copy that stands up well over a several month period. So the few days lost mailing the query letter are insignificant. It seems more prudent to indicate in your query that you have a fax (and its number). That way, should editors be so moved by your letter, they can beg you, by fax, to get the promised prose in their hands as quickly as possible. In other words, write a clean, solid query the old-fashioned way, mail it, and give the editor a reason for faxing you back! (I'd also include an S.A.S.E. should the editor prefer to respond the old-fashioned way.)

2. Are the editors linked to e-mail, so you can send your query to them via modem? Will the editor respond the same way?

Again, this would be indicated in the current

Writer's Market. Do what that editor wants.

Some listings currently state that "writer's guidelines" are available through e-mail, with the publication's code listed for those eager or able to find and download the copy.

Be certain to include in your query or cover letter any codes or numbers the editor should know to use any new form of contact, just as you do now by including your return address and your phone number.

What if the editor prefers contact by modem and you have no modem? First, check your directory to see if your software doesn't include a modem, even though you may never have used it. Then contact a local computer firm, tell them what you have and what you want, and ask if they can provide any needed linking software. The kind of computer you have is immaterial here; such software is often available on discount for as little as $50.

Since faxing can be done at most local copy shops, it is accessible to almost any writer.

3. **If your manuscript is accepted, should you send it on paper, by fax, by modem, or on a mailed disk?**

One would imagine that every editor would prefer copy by disk or modem, assuming that all major commercial publications are now prepared by computer. The copy is available immediately, rewriting or correcting are simple, and the time saved for all is considerable.

Yet only a small fraction of the magazines offer the option of paper versus disk copy in the *Writer's Market.* Editors still seem to want the query on paper, with the manuscript, if requested, to follow in the same fashion.

My experience validates this preference. How-

ever, once the editor has responded positively
(knowing that I can send the material by disk, as
I said in the query—see Figures 10, 11, and 22)
I have been asked about 60% of the time in the
past two years to send the disk with the printed
manuscript!

Only once has fax been an issue: a sidebar containing last-minute facts was sent hours before the
deadline, to be typeset there just as the magazine
went to print.

4. **If sent by modem or disk, doesn't the hardware/software
issue enter in?**

Most publications seem to be able to accept any
copy, as is or converted into ASCII. If they want
copy by disk or modem and you are uncertain, call
and iron out the details. Or send the text, then call
to see if it arrived in usable fashion. Remember to
include your name, address, and phone/fax numbers prominently located on the copy itself, as
well as on the disk label.

5. **When submitting copy directly to newspapers, without a
query, should it be sent on paper, by fax, via modem, or on
disk? Again, does it matter which computer and software
you are using?**

Many newspapers will later request the copy on
disk or by modem, yet few if any want the initial
submission except by mail in printed form. That
will change, and many writers, once they are
known to the editor, will be individually in-
structed otherwise, but at the outset simply submit to newspapers as described in Chapter 12, then
do as the editor directs.

Fax comes into play for fast-breaking news sent
by those without access to computers, to be

proofed and typeset at the newspaper and used immediately. But that will rarely affect the travel section. The editor will tell you if or when this kind of immediacy is needed.

The kind of computer or software seems to be unimportant to most newspapers: they can convert all conventional formats or accept the text in ASCII.

CHAPTER 17

Air Couriers

Want to travel abroad at a 50–85% discount, be assured a seat both ways on the best nonstop airlines, and be met at both ends to help expedite your passage through customs? Become an air courier!

Contrary to popular assumption, you won't be smuggling drugs, gems, or radioactive isotopes. But you will take the last flight of the night, must dress conventionally and stay sober, and had better guard a manifest container with your life or you will swim home!

Mostly you will be a body accompanying baggage, since the courier firms can't send personal baggage unaccompanied, yet they must transport 70-pound containers overnight. The baggage—mostly paper contracts, computer disks, small repair parts, and backup systems—becomes yours while you are in-flight, though it's safely below and you are in the last open seat in the passenger section.

What about *your* baggage? Well, there are some sacrifices or conditions you must make or meet to save $300–800 or more in flight costs.

First, you should live near the departure airports: a vast majority of the flights leave from New York, Los Angeles, San Francisco, or Miami.

Next, you must match the U.S. hub with a city you want to visit. Most New York flights go to Europe (London, Frankfurt, Paris, Rome, Brussels, Zurich, and more) or South America. Miami flights head south, particularly Caracas, Mexico City, Buenos Aires, and Montevideo. And most California flights head west to the East: Hong Kong, Singapore, Sydney, Seoul, Tokyo, and others.

So you must find the courier firms that serve your airport and desired destination, then usually book well in advance. Forget the *Yellow Pages*. Check Hogsett's *Bargain Travel Resource Book*, with an excellent explanation of the process and full list of firms, or Jennifer Basye's *The Air Courier's Handbook*, a more anecdotal rendition that also includes a frequently updated list.

You must figure out how to carry the bare essentials for a visit of seven to sixty days (the length of stay you arrange with the courier firm in advance) in a 9" x 14" x 21" bag (plus another small container, like a purse or camera bag). Check Hogsett's Travel Easy Bag, just this size and a courier's favorite.

Finally, you must be at the airport on both sides well in advance of the departure hour, which means when you are overseas you will probably return to the airport city at least a day in advance and be in the airport hours before. If you are a no-show, you lose any deposit the courier firm has demanded plus your return ticket.

The biggest sacrifice for most is that couriers travel alone, unless your mate or friend can arrange a trip with another courier at the same time! Or you want to buy a ticket on the same flights directly from the airline or a consolidator, whichever is cheaper.

The best part of being an air courier? Once you arrive, you are on your own at a sliver of the usual cost in air fare! Plenty of time to explore, interview, experience, and photo. Just stay out of jail—or at least be free in time to return on the flight. There can be extra bonuses. Sometimes—rarely, usually on a standby basis—you can fly free. Often you can get frequent flyer miles. And you will know at the time you sign the contract exactly when you will fly, how, and where, so it's easy to work up a travel writing schedule around the trip.

The worst part, in addition to the shortcomings mentioned above? It's not for the aged, infirm, or anybody in who change provokes the vapors. Sometimes couriers are bumped to the next flight. Rarely, the trips are canceled altogether. And if that writing haven so electric on paper turns out to be a festering hellhole that no sane person would encourage others to visit in print, you are there to fester until your ship comes home!

CHAPTER 18

365 Ideas for
Travel Articles

Some travel writers have more ideas than a lifetime
of article writing could match. If their ideas were
falling leaves, life for them would be a perpetual autumn
in the woods.

But for other writers life is Antarctica. No leaves for
a thousand miles! Such writers need help until their
eyes and minds learn to see that travel ideas abound
at every turn.

So here are three hundred ideas that should work
for almost anywhere (except maybe for Antarctica). In
some cases one idea will be sufficient to create a full
article. In others several ideas might be combined to
produce one piece.

The easiest way to structure a selling article is to ask
a question first, then make the article answer it, through
facts, quotes, anecdotes, and perhaps photos. Full of
excitement, information, gusto, and accuracy.

Therefore, the ideas in this list are posed as questions.
This requires you to determine who would most benefit
from knowing the answer, and why. This, in turn, suggests
which publications would be most likely to buy your

article (once you've determined who would be interested you can determine what publications they read).

Enough preamble, there's writing to do. Best wishes for happy traveling, good writing, and bountiful selling!

1. What are the ten "hottest" travel destinations this year or season, and why?

2. Of those top ten, which of those at or near the top of the list are new? Why are they at the top? Why would travelers want to go there?

3. If one wanted to visit all ten, what is the best route, season, and means?

For each or any of the ten:

4. What are the five most interesting things to do there? Why? How can each be done? When is the best time?

5. What are the five best hotels or accommodations? Why? Describe each: cost, location, attractions, restaurants, etc.

6. What are the five best restaurants? Why? Describe each in detail.

7. What five places should one visit at night? Why? Should visitors plan to spend a whole evening at each or can they go to several? Describe the best itinerary and give details for each location.

8. What should visitors do during the daytime? Why? What itinerary allows them to do the most and reap the greatest benefits?

9. What are the best athletic facilities open to the public? Describe each: cost, accessibility, availability of equipment, friendliness, condition of the facility, etc.

10. What is the shopping like? What are the best stores? Bargains? Things to avoid? "Must" buys?

11. What would children most enjoy doing there? Describe each activity fully.

12. What would seniors most enjoy doing there? Are there conditions like terrain or altitude that might limit older people? Describe each activity fully.

13. What is there to do in the way of cultural activities? To what age group are these directed? Describe and evaluate the quality of the activities.

14. Using each site as the center, what of interest can the traveler see within a day's range? Describe each major attraction and how it can be reached. Rank the attractions.

15. Again using each site as the center, how can an exciting weekend be spent in that area? Suggest an itinerary, explaining each item in detail and why it is included.

16. How could an exciting weekend itinerary best be expanded to a full week? Two weeks? A month?

17. How would you rank the top ten, or any combination of the top ten sites, by any of the mentioned criteria: hotels, restaurants, activities, etc.? Why?

18. As you rank the top ten by a chosen criterion, what other sites not mentioned must be included? Why?

19. What were the top ten sites last year or season? Which ones are not included this year? Why?

20. Historically, which sites have remained at or near the top for many years? Five years? A decade? What makes them perennial favorites?

21. What other sites have many or most of the same qualities or characteristics but are not presently among the top sites? What are their prospects for the future?

22. What are "travel spots to watch" in the short or long range? Why?

23. Since many travelers are interested in investments in prime travel locations, what places look promising for present or future investments? Why?

24. How might travelers' money best be invested? Hotels? Restaurants? Services? Other?

25. What is the local climate like for foreign or outside investment? Should or must the investor live on-site?

26. How can travelers get more information about investing in a particular place?

27. How can travelers get details on the local currency? Current exchange rates? Where it is best exchanged? Long-term prospects? What to do with extra pocket money after returning?

28. Where can travelers learn the customary tipping practices of various countries? Of cruises? In dining and social situations?

29. Why should—or shouldn't—a traveler get tickets from a travel agent? How can an agent minimize a traveler's risk while increasing the service supplied to the traveler?

30. How can travelers find the best (and the best type of) agent for their various travel needs?

31. What recourse does a traveler have when a travel agent acts dishonestly, unfairly, suspiciously, or in any other way seemingly improperly?

32. Along that line, how can one select the best carrier—air, sea, whatever—for the trip planned? Describe the various criteria one could use: safety, comfort, adherence to schedule, price, food, service, appearance, prestige, etc.

33. How can travelers secure guarantees that the criterion or criteria will be met??

34. If the guarantees are secured but not fulfilled, what recourse do travelers have? How do they exercise that recourse?

35. Lost or damaged baggage is a common problem while traveling. How can one find out the incidence of this for the various carriers?

36. If one's baggage is lost or damaged, what recourse is there? How does one initiate that action?

37. What should travelers do if their tickets are lost? When? If that brings no results, is there any recourse?

38. One reads of extraordinarily low-priced tickets in the newspaper classifieds. Are these generally legitimate? How can one check before buying? Any recourse later?

39. One also hears of "bucket shops" where low-priced tickets are found. What is the story here? Legitimate? How do they do it? What risk does the traveler run?

40. Some carriers are completely unknown. How can one check on their legitimacy, reliability, safety record, adherence to schedule, etc.?

41. Which U.S. carriers have foreign branches or affiliations? What are the names of their other lines? Will tickets from them be honored, or accepted for credit, by the U.S. firms? Will the U.S. firms accept full responsibility for their actions?

42. What should the traveler know about purchasing airfare before leaving? How much in advance? Round trip?

43. Some airlines charge considerably less than others. Is there any danger implied in the lower costs? What questions should the buyer ask?

44. Often a ticket has additional air mileage included beyond the stated destination. When is this the case? How can the flyer know this and plan for it?

45. Do all airlines serving food make special dietary arrangements? Which do not? Why?

46. How can travelers arrange for special-diet meals? How can they be assured that this request is met?

47. Are there items that one should not use while flying? Do portable computers, for example, interfere with the plane's radio transmission?

48. How does one travel with prohibited items when these are needed at the destination? For example, hunting rifles and camping knives?

49. How does one carry delicate but odd-sized baggage, such as cumbersome carvings or large, mounted display boards?

50. Are there ways to streamline the registration, exiting, and baggage retrieval process?

51. What does "standby" booking actually mean? Is it less expensive? Are there levels of priority for standby customers?

52. What are the services customarily performed by flight attendants? What additional services can the customer expect but not know about? Is tipping ever expected or accepted?

53. Does the flyer have recourse if seatmate(s) are abusive, drunk, excessively noisy or troublesome, or otherwise unpleasant?

54. If a movie or other service is advertised but not provided on a flight, does the flyer have any recourse, financial or otherwise?

55. What is the air industry's policy regarding flying with children? How does this vary by airline?

56. What regulations prevail concerning minors flying unaccompanied? How does this vary by airline?

57. When a plane arrives behind schedule and connections are missed, what must the airline do in the way of accommodations, meals, transportation, and rescheduling?

58. How has the air industry changed over the past 50, 25, 10, 5 years? What does that mean to the traveler?

59. How do the various airlines compare in fares, time spent traveling, comfort, and in other ways between the U.S. and a particular destination?

60. If you miss a flight and did not cancel the ticket, can you receive a full refund? How do the airlines differ on this? What questions should the buyer ask in advance?

61. How can one travel and earn U.S. tax benefits at the same time? By conducting business? Writing? Attending conventions? What are the current tax laws in these areas?

62. To receive U.S. tax benefits, what kind of paperwork and/or proof of activity or intent is required before or after the trip?

63. Is the U.S. traveler ever taxed by the country or countries visited abroad? How? Where? How much? Can it be avoided?

64. If the U.S. traveler pays taxes abroad, direct or indirect, can these be deducted on the 1040 tax form later? What kind of validation or paperwork is required?

65. Which countries charge an exit fee at the airport? Prepare a list of these countries by continent and indicate the cost. Payable in U.S. or local currency? Is it also payable if you are in transit?

66. Is there a way to avoid paying exit fees? Where? How?

67. Are there any other official "hidden" fees at airports or in overseas countries that the traveler would likely be unaware of? Where? How much? For what?

68. Which countries require tourist visas? Prepare a list of the countries by continent, stating where such visas can be obtained, how much they cost, and what is required to receive them.

69. How can one obtain a tourist visa if one is abroad and wishes to travel from one country to another?

70. What other kinds of visas, besides tourist, are available? Are any preferable, if the traveler qualifies? What is their cost, how are they obtained, and what is required to receive them?

71. With a tourist visa, does any foreign country require additional paperwork before exiting? Do any require tax or police clearances?

72. What happens to tourists who remain in a foreign country beyond the expiration period of their tourist visa?

73. In planning an extended stay abroad, what potential visa-related problems should be considered? Are there actions that can be taken in advance to alleviate or reduce these potential problems?

74. What should every traveler know about U.S. customs before traveling?

75. How can the traveler find out the most recent information about customs before each trip?

76. How can travelers speed up their customs inspection? What should they do beforehand? What papers and receipts are necessary? Must these be in English? What if these are lost?

77. What are the penalties for exceeding the customs limits? Are all enforced? What do travelers do if they can't pay the penalties?

78. In general, what kinds of items are most likely to give travelers difficulties with foreign customs?

79. What are the most common restrictions enforced against U.S. travelers by different nations? Prepare a list of countries by continent.

80. What are the most common requirements for driving a car or truck from country to country? Flying a plane? Docking a watercraft?

81. Can one use a U.S. driver's license in a foreign country? Prepare a list or chart explaining the regulations in each country by continent. Where local licenses are required, what must a traveler do to obtain one?

82. Is U.S. car insurance applicable in foreign countries? If not, can an extension be secured? Or is insurance available there?

83. Is U.S. health insurance applicable in foreign countries? How can travelers best secure similar protection abroad?

84. Who is responsible for injury and health care payments, the person or the country? If the country, does that apply to U.S. tourists? Whom does one contact? Prepare a list of countries by continent.

85. How can one find English-speaking doctors or dentists when traveling outside the U.S.?

86. In what countries would it be advisable to seek medical attention from doctors or dentists trained in the U.S. or another nation with similar training standards?

87. In some countries injections are customarily given in pharmacies. What are the dangers to be avoided in this situation? How can they be avoided?

88. In which countries should travelers return home for particular operations or treatments of a non-emergency nature?

89. How can a traveler bring medications and neither be detained nor have the medicine confiscated by customs?

90. What medical conditions might make the traveler unacceptable by carriers or for admission into other countries? Are there ways in which that unacceptability can be modified?

91. How can travelers learn of unsafe health conditions in areas they wish to visit?

92. What are the most serious health threats in the world today? Where are these primarily found? Can travelers take precautions against them, other than staying out of the area altogether?

93. What is jet lag and how will it affect travelers?

94. What can be done to lessen the effects of jet lag or to alleviate or avoid them completely?

95. What consequences can many travelers expect in high-altitude sites? What can be done to lessen or alleviate these consequences?

96. What care should a traveler take when drinking local water? Why? Where is this not a concern? What precautions are possible?

97. Are there areas where freshwater swimming or bathing can be health threatening? Where? Why? Any precautions possible?

98. What should the traveler be concerned about when swimming in unknown waters? What precautions are advisable?

99. Often the sun is more direct and intense in sites closer to the equator. What concerns should

travelers have and what precautions should they take?

100. How can travelers learn of local health threats (such as the Chagas disease in Salvador, Brazil) so they are neither unduly frightened or inadequately prepared?

101. Are there local foods that should be avoided as potential health threats? Which ones, and where are they found?

102. For those with breathing difficulties, which cities or areas are the most polluted in the world?

103. Which cities are held to have the cleanest air in the world?

104. Which parts of the world house the oldest living people? Describe the evidence, life-style, food, explanation(s). Can the areas and people be visited?

105. Where are the most healthful spas in the world? Says who, and on what evidence? Give details, costs.

106. Where are the most popular spas found? Give details, costs. How do these compare with the most healthful spas?

107. How are the world's time zones determined? How do the various countries alter this (with daylight savings, etc.)?

108. What consequences can the time zones have on scheduling, telephoning, transacting business, etc.?

109. What parts of the earth have the longest and shortest nights? How are these celebrated? Can visitors participate in these activities? How?

110. How can travelers synchronize their biological clock with the local time of day to diminish the negative effects of disharmony between the two?

111. Is time, in the sense of a 24-hour day, told the same worldwide?

112. In what areas of the world are different calendars used? How does this affect the traveler?

113. Winter and summer are reversed in the two hemispheres. What should travelers know about this, and how might it affect their planning?

114. Holidays vary from country to country. Are there any holidays that are honored worldwide? Which? When do they occur?

115. What are the major holidays celebrated in each nation, the date(s), the occasion? What ceases to function during those times? Make a list of countries by continent.

116. In much of the world, pharmacies take turns staying open 24 hours a day. How can the traveler find out which pharmacies and which other vital services are open around the clock?

117. Are there areas of the world offering the kind of relief that the desert Southwest does for people allergic to the more common pollens in the U.S.?

118. What are the most humid areas of the world? How does this affect traveling in the area?

119. Where are the highest tides in the world? Can these be seen by travelers? When? From what viewing point?

120. For traveling golfers, which are the ten most enjoyable courses in the world? Why? Give details, including the best season to play.

121. What equipment should the average golfer bring on a trip? Is there any country that won't allow golf equipment through customs or charges extra for it? Why, and how much? What equipment is available locally? How can golfers find out about the best local courses?

122. Does golf etiquette differ in other countries? How? Any other peculiarities the traveler should know?

123. Is golf played and scored the same in every country?

124. For the traveling businessperson, is business conducted on the golf course in foreign countries as it is in the U.S.? Where? How does it differ?

125. What are the ten wildest courses in the world? Why? What should the traveler know to play on each or all?

126. Golfers on vacation might enjoy watching tournaments elsewhere. When and where are the major golf tournaments held outside the U.S. each year? How can one obtain tickets to watch?

127. When playing outside the U.S., do golfers have access to the clubhouse? How does this differ from country to country?

128. How much can a golfer expect to pay elsewhere? Are there green fees? Are caddies required? Golf carts? Special shoes or attire? Other costs?

129. Which major golf courses outside the U.S. are connected to hotels? Is access guaranteed to hotel guests? The public? Supply costs and details.

130. How does playing tennis in a foreign country differ from playing tennis in the U.S.?

131. Do travelers have access to the major tennis tournament courses outside the U.S., such as Wimbledon? How do they make advance arrangements?

132. How do travelers arrange temporary use of tennis clubs and courts in foreign lands? How do they find out about them?

133. Is there any country where tennis equipment cannot be brought through customs, or where it will be charged extra? Why, and how much?

134. Where in the world can the traveler expect to see baseball played professionally as it is in the U.S.?

135. How does a professional baseball game played in a particular country differ from one played in the U.S.? What presumably American traits are practiced there?

136. How can U.S. tourists find out the playing schedule in a particular country so they can watch a game while there? Can they reserve seats in advance?

137. Which former American major leaguers could a traveler watch play in the professional leagues outside the U.S.? Where do they play?

138. How and where can a visiting American practice or play baseball abroad? Softball?

139. Does the American community in the larger cities abroad have regular outings that tourists could join to play ball? Where and when?

140. Are there any cities that prohibit or discourage jogging and running in the parks? On the streets? Which, why, where, and when?

141. Must one wear attire different from that worn in the U.S. when jogging or running abroad? How does it differ? Where? Why?

142. Athletes regularly spit while exercising in the U.S. Is this prohibited or heavily discouraged elsewhere? Where? How is the offender penalized?

143. Is the etiquette of running different outside the U.S.? How and where?

144. How does one gain access to showers and locker facilities at major stadia or parks outside the U.S.? Must this be arranged in advance? How is that done?

145. How can runners find out the schedule of competitions in other countries so they can coordinate their visit with these activities?

146. Are requirements for running competitions abroad different from those in the U.S.? Doctor's form? Evidence of previous times?

147. Are there running events that last for days and or cross the country or cover long distances that the traveler could enter and thereby see much of the land? Where? When?

148. How could each of the running questions above be applied to triathloning, biathloning, marathoning, and ultramarathoning?

149. How does a visiting trackperson gain access to tracks abroad, for practicing, informal racing, and competition?

150. Are there track clubs and groups abroad that allow visiting American trackpeople to participate in their workouts? How can this be arranged in advance?

151. What are the ten prettiest running trails or roads outside the U.S.? Why? Any problems simply running on them?

152. What are the most exciting? Most difficult? Most daring?

153. How might one cross a country by running and walking a reasonable distance daily, stopping at super locations each night and seeing the best the land has to offer? Lay out such a trip, with details.

154. Are there any "Runs for Peace," or other runs for similar purposes, being planned outside the U.S. during the coming year that might attract travelers? Where and when? Whom should they contact?

155. How and where can one find good bicycles to use for seeing the countryside abroad? What might they cost? What kind of security would be required?

156. How do cycling regulations differ outside the U.S.? Are licenses required? Can one use all regular roads?

157. How can travelers bring their bicycles with them?
Do the carriers require special packing? Is there an
additional charge? Will customs allow them to enter?

158. Is special cycling attire required? Helmets? Are
these available for rent abroad?

159. How can travelers join cycling clubs and tours
outside the U.S.? How can they find out about them?
What is the customary charge to participate?

160. Where can traveling U.S. football fans find football
played outside the U.S.?

161. How does football played abroad differ from
football played in the U.S.?

162. How can travelers find out schedules, ticket
information, and whatever else they need to know
for football games outside the U.S.?

163. Where is rugby normally played and how can one
find necessary information about the schedule and
tickets?

164. How can spectators unfamiliar with rugby learn
the rules and intricacies of the game before seeing
a match?

165. The same for cricket: Where is it normally played
and how can one secure information about the
schedule and tickets?

166. Again, how can one learn more about it before
observing it?

167. Do rugby or cricket have a special etiquette that
the visiting spectator should know? What is it?

168. Soccer is widely popular. When are the major world
matches scheduled and how might this affect the
traveler's plans?

169. How does one learn the exact schedules of soccer
matches and the ticket information?

170. What might the traveler read to fully understand soccer before observing a match in person?

171. Is there a special etiquette for the spectators? Must they be careful about the color of their clothes to avoid the perhaps unpleasant or dangerous results of implied partisanship?

172. What other sports can be observed in the country in question? What should travelers know about these in advance? How can travelers view or participate in the event?

173. How can travelers arrange to visit a business similar to their own while outside the U.S.? What would be the proper way to do that in a particular country?

174. Once the business has been visited, is a gratuity expected? Would it be well received even if unexpected? How might that be done?

175. How can one get information on the kinds of business, trade, or professional associations of a particular country? Contacts (names and addresses)?

176. Is there a U.S. governmental agency that can help arrange a business visitation schedule for travelers with their counterparts abroad?

177. How can travelers visit the stock or commodities exchanges outside the U.S.? Where can they find information to read in advance to understand what they will see?

178. How can travelers learn about trade shows, or their equivalents, in the countries they wish to visit?

179. Is there a way to learn of fairs held outside the U.S., with the related ticket and schedule information?

180. Every nation has beauty contests. How can one find out when they are held, where, and what the visitor must do to attend?

181. What natural wonders or phenomena are there to see in a particular country? Why would the traveler want to see these?

182. Does the public have access to the phenomena? Are there fees? What arrangements must be made in advance? How can that be done?

183. What dangers, if any, can the traveler expect to encounter when viewing the natural phenomena? How can these dangers be protected against in advance?

184. Who would find viewing the phenomena difficult or inadvisable? Is it rigorous? Must one be at a particular state of training to participate fully or wisely?

185. How does a particular phenomenon fit into its natural setting? Is it singular or one of many such phenomena?

186. What is the geological history of the area or site? Is this typical or atypical of the surrounding area? If unique, what makes it so?

187. What is the history of human habitation in the area or site? To what degree is this a result of the geology?

188. What can the visitor see that shows the geological history of the area? Are there guided tours? Where? When? How does one participate?

189. What evidence can be seen of early human habitation? Are there archaeological digs there or nearby? Where? How and when can they be visited?

190. Are there guided tours of the digs? Can one participate in a dig? How can more information be obtained?

191. Is there a good museum display in the vicinity that shows the geological formation and/or the early

human habitation? Where? When is it open to the public? What does it cost?

192. When did the historical period of the site or area begin? How were the first writings made? Are copies still available for travelers to see?

193. What of significance has occurred in the site or area during the time of recorded history?

194. Which of those significant sites can be visited by the traveler? What physical evidence can be seen today? Where is it? Give details.

195. Can one read historical accounts of the events? Can one read actual historical documents while present at the site? How?

196. Are there symbolic re-enactments of these events today? When? Are they worth viewing? How can that be done?

197. Do ancestors of those involved in the historic events still live in the area? Who are they? Can they be visited? How?

198. Is the area currently undergoing a change of historical significance? What is it? How can it be viewed? Can one participate in it?

199. Who are the most famous personalities of the area or site? Where did or do they live?

200. If they have died, can the place(s) where they lived locally be visited? When? Cost? A guided tour possible?

201. If they are still living, can one meet with them? When? How does one make the arrangements?

202. Is it possible to visit the home where they are presently living? Where they used to live? When? How does one make the arrangements?

203. What would children enjoy doing at the site or area?

204. Are there programs solely for children, where they can be left and retrieved later, that will enlarge their understanding of the site or area?

205. If so, can the traveler's child(ren) participate? What does it cost? Can arrangements be made in advance?

206. If one visits the area during the school year, is it mandatory to enroll children in school during the visit? What are the regulations? Are they enforced?

207. How can the traveler's children get to know local children? What is the best means and setting for that interchange?

208. What dangers exist for visitor's children in the area? Is kidnapping common? What precautions should parents take?

209. Are there cultural activities specifically directed to children that are open to youngsters traveling in the area? What are they? Can newcomers participate? Can arrangements be made in advance?

210. What sports activities or facilities are open to traveler's children? Are they supervised and safe? What are the details?

211. For traveling parents with youngsters, are baby-sitters available? How trustworthy are they? How can one tell? How can they be hired? What is the going rate?

212. Are there any health precautions parents should know about before bringing children to the site or area? Anything they should do while the children are there? Or after they have returned home?

213. Are there any health care limitations such as inadequate hospital facilities or the absence of medical care that one should know about before visiting or bringing children?

214. Conversely, are there particularly healthful activities or locations that children (and probably adults) should avail themselves of while in the area?

215. Is there anything in the local diet that should be avoided by children? What? Why?

216. If the children are very young, is it possible to buy the necessary food and diapers locally?

217. If needed for infants, are reputable doctors available? How can they be contacted?

218. Are there summer camps in the area that will accept visitors' English-speaking children? How can a camp's reputation be checked? Provide details.

219. Are there similar camps or programs where visitors' English-speaking children can learn the local language and customs and associate with peers?

220. What are the local customs concerning children accompanying parents to social or cultural activities?

221. Can the visitor's children safely sightsee alone or with other children during the day? Play at the beach or at parks? What areas or activities are unsafe?

222. How safe is it for children to carry pocket money, cameras, radios, watches, or other items of value?

223. What phone numbers should every child visiting the area carry on a card in his or her pocket, on the remote chance the child gets lost, ill, etc.?

224. What clothes should parents bring for children to wear? What can be bought locally, if needed?

225. What kinds of shoes do children most need in this area? If needed, are the local shoes worth buying?

226. What would teenagers find particularly interesting to do in this area?

227. What can teenage girls see and do that is worthwhile yet different?

228. What advice should teenage girls receive before exploring alone or in pairs in this area? Where or at what hours is it always advisable to be accompanied or chaperoned?

229. How can they meet other girls roughly their own age and with similar interests?

230. How should teenage girls dress both to feel comfortable and to avoid sending the wrong message?

231. What would teenage boys find different yet worthwhile to do here?

232. Any advice they should heed to avoid trouble or problems? Any attire that should be avoided for the same reasons?

233. How can visiting teenage boys or girls participate in sports in this area? Can they make arrangements in advance?

234. What are the dating standards for teenage girls here? How much should a visiting girl adhere to those standards? Any outright taboos?

235. How do dating standards for boys differ here from the U.S., and what is regarded as proper behavior?

236. How prevalent is drug use among teens in this area? What are the penalties if caught, and how regularly are they enforced? Would they be stiffer for a tourist caught abusing the laws?

237. What are the regulations concerning alcohol or tobacco use as they apply to teens both local and visiting? Anything else prohibited that the visiting teen should know?

238. How does the local social dancing done by teens differ from that in the U.S.? Anything visiting teens should know, behavior they should avoid?

239. Where can visiting teens dance? Should they attend in pairs? Is chaperoning ever advised or required?

240. Should U.S. teens bring radios with them? Could they hear familiar music? Programs in English? Any advice on radio use there?

241. How much money should teens carry with them? In what form?

242. How much anti-Americanism is present in this area? How might it affect teens? How should they respond?

243. What are teen home parties like in this area? If invited, what would be expected, or desired, of U.S. visitors?

244. Can teens rent cars in this area? If so, what advice do they need to avoid injury, stay safe, and not run afoul of the law?

245. Given one full day in this area, what would be the best combination of things to see and do for teenaged girls? Boys? A mixed group?

246. Given two days? A weekend? A week? Two weeks? Give details.

247. Are there many extra-academic activities at the universities in this area that would interest visiting teens? How might they participate?

248. Are there academic activities, in or out of the university, that visiting teens might enjoy? Can they participate? How?

249. Are there secular or religious institutions in the area that encourage teen visitation and interaction? If so, give details.

250. In this area or society, what is the proper role of teens as they relate to the elderly, parents, teachers, and peers? Are visiting teens expected to act in the same way?

251. What would honeymooners enjoy doing in this area or at this site?

252. Are special provisions made locally for honeymooners? What kind of provisions? Should couples identify themselves as honeymooners at hotels, restaurants, other locations?

253. How do local newlyweds celebrate honeymoons? Could visiting honeymooners do the same? Explain.

254. What would be an ideal one-day schedule for visiting American honeymooners? Two-day? Weekend? Week-long? Two-week?

255. Is there anything commonly done in the U.S. that would be improper or embarrassing for visiting newlyweds? For any married couple?

256. What would be particularly interesting to do in the area for seniors, alone, in groups, or as couples?

257. Are there local accommodations for seniors (lower rates, elevators, special stairs in buses, etc.)?

258. Is there an age at which one can first avail himself or herself of these accommodations? Is there a local card or pass needed? How does one secure it?

259. Are there special tours for seniors to places that might otherwise be physically inaccessible or inconvenient? How can one learn of them? Can one participate?

260. Are there health facilities in the area of particular interest to the older traveler? Explain.

261. How can seniors meet their counterparts in this area? Is that to be encouraged?

262. For seniors dependent upon continued medical care or medication provision while traveling, how can arrangements be made in this area? How can this connection be established in advance?

263. What would constitute an ideal day for a visiting senior to this area? Two days? Weekend? Week? Two weeks? Describe.

264. What are the best months or seasons for visitors to come to this area? What can be done best during that period?

265. What is the next best season? What can be done best during that period? Which activities differ from those of the best months?

266. When shouldn't one visit this area? Why?

267. Are there special accommodations for the handicapped in this area? Explain.

268. Would visiting American tourists who are handicapped be looked down upon here? How would their treatment differ? Why?

269. Are there special telephone and TV accommodations for the hearing-impaired?

270. How do the deaf sign in this area? Anything the visiting deaf should know?

271. Are there any difficulties bringing Seeing Eye dogs to this area? Explain.

272. Which major sites in the area can be fully visited by those in wheelchairs? Which cannot? Explain.

273. What local religious centers or attractions would most interest the American visitor?

274. Must the visitor wear any special attire to see the local religious attractions? Is the attire available there? Any cost?

275. Are guided tours offered at the religious attractions? When? Open to anybody? Cost?

276. If a visitor wishes to preach or explain his or her religion to local residents, would this create any difficulties? Explain.

277. Are there activities or places that are inaccessible to those who are not believers of the national or official church or faith? Explain.

278. How can one find private guides in this area? Are they licensed? How can they be evaluated before hiring them?

279. Are there official taxi rates in this area? Where are those rates listed? How does one learn of the exceptions?

280. Is there a Traveler's Aid, or equivalent, in this area? Where is it located? How can one contact it by phone?

281. Where can one find maps in English of the region, city, or site? Are there various maps? Which is best? What does it cost?

282. What services does the closest U.S. consulate or embassy provide for visiting Americans? Who should be contacted there? What days/hours?

283. How can one receive mail in this area? What kind of identification is required to retrieve it?

284. What credit cards are commonly accepted in this area? What does one do if the cards are lost here?

285. Can the visitor bring pets? What shots or papers are required? What are the local rules regarding those animals?

286. If one buys a pet locally, what must be done to bring it back to the U.S.?

287. What are the most common local scams tried on visitors? What should the newcomer be particularly aware of?

288. Are there local bookstores or libraries with books in English?

289. Are there video stores with English-speaking films? Can one rent VCRs for use with hotel TVs? Do the hotels have TVs?

290. For the single visitor, what are the possibilities of meeting congenial peers of the opposite sex? Of the same sex?

291. What must the single visitor beware of in this area when socializing? Any absolute taboos?

292. How is the visiting single viewed by the local residents? Any way to reduce the discomfort that might create?

293. Are there precious works of art or legitimate artifacts available for purchase? Where might one find them? How can they be authenticated?

294. Must any purchase have a special antiquities release before it can be taken out of the country? If so, explain.

295. Can visitors pan, mine, or otherwise remove ores or metals from the ground, then sell them or take them home? What are the rules?

296. What can horticulturists take home of the plants or seeds they find in the area? How can they get permission to do so?

297. What local food should be tried by visitors? Where is it best prepared and available? Where might one find authentic recipes for preparation back home?

298. What sites or attractions are overblown and not worth the time or expense?

299. What deserves close attention but few outsiders know about? How can the visitor see it? What information should they have in advance?

300. If travelers want to write about this area, or any area, and later use their earnings to help offset the trip costs, plus deduct some or all of them for their taxes, what seminar should they attend or what tape series, with workbook, should they consult before taking the trip?

301. How has the fall of European communism changed European countries? Socially, economically, personally, educationally?

302. What happened to the more visual symbols, like the Berlin Wall and the mined fields along the boundaries? Have those totally disappeared? What can the visitor still see?

303. How have the former communist countries changed regarding border crossings, prohibited items one can carry, visa requirements? What should a potential visitor know?

304. Is there a commerce in memorabilia of those earlier regimes? Stores selling old communist posters, for example? How can one visit these? Any problems dealing in such matters?

305. Are there any tours built around the remnants or physical manifestations of the old communist rule? Describe them.

306. Along the same line, with the recent worldwide focus on the holocaust and World War II, what can be seen today of the earlier Nazi concentration camps? Which ones are open to visit? Describe them and details visitors should know.

307. Are there tours built around old Nazi buildings, monuments, or remnants, particularly in Berlin? Give details.

308. Where does communism still rule? What are the current regulations about visiting or touring?

Changes since the collapse of, say, the Berlin Wall?

309. Where in the world can gays visit without hassle? Where is it encouraged? Any stipulations? Anything outsiders should know to fit within the accepted range of freedoms?

310. Does this differ for gays versus lesbians? Where? How?

311. Where is the climate particularly negative to their visit and gathering? Why? What might happen to them?

312. How might gays find out about the local activities of places they wish to visit, either before the trip or once they are there?

313. Are there travel agencies that particularly cater to gays? Which?

314. Are there travel agencies that particularly cater to blacks? Other ethnic groups? Which? Will they also help others interested in the sites and activities of their focus group?

315. In the past few years ecotravel has become important. Describe that, how it has changed the travel scene, and what it means to the reader, with examples.

316. Where, for example, can the travelers most quickly and fully integrate themselves into the environment to sense and experience life to its fullest? List the top ten foreign ecotravel sites.

317. How does ecotravel affect the countries catering to it? What limitations does that have on the number and kind of visitors it can accommodate? How does that affect the cost?

318. How can the travelers keenly sensitive to the ecol-

ogy change their own activities to leave all sites they visit less ecologically damaged?

319. How are U.S. parks accommodating themselves to this new sensitivity? What can the traveler do to assist or provoke them into making more changes?

320. Which of the parks—national, state, or local—are the best ecotravel sites? What makes them so exceptional?

321. Which are the worst? What can Americans do to alter that?

322. Americans are becoming more conscious of the perils of city visitation. Which cities in the world are currently the worst to visit in terms of an individual's safety?

323. Which are the safest? Why? Is each likely to be as safe in the next five years? Ten?

324. The same questions for American cities: safest and least safe. Any predictions for the future?

325. What can tourists do in any large city to enhance their safety? What are the tips that seem to work anywhere in the world?

326. Are there specific things travelers can do in particular cities that will increase their safety? Cultural taboos that incite unsuspected response? Americanisms that put that person in exceptional, unknown danger?

327. What is the best way to carry money, passports, and other needed papers and documents so that they are unlikely to be stolen? Does this vary by sections of the world?

328. More people yearly rent cars abroad. What is the best way to find out the regulations, restrictions, and rates? How can you be certain the cost will be

the same when you arrive as it was when quoted at home?

329. Do you need anything beyond a U.S. driving license? Insurance? An international license? If so, give details.

330. How does driving differ in various parts of the world? For example, which countries drive on the left hand of the street, as in England? Do hand signals differ? Do all use red-yellow-green lights?

331. Explain how gas stations function in different countries. Self-service? Open at night? Does each handle repairs? What do you do if you are stranded in the middle of the night?

332. In which countries does it make sense to bring your own car for an extended visit? Explain the stipulations that entails.

333. In the U.S. it's possible to drive somebody's car for them from one site to another. Explain how this is done: where you find out about it, make the arrangements, and so on.

334. Travelers are intrigued by the prospect of becoming air couriers: flying at huge discounts in exchange for giving up their baggage space. Explain how this operates.

335. Where can they find more information about this activity: those air courier firms currently hiring, their routes, needs, rates.

336. How can they also find out about foreign air courier firms that will employ Americans?

337. How can one learn about working on steamers or cruise ships? What skills or talents are required? Who do they contact? Does it pay more than just getting to the destination? Must you work both ways?

338. Frequent flyer miles are a boon to many travelers who, by traveling, get to travel more at less charge. Explain how this whole phenomenon works and how it has changed over the years.

339. Which airlines offer this program? Do frequent flyer miles differ from line to line? How can miles be increased through hotel and car rentals plus taking advantage of bonus opportunities?

340. Explain the pitfalls of the system: what not to do, when it doesn't work, and how it can be used poorly.

341. Any tips you know that aren't common knowledge about how to use the frequent flyer system legally yet to its absolute maximum?

342. How does one "cash in" on unused frequent flyer miles? Can they be given to charity or be used for charitable means?

343. Where can credit cards be used abroad? Which cards? Any cards that simply have no use overseas?

344. What danger does the traveler have carrying credit cards? How can travelers safely store and use them? What do they do to get replacements if credit cards are lost or stolen?

345. Generally, overseas purchases are made in a foreign currency. How can the traveler be certain of the currency rate when the card is converted into dollars and that additional fees aren't added to the card?

346. Often cards in the U.S. act as warranties of product quality. Is that the same abroad? Should the item being mailed home prove to be a different one than purchased, for example, what recourse does the traveler have? Anything they can do there?

347. How difficult is it to use bank checks abroad? How

does one set up the proper conditions for their use before leaving? What do travelers do once they arrive?

348. Letters of credit can be created for use abroad. Explain how they work, where they are useful, and what the traveler must do both at home and overseas to put the letter in effect.

349. There has been a recent spate of interest in archeological digs, both abroad and in the U.S. How can one learn of digs where outsiders are welcome to participate?

350. Explain precisely what one does at a dig. The amount of work involved: digging, lifting, sifting, sitting, etc. Also, the living conditions and the time expectations.

351. When digging abroad, what additional requirements exist: registration in the sponsor's institution or programs, shots, waivers, etc.?

352. For archeological digs, who pays for what: airfare, food, local travel? Are the workers actually paid anything? When?

353. Often universities have overseas learning programs that travelers might include in their itinerary. Explain how one finds out about these and participates.

354. Sometimes university facilities go unused during part of the year, both in the U.S. and abroad. Since these can be rented at a nominal rate, how can you find out where these vacancies exist and how a traveler can fill them?

355. Many travel readers are interested in utilizing various travel means on the same trip. Explain, for example, how one might box a cycle, fly it to another city, unbox it, and ride to a campsite.

356. Expand that to any of the many combinations possible: trucking to the shore and canoeing into the wilderness; flying to a remote strip, then backpacking away, etc.

357. Explain how the traveler can pack for an overseas trip of several weeks' duration in one suitcase: what's needed, what isn't.

358. Do the same for travelers of varying ages: what must be brought for the youngster, teen, adult, senior.

359. Create a chart showing various things one might do in different countries, then the minimum attire one must bring to match each activity.

360. Another kind of chart could be created by season: what one does in specific countries, say, in spring. One for each season.

361. Travelers can compensate for underpacking by buying clothes abroad. Indicate what clothes are best bought where, with a possible price range.

362. Describe travel in the future: how will trips differ in 10, 25, 50 years based on what we know of the industry and the world?

363. Explain what effect the sub-Channel tunnel will have on travel from England to France. Give details at each stage of its development.

364. How much negative reaction already exists in specific countries to intrusion by foreign travelers? Where? How does it manifest itself?

365. As the world shrinks, how will that change travel in the future? Give specifics of current trends and future projections.

BIBLIOGRAPHY

BOOKS AND REPORTS

Travel Writing

Casewit, Curtis. *How to Make Money from Travel Writing.* Peter Smith, 1991.

Farewell, Susan. *How to Make a Living as a Travel Writer.* Paragon House, 1992.

Garfinkel, Perry. *Travel Writing for Profit and Pleasure.* NAL, 1989.

Milne, Robert Scott. *Travelwriter Marketletter* (monthly).

Zobel, Louise P. *Travel Writer's Handbook.* Surrey Books, 1992.

Travel Photography

Darling, Dennis C. *Chameleon with a Camera: A Unique Primer on Travel Photography and How to Survive the Trip.* Dorsoduro, 1989.

Engh, Rohn. *Sell and Re-Sell Your Photos.* Writer's Digest Books, 1991.

McCartney, Susan. *Photography: A Complete Guide to How to Shoot & Sell.* Allworth, 1992.

Purcell, Ann, and Carl Purcell. *A Guide to Travel Writing and Photography.* Writer's Digest Books, 1991.

General Writing

Brohaugh, William. *Write Tight: How to Keep Your Prose Sharp, Focused and Concise.* Writer's Digest Books, 1993.

Burgett, Gordon. *How to Sell More Than 75% of Your Free-lance Writing.* Prima Publishing, 1995.

Higgins, George V. *On Writing: Advice for Those Who Want to Publish.* Holt, 1991.

Meredith, Scott. *Writing to Sell.* Harper Collins, 1987.

Potter, Clarkson. *Writing for Publication.* NAL/Dutton, 1991.

Schumacher, Michael. *Writer's Complete Guide to Conducting Interviews.* Writer's Digest Books, 1993.

Finding Markets

Burgett, Gordon. "100 Best Travel Newspaper Markets." Report with addresses that can be copied for labels, Communication Unlimited, revised each September.

Burgett, Gordon. *Self-Publishing to Tightly-Targeted Markets.* Communication Unlimited, 1989.

Writer's Market, current edition, Writer's Digest Books, annual.

Query Letters

Burgett, Gordon. *The Writer's Guide to Query Letters and Cover Letters.* Prima Publishing, 1991.

Cool, Lisa Collier. *How to Write Irresistible Query Letters.* Writer's Digest Books, 1990.

Related Travel Publications/Air Couriers

Basye, Jennifer. *The Air Courier's Handbook.* Big City Books, 1993.

Hogsett, Suzanne. *Bargain Travel Resource Book.* Travel Easy, 1994.

Milne, Robert Scott. *Opportunities in Travel Careers.* NTC Pub. Group, 1990.

REFERENCE BOOKS

Biography Index. H. W. Wilson, current edition or appropriate volume.

Business Periodicals Index. H. W. Wilson, current edition.

Current Biography. H. W. Wilson, current edition or appropriate volume.

Encyclopaedia Britannica. Encyclopaedia Britannica Educational Corp., current ed.

Encyclopedia Americana. Grolier, current ed.

Encyclopedia of Science and Technology. Ed. Sybil P. Parker. McGraw-Hill, 1992.

Gale Directory of Publications and Broadcast Media. Gale, current ed.

Information Please Almanac. Houghton Mifflin, current ed.

Literary Market Place. Bowker, current ed.

Magazine Index. Microfilm.

New York Times Index. Microfilm.

Photographer's Market. Writer's Digest Books, current ed.

Reader's Guide to Periodical Literature. H. W. Wilson, current ed.

Webster's New Geographical Dictionary, Merriam-Webster, 1988.

Webster's New World Dictionary, various editions and publishers.

Who's Who, various editions and publishers.

Working Press of the Nation. National Research Bureau, annual.

World Almanac and Book of Facts. Pharos Books, current ed.

Writer's Market. Writer's Digest Books, current ed.

MISCELLANEOUS

Bunnin, Brad, and Peter Beren. *The Writer's Legal Companion.* Addison-Wesley, 1988.

Kane, Robert S. *Germany at Its Best.* Passport Books, 1988.

TAPES

Burgett, Gordon. "Finding Ideas for Articles and Books That Sell." Sixty-minute audio cassette, also available as a written report, Communication Unlimited, 1992.

Burgett, Gordon. "Research: Finding Facts, Quotes, and Anecdotes." Sixty-minute audio cassette, also available as a written report, Communication Unlimited, 1992.

Burgett, Gordon. "Writing Travel Articles That Sell!" Three-hour seminar on audio cassette, with workbook, Communication Unlimited, 1991.

SOURCES FOR TRAVEL WRITERS

Allworth Press
10 R. 23rd St., #400
New York, NY 10010
(212) 777-8395

ARTA (Association of Retail
Travel Agents)
Jefferson Davis Hwy., #300
Arlington, VA 22202-3402
(703) 553-7777

ASTA (American Society of
Travel Agents)
1101 King St.
Alexandria, VA 22314
(703) 739-2782

Big City Books
7047 Hidden Lane
Loomis, CA 95650

CLIA (Cruise Lines International Association)
500 Fifth Ave., #1407
New York, NY 10100
(212) 921-0066

Communication Unlimited
P.O. Box 6405
Santa Maria, CA 93456
(805) 937-8711
FAX (805) 937-3035

Dorsoduro Press
P.O. Box 3109
Austin, TX 78764
(512) 471-1973

Globe Pequot Press
P.O. Box 833
Old Saybrook, CT 06475
(800) 243-0495

Harper Collins
10 E. 53rd St.
New York, NY 10022
(800) 242-7737

Henry Holt
115 W. 18th St.
New York, NY 10011
(800) 488-5233

IATJ (International Association of Travel Journalists)
P.O. Box D
Hurleyville, NY 12747
(914) 434-1529

ICTA (Institute of Certified
Travel Agents)
148 Linden St.
Wellesley, MA 02181-0012
(617) 237-0280

IFWTWA (International
Food, Wine, and Travel
Writers Association)
P.O. Box 13110
Long Beach, CA 90803
(310) 433-5969

Macmillan Pub. Co.
866 3rd Ave., 7th Floor
New York, NY 10022
(800) 257-5755

Milne, Robert Scott
Waldorf-Astoria Hotel
Room 1850
New York, NY 10022

NAL/Dutton
375 Hudson St.
New York, NY 10014-3657
(212) 366-2000

NTC Publishing Group
4255 W. Touhy Ave.
Lincolnwood, IL 60646-1975
(800) 232-4900

Paragon House
90 5th Ave.
New York, NY 10011
(800) 727-2466

Prentice-Hall
Route 9W
Englewood Cliffs, NY 07632
(800) 922-0579

Prima Publishing
P.O. Box 1260
Rocklin, CA 95677
(916) 632-4400

Reference Software Intnatl
330 Townsend St.
San Francisco, CA 94107
(800) 872-9933

SATW (Society of American
Travel Writers)
1155 Connecticut Ave., NW
Suite 500
Washington, DC 20036
(202) 496-6639

Surrey Books
230 E. Ohio #120
Chicago, IL 60611
(800) 326-4430

TJG (Travel Journalists
Guild)
P.O. Box 10643
Chicago, IL 60610
(312) 664-9279

Travel Easy
3427 Thomas Dr.
Palo Alto, CA 94303
(415) 852-9952

The Writer
120 Boylston St.
Boston, MA 02116

Writer's Digest Books
1507 Dana Ave.
Cincinnati, OH 45207
(800) 289-0963

Write to Sell
P.O. Box 6405
Santa Maria, CA 93456
(805) 937-8711

INDEX

OTHER BOOKS FROM THE
GORDON BURGETT LIBRARY

Gordon Burgett books and audiocassette tapes have helped
tens of thousands of writers and speakers prosper. Here are
his hand-picked titles selected especially for readers of this
book.

BOOKS

Self-Publishing to Tightly-Targeted Markets

Subtitled "How to Earn $50,000 from Your First Book—Then
Double It!", this book shows you how to identify and reach
buyers who need specific information and are willing to pay
almost anything to get it. Includes all you need to know, from
book production to marketing. $14.95

Niche Marketing for Writers, Speakers, and Entrepreneurs

Applying his TCE (targeting, customizing, and expanding)
concept from *Self-Publishing to Tightly-Targeted Markets,*
here Burgett extends the niching process to writing (articles,
books, reports, newsletters) and speaking (talks, speeches,
seminars, audio and video cassettes, compact discs,
consulting) $14.95

Empire-Building by Writing and Speaking

If you have an exciting idea, you can have power—provided
you learn how to increase your sphere of influence through
writing and speaking. By widening your circle of influence,
your income will multiply, sometimes a hundred times. Here
are all the techniques necessary to take your idea, seminar,
or expertise and make it your guide to a six- or even seven-
figure income. $15.95

Writer's Guide to Query Letters and Cover Letters

This famous book is the best guide to writing exciting query
and cover letters—the kind that sell articles. The first edition
of this book was hailed by *Booklist:* "For new writers or
experienced ones looking for ways to multiply return on their
work, this manual is highly recommended." $12.95

How to Sell More Than 75% of Your Freelance Writing

Amateurs write, then try to sell....Professionals sell, then write. This is the theme of this revised and updated edition of Gordon Burgett's landmark book on the business of selling what you write. $12.95
Revised, updated version available January 1995

AUDIOCASSETTES

Here are the recordings of some of Gordon Burgett's own seminars as presented to his students. If they include areas of interest to you, you will find them of immense and permanent value as you listen to them again and again.

Writing Travel Articles that Sell! (3 tapes) $44.95

Before You Write Your Nonfiction Book
(3 tapes) $44.95

How to Self-Publish Your Own Book:
Preparation and Production (3 tapes) $44.95

How to Sell Your Book to General and
Niche Markets (3 tapes) $44.95

How to Set Up and Market Your Own Seminar
(3 tapes) $44.95

Producing and Selling Your Own Audio-Cassette
(1 tape) $9.95

Also Available From Prima Publishing

The Insider's Guide to Book Editors, Publishers and Literary Agents — 1995 Edition, *by Jeff Herman*

Updated annually. Here is the most comprehensive listing of book publishers and the names of editors and their specialty within each publishing house. Over 250 houses are included as well as the most complete information by top experts on what it takes to be successfully published. New to this edition are extensive details about more than 125 powerful literary agents. $19.95

And don't forget to order additional copies of
The Travel Writer's Guide $14.95

ORDER FORM

Please send me the following items:

Quantity	Title	Unit Price	Total
_____	_____	$____	$____
_____	_____	$____	$____
_____	_____	$____	$____
_____	_____	$____	$____
_____	_____	$____	$____
		Subtotal	$____

7.25% SALES TAX (California only) . . . . $____

SHIPPING ($3 for the first item, $1.50 for each additional item) . . . . $____

TOTAL ORDER . . . . $____

HOW TO ORDER

By telephone: With Visa/MC, call (916) 632-4400, Mon.–Fri. 9–4 PST.

By Mail: Just fill out the information below and send with your remittance.

I am paying by (check one): ☐ Check ☐ Money Order
☐ Visa/MC

My name is _____

I live at _____

City _____ State _____ Zip _____

Visa/MC # _____ Exp. _____

Signature _____

PRIMA PUBLISHING
P.O. Box 1260
Rocklin, CA 95677
(Satisfaction unconditionally guaranteed)